CONCEPTUAL CHANGE
AND THE CONSTITUTION

CONCEPTUAL CHANGE AND THE CONSTITUTION

Edited by Terence Ball
and J. G. A. Pocock

 *University Press of Kansas*

Published by the University Press of Kansas (Lawrence, Kansas 66045), which
was organized by the Kansas Board of Regents and is operated and funded by
Emporia State University, Fort Hays State University, Kansas State University,
Pittsburg State University, the University of Kansas, and Wichita State University

The preparation of this volume was made possible in part by a grant from the
Interpretive Research program of the National Endowment for the Humanities,
an independent federal agency.

Library of Congress Cataloging-in-Publication Data

Conceptual change and the Constitution.
  Includes bibliographies and index.
  1. United States—Constitutional history. I. Ball, Terence. II. Pocock, J. G. A.
(John Greville Agard), 1924-   .
KF4541.A2C56   1988   342.73'029   88-203
ISBN 0-7006-0369-7 (alk. paper)   347.30229

British Library Cataloguing in Publication Data is available.

Printed in the United States of America
10 9 8 7 6 5 4 3 2 1

The paper used in this publication meets the minimum requirements of the
American National Standard for Permanence of Paper for Printed Library
Materials Z39.48-1984.

To the memory of
Crawford Brough Macpherson
and
George Armstrong Kelly

Contents

Preface

The essays in this volume (with one exception acknowledged on p. 76) are revised versions of papers presented to a bicentennial conference bearing the same title, held in Washington, D.C., on 16–18 April 1987 and sponsored by the Conference for the Study of Political Thought and the Folger Institute for Renaissance and Eighteenth-Century Studies. We are indebted to the Folger Shakespeare Library and its director, Dr. Werner L. Gundersheimer, for warm hospitality; to the executive director of the Folger Institute, Dr. Lena C. Orlin, and her staff, for invaluable administrative support; and to the participants in a seminar concurrently conducted by the Folger Institute Center for the History of British Political Thought. We are equally grateful to the Research Programs Division of the National Endowment for the Humanities for their generous financial support. And not least, we are indebted to our audience and panelists. In addition to the editors and the authors appearing in the present volume, the latter included U.S. Solicitor General Charles Fried and Professors Charles R. Beitz, J. H. Burns, Stephen Holmes, Thomas Horne, Stanley N. Katz, Douglas Long, J. Donald Moon, James Moore, Anthony Parel, Melvin Richter, Lyman Tower Sargent, Gordon J. Schochet, and James Boyd White. To all of them, our heartfelt thanks for helping to make the occasion a stimulating and memorable one.

For unfailing helpfulness in getting this volume into print, we thank the staff at the University Press of Kansas. We would also like to thank

Lawrence Biskowski for preparing the index. Finally, each of the editors wishes to thank the other for the pleasure of the collaboration.

Terence Ball
J. G. A. Pocock

1

Introduction

Terence Ball and J. G. A. Pocock

I

Politics is a communicatively constituted activity. Words are its coin, and speech its medium. And yet, notoriously, the words that make up this medium have hotly contested and historically mutable meanings. Inasmuch as the concepts that constitute political life and language lose old meanings even as they acquire new ones, political discourse appears, in retrospect, to have been—and even now to remain—in a state of perpetual flux. Generally speaking, these changes are apt to occur gradually and at an almost glacial pace. Sometimes, however, such shifts in meaning and reference occur at a remarkably rapid rate, yielding unforeseen and often radical implications for future political thought and action. Such, arguably, was the case in early-sixteenth-century Florence, and during the English Civil War and the Glorious Revolution, the French Revolution, and other periods of political crisis and social change. At such times, conceptual innovations are brought about by action, practice, and intention, rather than by unintended structural change occurring in the historical context.

The same might also be said, and with even greater certainty, of the short span of years from the American Revolution through the debates over the ratification of the Constitution. This period of particularly intense political debate and disputation proved to be a period of profound political and conceptual change. The concepts of sovereignty, liberty, virtue, republic, democracy—even "constitution" itself—were virtually recoined. Others, such as "federalism," were scarcely less than novel American additions to the vocabulary of politics. Political innovation and conceptual change went hand in hand.[1]

These changes did not come easily or effortlessly. Conceptual disputes are almost never settled by uncontested definition or unanimous consent.[2] To the degree that conceptual disputes are political ones (and vice versa), they are apt to be hard-fought, in a most ungentlemanly way, with almost any weapon that comes to hand. Such changes as do occur are often the result of arguments *ad hominem*— rhetorical stratagems employed for temporary advantage and for narrowly partisan purposes—and of one side's sheer good luck in hitting upon an illuminating image or telling metaphor to make its case persuasive or at any rate palatable.[3] When the complex exposition of a carefully constructed argument contributes to the making of conceptual change—as it does in *The Federalist Papers*, for example—rhetoric and theory, polemic and philosophy, will characteristically coexist in the discourse.

One of the more remarkable features of the Federalist-Antifederalist debate was the degree to which the participants appear to have been quite self-consciously aware of the limits and possibilities of their own and their opponents' language. The extent and depth of their sensitivity to "conceptual" questions would hardly have been unusual if displayed by a philosopher or political theorist—a Hobbes or a Rousseau, say—but it is all the more remarkable when we recall that these were mainly men of affairs. Lawyers, legislators, military men, merchants, and planters, they nevertheless had an acute ear for the nuances of political idioms and languages. More than one Antifederalist critic of the new Constitution was heard to complain about the shameless linguistic license of their Federalist foes. The Massachusetts Antifederalist John DeWitt, for one, warned about the pernicious political consequences of linguistic laxity and imprecision. "Language is so easy of explanation, and so difficult is it by words to convey exact ideas, that the party to be governed cannot be too explicit. The line cannot be drawn with too much precision and accuracy."[4] The Federalists, for their part, contended that an older, essentially European stock of concepts and distinctions was woefully inadequate for describing and assessing the novel features of any post-Revolutionary American polity, particularly the one to be created by the newly drafted Constitution. Madison went so far as to offer a rather baleful reflection on the medium of language itself. To all the difficulties of drafting a constitution, Madison remarked,

> the medium through which the conceptions of men are conveyed to each other adds a fresh embarrassment. The use of words is to express ideas. Perspicuity, therefore, requires not only that the ideas should be distinctly formed, but that they should be expressed by words distinctly and exclusively appropriate to them. But no language is so copious as to supply words and phrases for every complex idea, or so correct as not to include

many equivocally denoting different ideas. Hence it must happen that however accurately objects may be discriminated in themselves, . . . the definition of them may be rendered inaccurate by the inaccuracy of the terms in which it is delivered.

Moreover, Madison added, "this unavoidable inaccuracy must be greater or less, according to the complexity and novelty of the objects defined." The "objects" with which the new Constitution abounded—the idea of a federal union, of the sovereignty of the people, of an extended republic, and the rest—were quite obviously both complex and novel; and no language, however perfect, could capture and convey their full meaning and import. Every language was at best, Madison concluded, a "cloudy medium."[5] On this much, at least, Federalists and Antifederalists could readily agree. Practical men of affairs they surely were, but they were also inhabitants of a sophisticated rhetorical and theatrical culture.

Add to this shared sensitivity both the obviously high stakes and the shortness of the time available to the participants to argue their cases publicly and persuasively, and one has the conditions under which profound political and conceptual changes can occur with almost unheard-of rapidity. Taken together, these conditions produced, almost overnight, a veritable flood of newspaper articles, broadsides, sermons, and pamphlets, some of which even today retain their sense of urgency and some measure of their persuasive power.[6] Although *The Federalist Papers* are usually cited as the premier example, many of the Antifederalist pamphlets were not lacking in rhetorical and argumentative powers of their own.[7]

Federalist and Antifederalist arguments centered not only upon the substance of their differences but also upon the very vocabularies in which their disagreements might be most suitably described and adjudicated. Both, for example, professed to favor a representative republican form of government; but each had rather different understandings of "representation" and "republic." Both, moreover, believed public "virtue" to be important, indeed indispensable; but each entertained different conceptions of civic virtue and had rather different views about where virtue might best be located. Should virtue reside in the individual citizen, as many Antifederalists maintained; or should civic virtue be built, as it were, into the system of government itself, as the Federalists insisted? Did institutions instill virtue into citizens or merely discipline their lack of it? And what of "representation"? Was it to be "actual" or merely "virtual"? Clearly, the answers that one gave to these and a host of other questions depended upon the choice, or the modification, of the particular political idiom in which one chose to think and speak and act.

Thus, theirs was not and could not have been what some might now wish to call a "semantic" squabble over the meaning of words—as though "words" scarcely matter or can mean anything one wishes them to mean. On the contrary, theirs was in no small part a *conceptual* dispute about the way in which American political life was to be constituted, lived, and justified. The upshot of this debate was that citizens of the fledgling republic ceased to speak a provincial variation of political English and began to speak in the terms of a political idiom that was distinctly and recognizably American.

II

Our common aim in this volume is to return to the political site at which these changes were wrought and this new language was created. We want, in particular, to examine two interrelated phenomena. First, we want to understand in a more general way the theoretical relationships between political (re)conceptualization and political change. Second, and more specifically, we seek to examine the particular changes in meaning that certain key concepts underwent during the debates in speech and writing, as well as the processes of drafting, amending, and ratifying that attended the creation and acceptance of the new United States Constitution of 1787–89. Or put another way, we want to analyze both the mechanisms of conceptual change and the ways in which the meanings of particular concepts changed during one particular period.

The first of these two tasks is undertaken by James Farr, who also attempts to clear a theoretical path for the detailed conceptual histories that follow. Farr contends that political debates disclose contradictions in the way in which (or the criteria according to which) concepts are employed. Criticism—that is, the discovery and public disclosure of such contradictions—then puts pressure on the participants to revise the meaning of the concepts in question (and/or the criteria of their application) in some supposedly noncontradictory direction. Such Socratic (or if you prefer, Popperian) rationality is rarely if ever realized in practice, because what is or is not contradictory is itself often in dispute.[8] Often, but not always; for otherwise the very point of our having at our disposal the concept of contradiction, as well as the sting attending the charge that one is contradicting oneself, would wholly disappear. Within the give-and-take of political discourse, the charge of contradictoriness retains its sting and its ability to shift the onus of argument. The critic's exposure of contradictions, Farr concludes, is the main, though not the only, means by which conceptual change occurs.

Political discourse is constituted not only by concepts and the kinds of statements and assertions that they make possible but also—and arguably, even more deeply—by the imagery that gives these concepts their place and point. This dependence is clearly evident, as Gerald Stourzh shows, in the evolution of the concept of "constitution." Given the older imagery of a body politic, the concept of its constitution was understood mainly, if not exclusively, in physical or medical terms (compare our still-intelligible paeans to someone's strong and healthy constitution—even though the reference in late-twentieth-century America is almost invariably to strong, healthy, and often narcissistic individuals, rather than to whole societies). Stourzh shows how and under what conditions the concept of constitution ceased to rely upon bodily imagery and came to refer, instead, to the sort of written document that is capable of establishing the political structure and the fundamental law of a state or nation. Stourzh traces the conceptual changes that made it possible for the Founders to conceive of a constitution in the way that they did and as we now do.

The concept of constitution is implicated in a network of other concepts, among the more central of which are "state" (in its more-or-less modern sense) and "union," or, more specifically still, "federal union." The question was often asked, How could the new Constitution bring into being a federated union of free and independent states? The query was at once political and conceptual. It could be asked and answered only if certain conceptual changes could be brought about. In the third essay in this volume, J. G. A. Pocock charts the changes that had to come about before such now-commonplace expressions as "federal republic" and "united states" could be rendered intelligible and meaningful. Where Stourzh focuses on "constitution," Pocock directs his attention to "federal" and "federative" and suggests that not only the structure of civil society but also the relations between civil societies were involved in the debate.

The concept of sovereignty, as Peter S. Onuf notes, remained an exceedingly problematic one. Under the Articles of Confederation the thirteen states had, for all practical purposes, retained their individual sovereignty. Antifederalists suspected, not without reason, that the Federalists wished to establish a national government that would effectively end the sovereign power of the states, transferring it to the central government. The original intent of the Founders aside, it became clear during the course of the framing—and clearer still during the ratification debate—that the states would never surrender every last remnant of their sovereignty. Onuf examines the ingenious rhetorical twists by means of which the Federalists disarmed their critics by defending the new design as necessary to the maintenance of state sovereignty. But in being defended in this unexpected and novel way, the concept of sovereignty—along with such allied concepts as "state" and "union"—took on a new and distinctively American meaning.

The theoretical and rhetorical weaponry employed in these politi-cal-cum-conceptual battles came from a variety of sources. One of the more surprising of these, as Garry Wills maintains, was Jean Jacques Rousseau, the "theoretic politician" *par excellence.*[9] The Pennsylvania Federalist James Wilson found in Rousseau a new notion of sovereignty, that of an essentially inalienable "popular sovereignty," to replace the older monarchical conception. In that older view, the people could not be sovereign but were, at best, a body crying for a head—that is, a sovereign. Clearly, this concept of sovereignty was singularly ill suited for service in republican discourse. Rousseau's genius lay in his having turned the tables on the absolutist-monarchist understanding of sovereignty by envisioning the people—as citizens, as subjects, and as individual selves—exercising sovereignty over themselves. And Wilson's genius, according to Wills, resided in his borrowing and amending this new Rousseauan-republican understanding of sovereignty to explicate the nature of the new American republic.

Another idiom in which Federalist authors defended the new design, Daniel Walker Howe tells us, was that of eighteenth-century faculty psychology. The view of human nature underlying and linking the arguments presented by Publius in *The Federalist Papers* derives from a more-or-less-coherent model of the various powers, or "faculties," possessed by human beings. These include not only the faculties of speech and reason but the potentially destructive emotions and affections as well. Just as a properly ordered individual constitution is one in which the tendencies toward self-destruction are kept in check, so, too, a rightly ordered public constitution would use the body politic's powers to check and control one another. Ambition, for example, must be made to counter ambition. By looking more closely at the concepts and categories of the language of faculty psychology, we see the rhetorical workings of *The Federalist* in a newer and arguably more illuminating light.

Among the concepts whose meaning was disputed during the ratification debate, none, as Terence Ball notes, was more hotly contested than "republic" and its cognates "republican" and "republicanism." Federalists maintained that the new constitution would create an extended republic; their Antifederalist rivals contended that the very concept of an extended republic was a veritable contradiction in terms. What was actually happening, Ball argues, was that several of the concepts constitutive of American political discourse were being disputed and changed during the course of the ratification controversy. Besides looking at the issue of size (can a large republic really *be* a republic?), he examines the Federalists' and Antifederalists' differing understandings of "representation" and "virtue" and concludes with some reflections on the increasingly "linguistic" turn taken by the protagonists themselves as the debate wore on.

Addressing another dimension of the dispute over who had proper title to the term "republican," Russell L. Hanson suggests that two quite distinct interpretations of republicanism coexisted uneasily in American politics during the late eighteenth century. One relied on "democratic" methods of popular control to limit the powers of government; the other, on constitutional mechanisms to reduce popular influence on government. Both claimed the mantle of republicanism. It was the struggle between these two interpretations of republicanism, Hanson contends, that defined the principal axis of political disputation during the Founding Era.

No concept is more central to republican discourse than is "virtue." In the concluding essay, Lance Banning critically reexamines a stock piece of conventional wisdom. It has often been held that James Madison and his fellow Federalists proposed to construct a new kind of republic, one in which civic virtue would occupy only a peripheral place. The older republican ideal of a virtuous and vigilant citizenry that would keep corruption at bay was to be replaced by the more pragmatic vision of a polity that would be kept vital and vigorous by individual ambition and contending group interests. And yet, as Banning notes, Madison— the author of those twin exemplars of hard-headed realism, *Federalist* numbers 10 and 51—quite clearly continued to insist upon the indispensability of virtue. The contradiction, Banning concludes, is more apparent than real, for Madison was relying upon what one might almost term a postrepublican understanding of "virtue." Madison believed that even in a well-designed polity, the few, at least, must remain virtuous and public-spirited, even if the many might not be counted upon to be so or to remain so for very long. Without that saving remnant, the vices most feared by earlier republican thinkers would reassert themselves, and corruption would descend upon the land.

III

The vocabulary in which we debate contemporary issues is descended but is very different from the idioms in which the Founders spoke and argued and, on occasion, agreed. Conceptual change is a more-or-less-continuous process, and time has hardly stood still since the Founding. This might seem merely an academic point, of some minor historiographical interest perhaps but utterly devoid of political import. A moment's reflection, however, reveals that this is not so. Consider, by way of illustration, only one of many ways in which questions about conceptual change are themselves important and highly charged political questions.

There is currently a call from some quarters for a return to a "strict construction" of the "original intentions" of the authors of the Constitution. This directs attention to some problems that are well known to historians of discourse and of jurisprudence in particular; and as historians and theorists of conceptual change, we would like to make a few observations on the matter. It is sometimes asked whether historical inquiry can recapture the "original intentions" of the author or authors of any text; the answer is that it can pursue them to great effect but rarely with finality. The reason is that utterances derive their meanings from the contexts in which they are made. These are contexts of language, of action, and of relevance; and any actor in history inhabits a number of such contexts at the same time. Consequently, he knows that his utterance is capable of bearing a number of meanings, and the act of intentionally imparting a certain meaning to it is an act of choosing and directing the context in which it is to be interpreted. Each of us, in uttering a statement, seeks to direct the manner in which it is to be understood, enjoining some ways of reading it and excluding others; but none of us possesses final or absolute authority over those who are to interpret or accept it.

The authors and ratifiers of the Constitution achieved highly authoritative utterance; they left to posterity a strongly worded text, containing equally strong indications of how it was to be interpreted; and to that extent, historians and jurists can pursue the "original intentions" of the text's authors with high hopes of agreeing on explicit statements about them. But these statements cannot be made incontestable; there may be legitimate debate between alternative readings of the text and its intentions. When this happens, the attempt to go behind the printed word, in search of the "intentions" that it communicates, may entail a debate between alternative readings and between alternative contexts in which the text is to be read. Alternatives of the latter kind may be of equal legitimacy, in the sense that the authors, as historical actors, may be seen to have inhabited and responded to several such "contexts" at the same time and may not have left or desired to leave any plain indications that they were to be read in one way and not in another. Language is ambivalent, and it is often important to keep it that way. It may happen, therefore, that the historian will be found pointing out that the authors of the Constitution expressed more than one set of "original intentions" and did not determine finally between them. When this happens, the decision to follow one reading instead of another is a judicial decision, rather than a historical statement. It is a decision to privilege one context of interpretation above another, to ascribe authority to one set of "original intentions" instead of another. Such a decision is normal and proper in jurists, whose business is to search for authoritative statements and for ways of ascribing authority to statements; but there are limits to their ability to claim the authority of history for what they pronounce, because the point must be reached at which the historian is no longer their partner in the search for authority. After that point, jurists are on their own, although they may still seek and find allies.

It can also be pointed out that to the extent to which we may be able to validate a series of statements about the "original intentions" of the authors of the Constitution, these intentions will prove to have been formulated in historicized contexts belonging to the late eighteenth century. Clearly, this does not prevent the text of the Constitution or the intentions that it embodies from retaining and exercising authority in the late twentieth century; the Constitution is one of those texts that continue to exercise authority and to display considerable continuity of meaning over long periods of time. Indeed, at least one of the authors in this volume argues that the Constitution expresses principles of early modern politics in early modern language (republican constitutionalism, the separation of powers) and is none the worse for that as a document governing a modern or postmodern society; indeed, if anything, it helps the United States maintain high levels of liberty and legitimacy, which were concerns of early modern politics.

But the more we "contextualize" the text—going behind it in search of the "original intentions" that it embodies—the more we shall find that the Founders were inhabiting eighteenth-century contexts and were thinking in eighteenth-century terms. We shall at the same time be made aware that processes of conceptual change and consequent interpretation have occurred, by means of which eighteenth-century language has acquired twentieth-century meanings (the Second Amendment offers an obvious example). Given that interpretation of the text has gone, is going, and must continue to go on, the call for a jurisprudence of original intent cannot be a call for the abolition of interpretation; it must, rather, be a call for interpretation to be conducted according to certain rules. Let us consider a historical analogy that may help in discerning what these rules might be.

The analogy is that of the succession of "Bartolists," "grammarians," and "Neo-Bartolists" in the civil jurisprudence of the sixteenth century. The Bartolists had evolved an elaborate technique for applying the rules of Roman law to the judicial problems of late-medieval Europe; but this was in turn challenged by the Renaissance grammarians, who with the aid of advances in classical philology claimed to be able to restore Roman law to its original Roman meanings.

Initially, they claimed that these original meanings would possess authority, enhancing that of the law, in the Europe of their own times; but it was found on further inspection that these original meanings often presupposed historically remote contexts, those of imperial or republican Rome, which no longer obtained. There was a perceived danger that Roman law might recede into history and cease to be of any practical value. The solution that the Neo-Bartolists proposed was that after philological reconstitution had done its work, the enterprise of applying Roman law to modern conditions could be resumed, informed by a far more sophisticated awareness of what it entailed. Jurists would not become historians; but history would inform them about the conditions under which the law had once possessed meaning, of the difference between those conditions and those under which he was himself practicing, and of the changes in the interpretation of the law which he must apply in order to continue using its language in rendering decisions.

This increase in historical awareness would, for any lawyer, have one plainly conservative practical consequence. The former state of the law would retain authority even as it was being shown to be obsolete. The presumptions would be in its favor, and good reasons would have to be given for changing received interpretation. Certainly, the better its obsolescence was understood and could be stated, the better equipped jurists would be to give reasons for changing their interpretations. But at the same time and with no less force, the better they understood the conditions under which the law had formerly been valid, the better would be the chances that some of these conditions would persist or might be restated at the present time and the better the reasons for changing its interpretation would have to be. The tensions between text and interpreter were simply being reformulated at a new level of sophistication, and the historical exposition of the law was being proved compatible with the character of judicial activity as a search for rules that was itself governed by rules, which is the constant pursuit of any jurist.

This analogy enables us to present the call for a "jurisprudence of original intentions" as a straightforward conservative strategy. By knowing more about the Founders' intentions, one proposes to privilege them and so to demand a highly detailed and disciplined statement of the reasons for setting aside any reading of a constitutional provision that historical inquiry may be able to present as intended by the Founders. One does not, because this cannot be done, propose to render it impossible to set aside "original intentions"; one proposes only to make this more difficult. We will not attempt to determine whether such a conservative strategy is called for in the present state of American jurisprudence. We will confine ourselves to pointing out that a jurisprudence based on historical inquiry is in two senses a double-edged weapon. More than one reconstruction of "original intentions" may be possible, and the historian may decline to help the jurist choose between them. And the information that renders it more difficult to depart from a received interpretation may render the decision to do so, once it has been taken, more authoritative and dynamic—even more revolutionary—than it would have been without this heightened awareness of history. Perhaps this is part of the history of constitutional debate, at Philadelphia and subsequently.

The call for Supreme Court justices, if not for the rest of us, to return to the thoughts and intentions of the Founders would require that one recover and return to the vocabulary in which those thoughts and intentions were framed in the first place. It would mean, in short, that the law of the land would perforce be couched in a language that we no longer speak. The language of the law would, that is, be sundered from the language of the marketplace and from the language of morality and politics in which we talk and think about and act upon matters of common concern.

Even if it could succeed, which seems highly unlikely, the result of any Canute-like attempt to turn back the tide of linguistic and conceptual change would doubtless be to render the language of the law largely irrelevant to the cares and concerns that the law and the courts have traditionally attempted to address and adjudicate. Discourse about justice would be about as meaningful to most Americans as the Latin mass is (or rather was) to many Catholics. It would have a hollow ritualistic ring, of some comfort to the faithful perhaps but of little legal or practical value for the perplexed and troubled people who take their cases to court. Thus, in these and in other ways, the doctrine of Original Intent flies in the face of much of what we know about the phenomenon of conceptual change.

As this single illustration suggests, older political vocabularies are difficult to recover, although doing so is the job of the political theorist and the conceptual historian; but they are almost impossible to resurrect and revitalize. Politically speaking, the moral may be that earlier political languages are better studied and appreciated than revived. Such studious appreciation is our common aim in the ensuing essays.

NOTES

1. On the connection between political innovation and conceptual change see Quentin Skinner, "Language and Political Change," and James Farr, "Understanding Conceptual Change Politically"—both in *Political Innovation and*

Conceptual Change, ed. Terence Ball, James Farr, and Russell L. Hanson (Cambridge, Eng.: Cambridge University Press, 1988); J. G. A. Pocock, "The Concept of a Language and the *Métier d'historien:* Some Considerations on Practice," in *The Languages of Political Theory in Early Modern Europe,* ed. Anthony Pagden (Cambridge, Eng.: Cambridge University Press, 1987); and Terence Ball, *Transforming Political Discourse* (Oxford, Eng.: Basil Blackwell, 1988).

2. See, e.g., Alasdair MacIntyre, "The Essential Contestability of Some Social Concepts," *Ethics* 84 (Oct. 1973): 1–9; and William E. Connolly, *The Terms of Political Discourse,* 2d ed. (Princeton, N.J.: Princeton University Press, 1983).

3. See Clifford Geertz, "Ideology as a Cultural System," in his *The Interpretation of Cultures* (New York: Basic Books, 1973); and James Boyd White, *When Words Lose Their Meaning: Constitutions and Reconstitutions of Language, Character, and Community* (Chicago: University of Chicago Press, 1984).

4. In *The Complete Anti-Federalist,* ed. Herbert J. Storing, 7 vols. (Chicago: University of Chicago Press, 1981), vol. 4, sec. 3.7, p. 21.

5. James Madison, *Federalist* no. 37, in *The Federalist Papers,* ed. Garry Wills (New York: Bantam Books, 1982), pp. 179–80.

6. For a generous sampling of the pamphlet and other literatures see *American Political Writings during the Founding Era, 1760–1805,* ed. Charles S. Hyneman and Donald S. Lutz (Indianapolis, Ind.: Liberty Press, 1983); and the gargantuan *The Founders' Constitution,* ed. Philip B. Kurland and Ralph Lerner, 5 vols. (Chicago: University of Chicago Press, 1987).

7. See Storing, *The Complete Anti-Federalist.*

8. Except, perhaps, in the clearly counterfactual "ideal speech situation" imagined by Jürgen Habermas, in which all participants recognize and are guided solely by "the forceless force of the better argument" (see "Wahreitstheorien," in *Wirklichkeit und Reflexion* [Pfullingen, W. Ger.: Neske, 1973], p. 239).

9. Madison, *Federalist* no. 10, p. 46.

2

Conceptual Change and Constitutional Innovation

James Farr

I

In *Federalist* number 37, James Madison set himself the task of conducting "a more critical and thorough survey of the work of the Convention." Clever rhetorician that he was, he pretended not to have been in attendance and claimed only to be addressing those honest readers who would admit that a "faultless plan was not to be expected." Madison then warmed to his topic and played upon his readers' sympathy by listing a number of the "difficulties" that the Philadelphia Convention had faced the preceding summer when drafting the Constitution.[1] Some were straightforwardly political. "A very important one must have lain, in combining the requisite stability and energy in Government, with the inviolable attention due to liberty, and to the Republican form." The difficulty of such combining was attended by another, that of "marking the proper line of partition, between the authority of the general, and that of the State Governments." And these difficulties were attended by yet others of a different sort; among them Madison included the delegates' shared recognition of the sheer "novelty of the undertaking" and the difficulty of adequately expressing this novelty in language, because "the medium through which the conceptions of men are conveyed to each other, adds a fresh embarrassment." "No language," he went on, "is so copious as to supply words and phrases for every complex idea, or so correct as not to include many equivocally denoting different ideas." This, Madison averred, is an "unavoidable difficulty" rendered all the "greater . . . according to the complexity and novelty of the objects defined." The linguistic difficulties and embarrassments faced by the Framers, moreover, could have not have been alleviated by gazing—or rather listening—heavenward. "When the Almighty himself condescends to address mankind in their own language, his meaning, luminous as it must be, is rendered dim and doubtful, by the cloudy medium through which it is communicated."

In this bicentennial year, *Federalist* number 37 merits our attention not only as an artifact of the ratification debates but also as a continuing reminder of how deeply rooted in language are many problems of politics and of how thoroughly political are many problems of language. Indeed, in trying to understand the Constitution and the innovations it enacted two hundred years ago, we find in documents such as *Federalist* number 37 a point of departure for considering a problem of heightened contemporary interest: the problem of conceptual change and political innovation.[2] This problem is one of special concern for those political theorists who espy a strong connection between language and politics, as well as for those historians who understand history to include the transformative powers of political theory and who further understand the history of political theory to be nothing other than "the history of change in the self-conceptualization of political societies."[3] Putting these concerns together, we might say that the attempt to theorize politically about conceptual change—to explain why and how conceptual change comes about amidst political innovation—in part turns on the attempt to capture in general terms what historians often do in particular terms when they trace changes in language and political life.

The theoretical and historical enterprises, in short, jointly converge on the problem of understanding the *mechanisms* of conceptual change and political innovation—to use language that our eighteenth-century Newtonians would have well understood, given their machines, engines, and mechanical principles.[4] I want to suggest that those mechanisms are triggered, as it were, by *contradictions* and the criticism of them. Conceptual change is one very imaginative consequence of political actors, in concert or in conflict, criticizing and attempting to resolve the contradictions that they either discover or generate in the complex web of their beliefs, actions, and practices as they try to understand and change the world around them.

This perspective would not have been alien to the Founders themselves. Reminding the "writers on the other side" of the failures of the Articles of Confederation, Alexander Hamilton said: "Let us not attempt to reconcile contradictions, but firmly embrace a rational alternative."[5] The alternative to which Hamilton referred was, of course, the Constitution and the authority that it granted to the central government in an extended, compound federal republic. But this political alternative, soon to be realized, already presupposed a novel reconceptualization of the nature of authority and of republican government itself—a reconceptualization to which he was party and was then in the process of popularizing. Constitutional innovation partly depended, in short, on conceptual change. Changes in the concepts that constitute American political thought and discourse—such as "republic," "constitution," "constituent power," "sovereignty," and "federalism"—marked, then, no mere semantic busyness in and around 1787. They were essential to the actual, practical constitutional changes that were then under way and under dispute.

The language of the Constitution and its enactment as fundamental law provide, then, a dramatic example of a more general understanding of conceptual change and political innovation. The language of the Constitution must be understood to cover not only, or even mainly, the words of the document but also the debates between Federalists and Antifederalists over its composition and ratification, as well as the broader language of political argument from which these debates drew their fiery breath. Dates are more easily fixed here than in other areas of historical inquiry, though one could choose differently, say from 1781 to 1787 or from 1776 to 1789 or from 1774 to 1800. There is also not just one language, but several; and these operate at different levels, not all of them consistent. Conceptual fissures and fault lines ran everywhere. Here is but one source for contradiction and change.

Let me begin by looking at some of the relationships between language and politics that should incline us at the very outset to deem that the question of conceptual change is a political one. Before the end of this chapter, I hope to forestall certain misunderstandings that might arise on this score; to canvass briefly the profound conceptual changes that occurred in and around 1787; to analyze contradictions and the criticism of them in somewhat general terms; and to make this analysis concrete with the help of contemporary historians and the Founders themselves. In this way, I hope, we may continue to have a conversation with our constitutional past, as the bicentennial extravaganzas roar around us.

II

Politics as we know it would not only be indescribable without language; it would be impossible. New nations could not declare independence, legislators could not promulgate laws, courts could not sentence criminals, leaders could not instruct partisans, citizens could not protest against war and standing armies. Neither could we criticize, plead, promise, argue, exhort, demand, negotiate, bargain, compromise, counsel, brief, debrief, advise, or consent. To imagine politics without these linguistic actions would be to imagine no recognizable politics at all. At best, there would be silence; at worst, a politics rather like Hobbes's war of all against all—missing only its taunts and insults.

Few would wish to take exception to this characterization of the impossibility of politics without language. The Founders, whether Federalist or Antifederalist, certainly did not. However, the general view of language that most of them espoused seemed inadequate to express why. Consider, for example, that in *Federalist* number 37, Madison gave vent to the widely held Lockean and Humean view that "words . . . express ideas," and he implied there and elsewhere that ideas in turn function to describe or to refer to things. Such a purely descriptive view of language and meaning fails to capture the political and rhetorical activity that language makes possible. This is somewhat ironic, because Madison and everyone else were then very heatedly engaged in just this sort of rhetorical activity. The later Federalist Thomas G. Fessenden came somewhat closer to the mark when he said that linguistic partisans of his sort "believe . . . that 'words are things.' If false, they give a wrong direction to the public mind, and of consequence to the physical powers of the community."[6] But words, as we now better appreciate in the wake of philosophy's linguistic turn, are not things. Their functions are not merely or even mainly descriptive or referential. And indeed, to reverse Madison's order, ideas express words.

For political theorists and historians of the Constitutional era, the discussion of language can and should be recast in order to accent what we might call its *activating* and *constituting* dimensions. First, language should be seen as an arena of usage in and through which political actions are undertaken, above and beyond the activity of describing or referring. In speech, pamphlets, and treatises, political actors struggle to realize strategic or partisan ends of some kind by playing or preying upon the needs, interests, and powers of one another. For example, in signing the Declaration of Independence, the signatories obviously declared but did not describe independence. And through their declaration they performed still-other political actions. They warned Britain about armed resistance and sought to inspire American colonists to change their very identities and so forge "one people."[7] Eleven years, several state constitutions, and numerous civil disturbances later, the Framers of the Constitution did not so much describe a new set of institutions (though they did that as well). They constituted and created it (or at least expressed an intent to do so). Should the Constitution weather the fight over ratification, it would further act, as Federalists hoped and Antifederalists feared, to suppress the "excess of democracy," facilitate the expansion of a "commercial republic," and much else besides.[8] Here, then, to adapt J. L. Austin's apt phrase, is an object lesson in how to do constitutional things with words.[9]

Political actions of this sort—those, that is, that happen in and through the use of language—presuppose shared understandings among political actors, understandings that are deeply embedded in social and political practices. Among other things, this presupposes shared agreements—when, of course, there *are* shared agreements— about the use of political words and concepts.[10] This implies agreement about (1) the criteria for applying political concepts—their sense; (2) the range of things to which these concepts refer in the political world—their reference; and (3) the range of attitudes that these concepts express— their attitudinal expressiveness.[11] For example, for the Declaration to realize the actions that its signatories intended, there had to be (at a minimum and without guarantees of ultimate success) a large measure of agreement between authors and readers that certain usurpations and abuses would amount to calling some policies "tyrannical"; that George III's policies were indeed "tyrannical"; and that calling them "tyrannical" was to condemn them and to commend actions to resist them. For the Constitution to realize the actions that the Framers intended, there had to be (at a minimum and without guarantees of ultimate success) a large measure of agreement between authors and readers that certain forms of collective self-governance and certain individual rights against government itself amounted to "liberty"; that the proposed instrument of government referred to these forms and rights of "liberty"; and that "liberty" was a blessing deserving of the highest commendation. It had been hard won by the blood of patriots and it required, then and forever, that the citizens be constantly vigilant for its protection. For Antifederalist writers to even begin to realize their actions (again at a minimum and obviously without any guarantees of success), there had to be a large measure of agreement between them and their readers that certain (new) forms of wealth and privilege amounted to an "aristocracy"; that the Federalists indeed intended to form and that they themselves composed an "aristocracy"; and that calling them partisans of an "aristocracy" was to condemn them and to commend actions resisting the ratification of the Constitution. That the Federalists well understood the meaning and the full sting of this attribution is attested to by their heated denials of it and by their frequent attempts to sound more oriented to "the people" than did their opponents, whom they characterized as narrow-minded spokesmen for local interest. Everyone understood the stakes of the conflict, for they were in essential agreement on the meaning of fundamental concepts: that is, on their sense, reference, and attitudinal expressiveness.

This point about shared agreements even amidst conflict has its converse as well. To appreciate this, we might introduce the other dimension of language that the very notion of shared understandings invites. Political concepts—among them "tyranny," "liberty," and "aristocracy"—partly *constitute*, and so make possible, the beliefs of political actors. That is to say, just as certain rules constitute certain games, in that without these rules, certain games cannot possibly be played,[12] so, too, do certain concepts constitute certain beliefs, in that without these concepts, certain beliefs cannot possibly be held. Beliefs, in turn, constitute certain practices, in that without these beliefs, certain political practices cannot be undertaken or preserved. (Beliefs are particularly important here, for they mediate between the concepts in language, on the one hand, and the practices of politics, on the other. This proves to be important when discussing contradictions and change.) For example, how revolutionaries will respond to the standing government will depend upon their shared beliefs about what practices the revolution requires. And these beliefs are partly composed of a number of concepts, principal among them being the concept of "revolution" itself.[13] Some practices will be believed to be "revolutionary"; others, "reformist"; still others, "counterrevolutionary." Shared agreements are here necessary. Of course, different revolutionaries at the same, much less at another time, may disagree and hold fundamentally different beliefs about these practices. (Compare the Patriots of 1776 with the Jacobins, and think of the difficulties that this posed for many Americans, Thomas Paine foremost amongst them. And then broaden the horizon to include the Whigs of 1689, the Bolsheviks, and the Iranian Republicans.) These differences express themselves as differences over the concept of "revolution," among others. Thus the concepts in language provide for agreement or disagreement, for unity or conflict.

Similar things may be said about republicans, federalists, constitutionalists, or even educators and scientists. Their practices depend upon—that is, are partly constituted by—their beliefs; and these beliefs depend upon—that is, are partly constituted by—their concepts, among them most pointedly the very concepts that pick out these practices, here "republican," "constitutionalist," "federalist," "education," and "science." By now it should be clear that there must be shared agreements about these concepts if relevant beliefs and practices are to exist. It should also be clear that these concepts and therefore the relevant beliefs and practices might be contested or might occasion conflict. One need only consider, for example, the case of Loyalists versus Patriots on what a "constitution" is and what "constitutional" government requires; or Federalists versus Antifederalists on what a "republic" is and what "republican" practices require.

III

Speaking, as I have, about the conceptual "constitution" of political beliefs and practices might seem to be a rather poor pun on the occasion of the bicentennial. Worse still, it might seem to some either to subscribe to a kind of linguistic determinism or to prejudge an answer to a question about the causal role of economic interests or to underwrite the utterly naïve strategy of believing everything that historical actors have said about themselves. None of these need be entailed by what I have written so far.

First, no pun is intended, because the notion of conceptual constitution has been frequently employed in philosophical discussion in our time by Charles Taylor, Alasdair MacIntyre, and others.[14] This had its origins in the distinction between constitutive and regulative rules. I do not know why the image of "constitution" was appropriate for this distinction in the first place, although related distinctions and images have been staples of continental philosophy since Immanuel Kant. It is not inconceivable that Kant's philosophical use of the notion of "constitution" was prompted in part by the constitutional craze and the rush of political events during the late eighteenth century. It would be an ironic, though exceedingly interesting, circuit if the United States Constitution, among other things, was formative in Kant's philosophical imagination, an imagination that now helps us better understand the constitutive relationship of language to politics, including the language and politics of the United States Constitution. "Constitution" awaits its history to see this matter through.[15]

Second, no linguistic determinism lurks here.[16] Determinism in its various forms turns on causality; but a constitutive relationship is one of possibility: of a rule that makes a game possible, of a concept that makes a belief possible. Furthermore, the causal relationships that are of concern to us as political theorists and historians are hardly ever law-governed, much less preordained. Still, when we ascribe causality in the context of historical and political explanation, it is usually, if not always, between two or more conceptually constituted beliefs, actions, or practices. Consider the extremely complex web of concepts that is required for both actors and historians in order to forward the causal claim that "Shays' rebellion caused the calling of the Philadelphia Convention," quite apart from the question of whether this causal claim is true or false, much less whether it is the whole story. Neither *explanans* nor *explanandum* is a brute event. Both compress very complex sets of beliefs, actions, and practices that are conceptually constituted. The question of causality is not prejudiced either towards "ideology" or so-called material events, as it were, when one attends to the constituting dimensions of language.

Nor does the picture change if we come to consider the role of economic interests. For present purposes we may waive any objection to a general theory that insists that economic interests can appropriately be introduced in *all* explanatory contexts, particularly perhaps in those concerning the Constitution.[17] Quite simply, economic interests are themselves conceptually constituted. Take the relatively simple causal claim that "interests in commercial property caused the Federalists to compose and campaign for the ratification of the republican Constitution." This claim requires an enormously complex set of concepts for both Federalists (to have been able to have had the interests in the first place) and historians (to be able to explain actions as a consequence of these interests). These concepts include what rhetorical and political practices a "constitution" required and what comprised "property" in and among mercantile, agrarian, and slave-owning states on the eve of consolidation into a "commercial republic." And all of this is so quite apart from the question of whether the causal claim is true or false, much less of whether it is the whole story. In short, the question of causality *cuts across* the question of the conceptual constitution of economic interest or other sorts of belief. These questions do not collapse one into the other.

Interests are interesting, moreover, in that they are often not expressed publicly: they are "hidden" or are "behind" what is going on. It is important to note that the time-honored practice of public dissimulation is an act that is carried on in and through language. It may be a perennial favorite of politicians, but it is no less a language game, for all of that (and its success depends upon a mastery of the public language, even of a changing public language).[18] In any case, dissimulating to cover up one's real economic interests requires a very complex web of beliefs and practices that are themselves conceptually constituted. To posit that economic interests are "behind" what is going on requires, not less conceptual work, but more. We must be able to articulate the distinctions between the linguistic practices spoken in public and the hidden language of private interest, as it were. And we must be able to specify those concepts that constitute unspoken private interests from those that constitute public discourse and rhetorical practices in any particular era.

None of this would need to be mentioned if some historians and political theorists did not think that attention to language commits us to some naïve methodological strategy: namely, believing everything that actors say about their practices and beliefs. Saying so does not make it so, and what is *said* by political actors is neither all that can be said nor what may actually be believed or intended by them. Nothing that I have said about the activating and constituting dimensions of language prejudges these important issues. Nothing that I have said provides abstract rules for determining when we should or should not believe what actors say either. This is a problem of practical judgment and one of considerable moment for historians, especially perhaps for historians of political thought in the commercial era. But I trust that this will not be seen as a liability to the case presented so far, because I doubt that abstract rules of this kind are possible at all, no matter what one's philosophical principles, political prejudices, or economic interests.

IV

Conceptual change attends political change. Revolutions and civil wars—those periods in which the world seems to be turned upside down—reveal this in a particularly dramatic if painful way. For these are often the crises during which, as Thucydides said of the Peloponnesian War, "words lose their meanings."[19] Fearing secession and civil war in the 1850s, Francis Lieber—the author of that nearly forgotten classic of constitutional interpretation *Legal and Political Hermeneutics* (1839) and the first professor of political science in the United States—felt painfully that "what Thucydides said . . . applies to us."[20] "The greatest link and tie of humanity, language, loses its very essence, and people cease to understand one another."[21] The early years of the American Republic had also witnessed the loss of meaning and the corruption of republican discourse. Certainly Rufus King thought so. As a delegate who had repeatedly made observations about language at the Constitutional Convention, King put the point this way a few years later: "Words without meaning or with wrong meaning have especially of late years done great harm. Liberty, Love of Country, Federalism, Republicanism, Democracy, Jacobin, Glory, Philosophy, and Honor are words in the mouths of everyone and used without precision by anyone; the abuse of words is as pernicious as the abuse of things."[22]

But conceptual change need not always be pernicious or an omen of corruption in a world turned upside down. Meaning may be gained, as well as lost, amidst change. To the extent that our concepts constitute the political world, we can say that *conceptual change* attends any *reconstitution* of the political world. In short, our concepts, beliefs, and practices go together and change together. Sometimes these collective changes find expression in new words.[23] It is as if new worlds are being announced. Consider the announcement that newly liberated Americans made about the matter of popular sovereignty in the years between the Revolution and the first state constitutions. As Willi Paul Adams tells it, "the concept underlying the distinction between legislation and constitution-making, that of a fundamental 'constituent power' "—that is to say, the extralegislative power of the sovereign people to frame a constitution by the process of convention and ratification—"was formulated in these years. . . . Americans invented not only the thing, but also the name for it."[24]

Conceptual change, however, need not be signaled only by newly invented names. We find conceptual change whenever we find changes in any of the interrelated features of a concept as outlined above: in its criteria of application, its range of reference, or its attitudinal expressiveness. These changes happen beneath the surface of vocabulary, as it were. Conceptual change, accordingly, varies from wholesale changes across an entire constellation of words and concepts, to more localized changes in the sense, the reference, or the attitudinal expressiveness of a single concept.

As it happens, the Constitutional period in and around 1787—or better still, the last quarter of the eighteenth century—teems with conceptual change amidst political innovation. These changes have been amply documented of late, particularly by historians who have taken what we might call the "ideological turn." Among them we might include Bernard Bailyn, Gordon S. Wood, Gerald Stourzh, J. G. A. Pocock, Michael G. Kammen, John P. Diggins, Forrest McDonald, Willi Paul Adams, Linda K. Kerber, Lance Banning, Garry Wills, Isaac Kramnick, Russell L. Hanson—to begin a long, long list.[25] Despite their many differences, all agree on the magnitude and importance of the conceptual changes and political innovations in the early American Republic. And all would probably consent—amidst other matters of dissent, no doubt—to the way in which Forrest McDonald has recently summarized these changes, at least insofar as the language of classical humanism goes. This was the language, or at least one of the most important languages, that the delegates brought with them to Philadelphia in May 1787. They "departed four months later having fashioned a frame of government that necessitated a redefinition of most of the terms in which the theory and ideology of civic humanism had been discussed. Into the bargain, they introduced an entirely new concept to the discourse, that of federalism, and in the doing, created a *novus ordo seclorum:* a new order of the ages."[26]

Those four months had plenty of momentum behind them: the preceding decade had witnessed an enormous number of changes in concepts and redefinitions of terms. The concepts of "virtue" and "corruption," "tyranny" and "aristocracy," "sovereignty" and "the people," "rights" and "bills of rights"—all had gone through substantial changes.[27] The meaning of "power" had changed, especially in terms of the mechanisms of how it could be "balanced" and "separated.''[28] "Liberty" and "property" had ceased to find invariably natural republican allies in each other.[29] The concept of "constitution" itself had changed. As the unwritten British constitution receded from the patriotic imagination, "constitution" came increasingly to refer to a written document, though more particularly to higher law and natural rights, which a written document embodied and attempted to express. The connection between this changed concept of "constitution" and the subsequent written state constitutions, and at last the United States Constitution itself, suggests the important, if obvious, connections between conceptual change and political innovation.

The ratification debates saw still-further conceptual changes. Those proposing the "novel undertaking" of the Constitution were at the forefront of these changes. Alexander Hamilton had already been well practiced in redefining key terms, such as "democracy" and "republic"—and probably coining others, such as "representative democracy"—when Madison tried his hand with the same set of words and concepts.[30] Complaining in *Federalist* number 14 about the "confusion of names" and in number 39 about the "extreme inaccuracy with which the term [republic] has been used," Madison simply asserted that a "republic" was "a government in which the scheme of representation takes place." "Democracy" thereby became a government of direct self-rule.[31] While this hardly met with universal acceptance, it was still a bold and very self-conscious effort at conceptual change.[32] And this change was accompanied by others that furthered what we might call the mechanization or systemization of "virtue," a process that Montesquieu had started.[33] "Interest" and "commerce" found new meaning and attitudinal expressiveness, freed from their role as antonyms to "virtue." And "commercial republic" no longer sounded like an oxymoron.

V

This scene of conceptual and political restlessness poses a theoretical question: How, if at all, can we explain it? Can we begin to generalize about the mechanisms by which conceptual change occurs amidst political innovation? I believe that the notions of contradiction and criticism can help us take some first steps; that is, conceptual change may be understood as one imaginative consequence of political actors, in concert or in conflict, criticizing and attempting to resolve the contradictions that they either discover or generate in the complex web of their beliefs, actions, and practices, as they try to understand and change the world around them. I am not yet sure how far or how fully this will take us in understanding the overall dynamics of conceptual change, although to date there have not been many attempts to understand conceptual change at all, much less to understand conceptual change politically.[34]

Contradictions form a special class of problems; and the criticism of contradictions and the attempt to overcome them form a special class of attempts to solve problems. The idea of problem solving figures in many contemporary accounts of scientific change, which offer some initial though limited help in understanding conceptual change more generally. Whereas "problem" covers an enormous range of readily solvable difficulties, a "contradiction" implies manifestly *inconsistent* propositions either *within* a theoretical system or *between* a theoretical system and an observational system, so that holding or asserting one proposition implies the denial or negation of another. Contradictory propositions require resolution by eliminating one of two (or more) propositions or by making changes in the theoretical or observational system(s) that generates them in the first place. Karl Popper has elevated this insight into a wholly general and expressly dialectical principle about scientific change: "Without contradictions, there would be no rational motive for changing our theories."[35] Criticism rationally moves science from contradiction to change, including conceptual change. As Popper put it elsewhere, "concepts are partly a means for formulating theories . . . and may always be replaced by other concepts."[36]

Criticism plays an altogether more *political* role in the kinds of contexts that interest us. Criticism—which is itself a political action undertaken in and through language—will not just be directed against the contradictions embedded in abstract theoretical propositions, as in science. (It can be, of course, as in the criticisms lodged against the great political theories; in the Constitutional period, these criticisms were quite important.) Instead, criticism usually will be directed against contradictions that are embedded in or between beliefs, actions, and practices in the political domain—all of which, I argue, are conceptually constituted features of political life. Contradictions may be discovered or generated in any number of concrete ways, but contradictory *beliefs* are central to most of these ways. Beliefs have propositional content, one might say, and thus are not utterly unlike scientific propositions, though they are seldom fully articulated or codified, much less systematically assessed in the way required by the rather more pristine rationality of science, which was never a matter of pure logic, but was always less pristine than the textbooks said.

Contradictions are rarely found in the simultaneous profession of two directly and glaringly incompatible or negating beliefs. Rather, contradictions emerge in the extended implications or unintended consequences of two or more beliefs within a belief system; or they emerge in the confrontation between beliefs and certain actions or practices, including the unintended consequences of those actions or practices; or they emerge in the fault lines between two belief systems that are competing for the allegiance of those who struggle to hold them simultaneously; and so on and so on. The concepts that constitute these various beliefs, belief systems, actions, and practices are thereby implicated in the contradictions. Criticism brings these contradictions to the surface—that is, to the level of reflection and articulation. In the face of contradictions—those that one discovers or those that one is accused of—one feels forced to change. Contradictions may subsequently be resolved by changes in belief or action or practice. But change can also come in one's language and in the concepts that one holds, for these constitute our beliefs, actions, and practices, and so they help make political life what it is. Conceptual change and political innovation will go together.

In this attempt to understand conceptual change politically, I have tried to steer clear from an exclusive dependence on logic and science and thus from a too rationalistic account of contradiction and criticism. But I have also intended to steer clear from any sort of structuralism that claims to discover and criticize contradictions in a political or social structure independently of language or political belief. In the context of the Constitution or of the law more generally, the most problematic of these structuralisms is Critical Legal Studies, at least as given an early methodological formulation by Duncan Kennedy. In a law-review article on "The Structure of Blackstone's Commentaries"—an article in which the "hidden political intentions" of Blackstone are brought to light, "structures" have "motives" attributed to them, and "all [categorical] schemes" for interpreting the law turn out to be "lies"—Kennedy claimed to have unearthed not only structural contradictions (in the plural) but also "*the* Fundamental Contradiction" of all social life—namely, that "relations with others are both necessary to and incompatible with our freedom."[37] The Fundamental Contradiction, therefore, is in the nature of things; it exists irrespective of individuals' beliefs or their experience of it; and it cannot be resolved, not even by Critical Legal Studies.

Plenty of problems are worthy of close scrutiny and criticism here, but for present purposes we need only clarify differences. On the account sketched here, contradictions exist largely between beliefs (including beliefs about social connectedness and individual freedom); and structures (like "practices," a term that I prefer) may be said to be contradictory only to the extent that the beliefs that constitute them are contradictory. Moreover, contradictions between beliefs beget "motion," if you like, but it is a motion of reflection and discourse that tries and often succeeds in propelling us beyond the particular contradiction of its motivation. This suggests—contrary to the claims of Critical Legal Studies—that contradictions are historically contingent and may be resolved. And in resolving them, others doubtless will occur, even in a world of modest change, much less in a world of conceptual and practical turbulence of the sort that 1787 symbolizes.

Some will say, rightly enough, that not all contradictions get resolved. There is in the early American republic, of course, the standing contradiction of slavery. Although slavery actually did motivate some changes in concept, belief, and practice, these differed in various parts of the Union;[38] and overall they hardly amounted to much of an answer to Samuel Johnson's barbed query on the eve of the Revolution: "How is it that we hear the loudest yelps for liberty among the drivers of negroes?"[39] Thus, the example of slavery suggests an important limitation: not all contradictions generate corresponding or uniform efforts to criticize, much less to resolve, them. Indeed it appears to be a fact about the human condition that all of us some of the time and some of us all of the time live with contradictions. This did not trouble Walt Whitman:

> Do I contradict myself?
> Very well then I contradict myself.
> (I am large, I contain multitudes).

However, this does or should trouble political theorists who desire to explain conceptual change in the midst of political innovation. Contradictions figure, at best, as need, not necessity; as determinant, not determinism.[40]

Yet even with this important qualification in mind, the notion of contradiction is essential to a political theory of conceptual change, *especially* in the absence of alternatives. A political theory of conceptual change should also recognize what might at first sight seem to be a paradox, at least when judged by the usual promises or aspirations to generality that attend theories. Its value resides, not in generality as such, but in the *historical understanding* that it makes possible, indeed demands and underwrites. This is so because contradictions must be identified in terms of the concepts of those whose contradictions they were or are. Of necessity, this requires that we locate them in their particular historical contexts and, over time, in the changing historical contexts that follow from the criticism and attempted resolution of them. Thus, *conceptual histories* will be the vehicles for the sort of historical understanding that the study of conceptual and political change demands. They promise to bring out the political importance of conceptual change and the conceptual importance of political change.

VI

We need a number of conceptual histories to see this matter through; and these are either under way or completed, in this volume and elsewhere. But some other encouragement for the political theory that I have been sketching comes from two sources—from historians and from historical actors of the Constitutional era. This is important for methodological reasons, because every political theory—besides hoping to be true—tries to capture what historians do and what historical actors emphasize, as well.

Consider some of the explanatory asides made by historians of the early American republic. Bernard Bailyn unveiled the "striking incongruities and contradictions" that went into the making and changing of "the Revolutionary frame of mind." "In the course of a decade of pounding debate," he went on, "the word 'constitution' and the concept behind it . . . was forced apart, along the seam of a basic ambiguity, to form the two contrasting concepts of constitutionalism that have remained characteristic of England and America ever since."[41] Gordon S. Wood made us see how "the need to institutionalize American experience [in the Constitution] . . . had the effect of accelerating and telescoping intellectual developments and of exposing the ambiguities and contradictions of American thought."[42] J. G. A. Pocock revealed that "the foundation of the republic" constituted "an ambivalent and contradictory moment within a dialectic of virtue and corruption," which was particularly evident in "a flight from modernity."[43] These and other historians *presuppose* a political theory of conceptual change as being triggered by contradictions and criticism when they make such explanatory asides.

Historians such as Bailyn, Wood, and Pocock do not impose their understanding of contradiction and criticism on those whom they study in the Constitutional era. It would be more accurate to say that they discover the rudiments of it as a consequence of sympathizing (to use the methodological advice of Hume and the Scottish Enlightenment) with them.[44] For these historians sympathize with the inhabitants of a contradictory world, to say the least. Contradictions were generated virtually everywhere and in all directions by those who tried to promote country partisanship without a court; to face the disparities between the legal guarantees of the Articles of Confederation and the actual practices between the states; to create a republic in a large extended territory; to reconcile the classical scheme of three forms of government with the modern system of representation; to celebrate Montesquieu and yet follow Hume; to want a balance in constitutional government without a society of estates; to square natural right with constitutional law; to love freedom and support a proslavery Constitution; to desire virtue in a commercial republic of interested men who were prone to faction. These contradictions were generated multifariously; and in resolving some, others emerged. There was, in the nature of the case, the contradiction-generating enterprise of applying English (and/or Continental) concepts, beliefs, and principles to American circumstances. Any belief system as complicated as republicanism, designed to adapt to the fortunes of virtue and corruption, would generate its own internal contradictions, as well as its own resources for change. Moreover, there were still other belief systems competing for American allegiances. Conceptual fissures and fault lines ran everywhere, what with the competing languages of classical humanism, natural and common law, Puritan Calvinism, Lockean radicalism, Enlightenment rationalism, and Scottish political science. These fissures and fault lines exposed many contradictions, and along these lines, conceptual change and political innovation traveled.

The Founders heartily felt and fully understood the pressures posed by these contradictions, just as they knew they had "broken through the conceptions of political theory that had imprisoned men's minds for centuries."[45] Collectively, they themselves pointed out these contradictions. Of course, someone else's contradictions deserved to be mentioned first, and always when in public. This only underscores an obvious point: the language of contradictions is not only a language that one uses to reflect upon and assess one's own beliefs and concepts;[46] rather, like the language of corruption, it is also a language of accusation. This latter sort of language generally dominated the debates that attended the ratification of the Constitution and the various political innovations of the early American republic. Hamilton's repeated charges of "contradiction" were met with nothing less than the same by Centinel, Brutus, and a host of other mock Romans.[47] Into the bargain they threw charges of "solecisms," "the mazes of sophistry," and the "unmeaning sentences" that issued from the "deranged brain of Publius."[48] Accusatory rhetoric notwithstanding, however, charges of contradiction (like those of corruption) often stick. Changes in concepts, beliefs, and practices that are so charged often provide one way out of the contradiction. Conceptual change often follows the criticism of contradictions, whatever the source.

Away from the rhetorical tumults of the public arena, Madison was much less heated and more candid when, in private correspondence with Jefferson, he acknowledged that his own views of "the true principles of Republican Government" were in "contradiction to the current opinions of theoretical writers."[49] Within the year, Madison moved beyond this contradiction, at least in his own mind, by boldly changing the terms that previously had seemed to invite the charge. Representation, he believed, constituted a republic, at least one that was fit for a large territory of diversely interested and potentially factious men. This was a novelty in word amidst the novelties of deed; but it all fit in with "the glory of the people of America," who suffered not a "blind veneration for antiquity . . . or for names."[50] Americans could change their language just as they could change their government and its instrument. Thus "contradictions" both charged the rhetorical atmosphere of debate and informed the quieter chambers of reflection. And they motivated changes in belief and in practice and in the concepts that made these beliefs and practices possible. So it was that most of the Founders were rather more impressed with the critical Hume than they would have been with the overly large Walt Whitman, especially when they found their convictions confirmed in Hume's *Essays:* "The Heart of Man is made to reconcile Contradictions."[51]

NOTES

1. Alexander Hamilton, James Madison, and John Jay, *The Federalist*, ed. Jacob E. Cooke (Middletown, Conn.: Wesleyan University Press, 1961). On the "difficulties" of the convention also see Madison's letter to Jefferson, in Michael Kammen, ed., *The Origins of the American Constitution: A Documentary History* (New York: Penguin, 1986), p. 66.

2. Two projects of major proportions are currently under way in Germany: *Historisches Worterbuch der Philosophie*, ed. Joachim Ritter and Karlfried Grunder (Basel/Stuttgart: Schwabe & Co., 1971–); and *Geschichtliche Grundbegriffe: Historisches Lexicon zur Politisch-Sozialer Sprache in Deutschland*, ed. Otto Brunner, Werner Conze, and Reinhart Kosselleck (Stuttgart: Klett-Cotta, 1972–). For English speakers, Melvin Richter has provided a helpful introduction to these projects in his "Conceptual History [Begriffsgeschichte] and Political Theory," *Political Theory* 14 (1986): 604–37, and in "Begriffsgeschichte and the History of Ideas," *Journal of the History of Ideas* 48 (1987): 247–64. In this connection also see Reinhart Kosselleck, *Futures Past: On the Semantics of Historical Time*, trans. Keith Tribe (Cambridge, Mass.: MIT Press, 1985). There is now also a volume consisting largely of conceptual histories of key concepts in the Anglo-American tradition: see Terence Ball, James Farr, and Russell L. Hanson, eds., *Political Innovation and Conceptual Change* (Cambridge, Eng.: Cambridge University Press, 1988).

3. J. G. A. Pocock, *The Ancient Constitution and the Feudal Law* (New York: W. W. Norton & Co., 1967; first published in 1957), p. 1.

4. Among other places see *Federalist* nos. 7, 9, 14, 15, 16, 19, 22, and 65. This mechanical language was not unique to the Federalists, as can be seen in the Antifederalist writings: see Herbert J. Storing, ed., *The Complete Anti-Federalist* (Chicago: University of Chicago Press, 1981), especially 2.6.24 and 2.7.11.

5. *Federalist* no. 23.

6. Quoted in Linda H. Kerber, *Federalists in Dissent: Imagery and Ideology in Jeffersonian America* (Ithaca, N.Y.: Cornell University Press, 1970), p. 195. Kerber's is an excellent study in rhetoric and imagery. In this connection, especially see chap. 5 on "Concepts of Law and Justice."

7. For discussion of these actions see James Boyd White, *When Words Lose Their Meaning: Constitutions and Reconstitutions in Language, Character, and Community* (Chicago: University of Chicago Press, 1984), chap. 9, esp. p. 239.

8. On this, among others, see Gordon S. Wood, *The Creation of the American Republic, 1776-1787* (Chapel Hill: University of North Carolina Press, 1969), chaps. 12, 13, and 15; and Forrest McDonald, *Novus Ordo Seclorum: The Intellectual Origins of the Constitution* (Lawrence: University Press of Kansas, 1985), esp. chaps. 6-8.

9. J. L. Austin, *How to Do Things with Words* (Cambridge, Mass.: Harvard University Press, 1962).

10. Jay suggests some of those other things in *Federalist* no. 2, when speaking of "one united people, a people descended from the same ancestors, speaking the same language, professing the same religion, attached to the same principles of government, very similar in their manners and customs, and who, by their joint counsels, arms and efforts, fighting side by side throughout a long and bloody war, have nobly established their general Liberty and Independence."

11. Here I follow the distinctions that Quentin Skinner makes in "Language and Political Change," in *Political Innovation and Conceptual Change*, chap. 1.

12. See John Rawls, "Two Concepts of Rules," *Philosophical Review* 64 (1955): 3-32; and John Searle, *Speech Acts: An Essay in the Philosophy of Language* (Cambridge, Eng.: Cambridge University Press, 1969); also see the extensive discussion of rules in Ludwig Wittgenstein, *Philosophical Investigations* (New York: Macmillan, 1953).

13. See my "Historical Concepts in Political Science: The Case of 'Revolution,'" *American Journal of Political Science* 26 (1982): 688-708.

14. See, e.g., Charles Taylor, *Philosophy and the Human Sciences* (Cambridge, Eng.: Cambridge University Press, 1985), and Alasdair MacIntyre, "The Essential Contestability of Some Social Concepts," *Ethics* 84 (1973): 1-9; also see J. G. A. Pocock, *Politics, Language and Time: Essays on Political Thought and History* (New York: Atheneum, 1971), chap. 1.

15. See the chapter in this volume by Gerald Stourzh; and also see Graham Maddox, "Constitution," in *Political Innovation and Conceptual Change*, chap. 3. For hints about Kant see Patrick Riley, *Kant's Political Philosophy* (Totowa, N.J.: Rowman & Littlefield, 1983), and Susan Meld Schell, *The Rights of Reason: A Study of Kant's Philosophy and Politics* (Toronto: University of Toronto Press, 1980).

16. This is John Patrick Diggins's worry as expressed in *The Lost Soul of American Politics: Virtue, Self-Interest, and the Foundations of Liberalism* (New York: Basic Books, 1984), p. 361.

17. This is too enormous a subject to treat here, save only to turn readers once again to Bailyn, McDonald, Wood, Pocock, and other critics of Marxism and of Charles Beard's economic interpretation of the Constitution. In the present context, consider only Alasdair MacIntyre's observation, cast in the terms of our discussion: "Conceptions of justice and allegiance to such conceptions are partly constitutive of the lives of social groups, and economic

interests are often partially defined in terms of such conceptions and not *vice versa*" (*After Virtue* [Notre Dame, Ind.: University of Notre Dame Press, 1981], p. 235).

18. Gordon Wood has rightly noted about the rhetorical skills of the Founders: "Language, whether spoken or written, was to be deliberately and adroitly used for effect, and since that effect depended on the intellectual leader's conception of his audience, any perceived change in that audience could alter drastically the style and content of what was said or written" (see his "The Democratization of Mind in the American Revolution," in *The Moral Foundations of the American Republic*, ed. Robert H. Horwitz, 2d ed. [Charlottesville: University Press of Virginia, 1979], p. 110).

19. Thucydides, *The Peloponnesian Wars*, ed. John H. Finley, Jr. (New York: Vintage, 1951), p. 189. For development of this notion see White, *When Words Lose Their Meaning*, passim.

20. A fear he expressed to his son, who was then preparing to fight (and soon to die) for the Confederacy, as quoted by Frank Freidel in *Francis Lieber: Nineteenth Century Liberal* (Baton Rouge: University of Louisiana Press, 1947), p. 301.

21. Francis Lieber, *Manual of Political Ethics* (Philadelphia: J. B. Lippincott & Co., 1911; originall' 1839), vol. 2, pp. 262–63.

22. Quoted in Kerber, *Federalists in Dissent*, pp. 196–97.

23. Quentin Skinner has rightly noted that "the surest sign that a society has entered into the secure possession of a new concept is that a new vocabulary will be developed, in terms of which the concept can then be publicly articulated and discussed." Such signs also give us the confidence to attribute certain beliefs and practices to agents (see *The Foundations of Modern Political Thought* [Cambridge, Eng.: Cambridge University Press, 1978], vol. 2, p. 352).

24. Willi Paul Adams, *The First American Constitutions: Republican Ideology and the Making of the State Constitutions in the Revolutionary Era* (Chapel Hill: University of North Carolina Press, 1980), p. 65.

25. For a select list see Bernard Bailyn, *The Ideological Origins of the American Revolution* (Cambridge, Mass.: Harvard University Press, 1967); Wood, *Creation of the American Republic*; Gerald Stourzh, *Alexander Hamilton and the Idea of Republican Government* (Stanford, Calif.: Stanford University Press, 1970); J. G. A. Pocock, *The Machiavellian Moment: Florentine Political Thought and the Atlantic Republican Tradition* (Princeton, N.J.: Princeton University Press, 1975); Michael Kammen, *Spheres of Liberty: Changing Perceptions of Liberty in American Culture* (Madison: University of Wisconsin Press, 1986), and *A Machine That Would Go of Itself: The Constitution in American Culture* (New York: Alfred A. Knopf, 1986); McDonald, *Novus Ordo Seclorum*; Diggins, *Lost Soul of American Politics*; Adams, *First American Constitutions*; Kerber, *Federalists in Dissent*; Lance Banning, *The Jeffersonian Persuasion: Evolution of a Party Ideology* (Ithaca, N.Y.: Cornell University Press, 1978); Garry Wills, *Explaining America: The Federalist* (New York: Penguin, 1982); Isaac Kramnick, "Republican Revisionism Revisited," *American Historical Review* 87 (1982): 629–64; Russell L. Hanson, *The Democratic Imagination in America: Conversations with Our Past* (Princeton, N.J.: Princeton University Press, 1985). For an earlier work that is carefully attentive to language see William Winslow Crosskey, *Politics and the Constitution in the History of the United States* (Chicago: University of Chicago Press, 1953).

26. McDonald, *Novus Ordo Seclorum*, p. 262.

27. For beginnings see Bailyn, *Ideological Origins*, pp. 77, 196ff.; Wood, *Creation of the American Republic*, p. 608; Stourzh, *Alexander Hamilton*, chap. 2; Adams, *First American Constitutions*, pp. 144ff.; Pocock, *Machiavellian Moment*, chap. 15; McDonald, *Novus Ordo Seclorum*, pp. 40–43.

28. Bailyn, *Ideological Origins*, p. 299; Adams, *First American Constitutions*, p. 257.

29. Adams, *First American Constitutions*, p. 161; for extensions see Kammen, *Spheres of Liberty*, pt. 1.

30. Stourzh, *Alexander Hamilton*, pp. 46–55; also see Wood, *Creation of the American Republic*, chap. 15, esp. pp. 595–96.

31. The classical papers for this site of conceptual change are found in *Federalist* nos. 10, 14, and 39. J. G. A. Pocock rightly calls attention to this "striking, not to say flagrant example" of innovation in *Virtue, Commerce, and History: Essays on Political Thought and History, Chiefly in the Eighteenth Century* (Cambridge, Eng.: Cambridge University Press, 1985), p. 16 n.

32. Consider John Adams's reflections when looking back from 1819: "Mr. Madison's . . . distinction between a republic and a democracy, cannot be justified. A democracy is really a republic as an oak is a tree, or a temple a building" (quoted by Stourzh in *Alexander Hamilton*, p. 55). During the later nineteenth century, however, Madison's distinction came to have its adherents (such as Francis Lieber, among others), particularly as *The Federalist* became the canonical source for the meaning of the Constitution. In our time, Forrest McDonald has said that although Madison was presumptuous in this matter, "he was also a prophet, for thenceforth *republic* would mean precisely what Madison said it meant" (*Novus Ordo Seclorum*, p. 287).

33. See Russell Hanson's remark that the Federalists spoke as if "virtue could be incorporated as a *systemic* feature of republican politics" (*Democratic Imagination*, p. 72); compare this with Madison's sentiments of a few years later, p. 74 n. For Montesquieu's part see Stourzh, *Alexander Hamilton*, p. 65; and more generally, see Melvin Richter, *The Political Theory of Montesquieu* (Cambridge, Eng.: Cambridge University Press, 1977), esp. pp. 85–97.

34. The accounts that do exist frequently treat conceptual change (or the related issue of change in ideas) as an effect, if not an epiphenomenon, of political innovation. One does not have to be a Marxist to believe this—indeed, Marx's own remarks on "language as practical consciousness" provide no support for this belief. One can even be a consensus liberal historian: consider Richard Hofstadter's view that "changes in the structure of social ideas wait on general changes in economic and political life" (*Social Darwinism in American Thought: 1860–1915* [Philadelphia: W. W. Norton & Co., 1945], p. 176). The above account of the constitutive relationship between language and politics suggests why this cannot be the first or the last word on the subject: see works cited in notes 2 and 14 above.

35. Karl Popper, *Conjectures and Refutations* (New York: Harper & Row, 1965), p. 316 (in the chapter on "What Is Dialectic?").

36. Karl Popper, *Objective Knowledge* (Oxford, Eng.: Oxford University Press, 1972), pp. 123–24. Of course, Popper is not very interested in concepts as such. For contrast and for much-greater elaboration on conceptual change in science see the excellent study by Stephen Toulmin, *Human Understanding: The Collective Use and Evolution of Concepts* (Princeton, N.J.: Princeton University Press, 1972). Toulmin's account of conceptual change is as good as it is, among

other reasons, because it periodically seizes upon examples drawn from social and political life in order to illustrate conceptual change in science (esp. see pp. 167–68, 238–39). At other times, however, Toulmin says that "factors such as conservatism and prejudice" are "entirely irrelevant" (p. 231) in order to understand conceptual change in science. This may be true of science, but it proves to be of little help when one wants to understand conceptual change in politics. These factors are entirely relevant; and then, of course, there is the question of conceptual change in things such as "conservatism" and "prejudice." Compare Burke and Paine in this context.

37. Duncan Kennedy, "The Structure of Blackstone's Commentaries," *Buffalo Law Review* 28 (1979), esp. pp. 211–16. For a better but still abstract view of contradictions from a perspective that is sympathetic to Critical Legal Studies see Roberto Mangabeira Unger, *Law in Modern Society* (New York: Free Press, 1976), esp. pp. 153–55, 243–62. These pages deal with contradictions between what is called the "ideal" and the "actual," particularly as found in liberalism.

38. See Bailyn, *Ideological Origins*, pp. 235ff.; and McDonald, *Novus Ordo Seclorum*, p. 53.

39. *Boswell's Life of Johnson*, ed. G. B. Hill (Oxford, Eng.: Oxford University Press, 1934), vol. 3, p. 201. Locke, too, was implicated in this contradiction: see my " 'So Vile and Miserable an Estate': The Problem of Slavery in Locke's Political Thought," *Political Theory* 14 (1986): 263–89.

40. Along with this goes any pretense to a predictive theory. The fine grain and direction of particular conceptual changes simply lie beyond the powers of prediction. Consider Popper's argument: "If there is such a thing as growing human knowledge, then we cannot anticipate today what we shall know only tomorrow. . . . No scientific predictor can possibly predict, by scientific methods, its own future results. Attempts to do so can attain their result only after the event, when it is too late for a prediction; they can attain their result only after the prediction has turned into a retrodiction" (*The Poverty of Historicism* [New York: Harper & Row, 1960], p. xii). Also see a more generalized version of this argument in MacIntyre, *After Virtue*, pp. 89–91.

41. Bailyn, *Ideological Origins*, pp. 33, 67; more generally, see chap. 5, "Transformations."

42. Wood, *Creation of the American Republic*, p. ix; also see Wood's discussion of how Shays' Rebellion "brought the contradictions of American politics to a head" (p. 455) and how, in general, "old words had assumed new meanings" under conceptual and political "pressures" (p. 524).

43. Pocock, *Machiavellian Moment*, pp. 545–46; also see the discussion of "the historical contradiction" in which "civic man" found himself "once land and commerce were placed in historical sequence" (p. 499) and of the belief of the Scottish School in the "contradiction between virtue and culture" (p. 503).

44. On the methodological implications of "sympathy" in Hume see my "Hume, Hermeneutics, and History: A 'Sympathetic' Account," *History and Theory* 17 (1978): 285–310.

45. Wood, *Creation of the American Republic*, p. 614.

46. It is a second-order language in this guise: see Pocock, *Virtue, Commerce, and History*, chap. 1, for remarks on the orders or levels of language.

47. See *Federalist* nos. 7, 22, 23, 32, 34, 80, and 81.

48. Storing, *The Complete Anti-Federalist*, 2.7.99; 2.7.136; 2.7.140; 2.9.62; and 2.9.76. Much of this was motivated by "the jealousy of innovation," a jealousy

attributed to the people and praised by Centinel (2.7.164). For discussion along these lines see Michael Lienesch, ''In Defence of the Antifederalists,'' *History of Political Thought* 4 (1983): 65–87.

49. Kammen, *Origins of the American Constitution*, p. 71.
50. *Federalist* no. 14.
51. David Hume, *Essays, Moral and Political* (London: A. Millar, 1748), p. 98.

3

Constitution:
Changing Meanings of the Term
from the Early Seventeenth
to the Late Eighteenth Century

Gerald Stourzh

The constitution of a state, Emmerich de Vattel wrote in 1758, is the fundamental settlement that determines the manner in which public authority shall be exercised: "Le règlement fondamental qui détermine la manière dont l'autorité publique doit être exercée, est ce qui forme la *constitution de l'Etat.*"[1] Vattel's work, which soon became widely known in the English-speaking world as well—among its early users was James Otis in Boston—is placed, as it were, at a turning point in the significance of the word "constitution."[2] With its emphasis on the fundamental settlement of public authority, Vattel's definition reflected traditional thinking in early modern Europe, which had been informed through generations by the categories and the vocabulary of Aristotelian political science and particularly by the meaning given to the term *politeia.*[3] Yet the meaning of *politeia*—as given in the most frequently referred to passage in *Politics* 1278 b—was for a long time rendered in English in terms other than "constitution." The earliest English version of the *Politics*, published in 1598, reads as follows: "Policy therefore is the order and description, as of other offices in a city, so of that which hath the greatest and most soveraine authority: for the rule and administration of a Commonweale, hath evermore power and authority joined with it: which administration is called policie in Greek, and in English a Commonweale." The commentary to this passage sums it up thus: "Policy is the order & disposition of the city in regard of Magistrats & specially in regard of him that hath soveraine authority over all, in whose government the whole commonweale consisteth." That was a translation from the French version of and commentary to the *Politics* by Louis Le Roy.[4] The first direct translation from Greek into English appeared in 1776. The translator, William Ellis, translated *politeia* by "form of government" and rendered the Aristotelian definition of *politeia* as a *taxis*, as "the ordering and regulating of the city, and all offices in it, particularly those wherein the supreme power is lodged."[5] It was not until the nineteenth century, with Benjamin Jowett's translation, that *politeia* was rendered as "a constitution," being "the arrangement of magistracies in a state, especially the highest of all."[6]

There are other indications as well that in early modern times, Aristotle-inspired political science did without the word "constitution." Englishmen of the Tudor age, applying their Aristotelian learning to England, did not speak of an English constitution. One of the best-known political scientists of the Elizabethan age, Sir Thomas Smith, consciously fashioned his survey of the *republica Anglorum*, of the "manner of government or policie of the realm of England," after Aristotle. In a letter, Smith indicated that he had written his book as he conceived Aristotle's lost works about the Greek *politeiai* to have been.[7] Yet he never spoke about the constitution of England; *politeia* was variously rendered as "commonwealth," "polity," or "government"; different kinds of *politeiai* were referred to as "kinds" or "fashions" or "forms" of commonwealths or governments—the last term, in the combination "form of government," was to be the most durable one, to last far into the late eighteenth century and the time of American constitution building. One might add, to enlarge a list of "negative evidence," that the *topos* of the *metabole politeion*, which was of such importance in early modern political thinking that was inspired by the Greek political tradition, seems to have been dealt with without the help of the word "constitution." One of the most important places in which the *topos* of the *metabole politeias* or *commutatio status rei publicae* was discussed—chapter 1 of book iv of Jean Bodin's *Six livres de la République*—makes no use of "constitution" at all. The English translation, done by Richard Knolles and published in 1606, speaks about the "Conversion of a Commonweale."[8] Alternative seventeenth-century terms for a *metabole politeias* are "change of government" or "alteration of government"—as used, for example, in the Rump Parliament's declaration on the reasons for changing England from a monarchy into a commonwealth in 1649.[9]

One of the most interesting items on a list of "negative evidence" is a document often called England's first (and only) "written constitution," the so-called Instrument of Government of 1653. Samuel R. Gardiner once referred to it as a constitution entitled "Instrument of Government";[10] that is, however, not an exact description of the document. Its official title was "The government of the Commonwealth of England, Scotland, and Ireland, and the dominions thereto belonging." "Government" is the central term, and the word "instrument" (from the Latin *instrumentum*) merely indicated "document." "Instrument of Government," then, merely meant, in contemporary parlance, the document that settled the supreme authority of the nation. "Instrument of Government," translated into modern parlance, means nothing other than "document of constitution" or "written constitution" (the German expression *Verfassungsurkunde* renders perhaps most precisely what "Instrument of Government" conveyed to contemporaries).[11] Let it be added, because it is little known, that the fundamental document drawn up by the Scottish estates in 1689, the "Claim of Rights" (which is analogous to the English "Declaration of Rights") was designated as an "Instrument of Government" and was published as such in the Scottish statute book.[12]

I would like to consider the significance of the term "government" during the late sixteenth and seventeenth centuries, because it is an important precursor of what "constitution" was going to mean later, in the eighteenth century. Two brief observations: first, government at that time had a much more inclusive meaning than merely "executive"; that restriction or reduction was to be the consequence of the breakthrough of the doctrine of separation of powers, less fully or less strictly carried out in the English-speaking world than in the German-speaking countries (*Regierung* is a narrower term than "government"; therefore the usual German translations of Locke's Treatises "of Government" with *über die Regierung* are faulty). Second, and more important, is the place of "government" within the tradition of political thinking inspired by Aristotelian terminology. Fundamentally, it is the most frequently used English equivalent to a *politeia* reduced to the *politeuma*—the ruling authority. The reduction of *politeia* to *politeuma* in *Politics*, 1278 b—which is rendered in Jowett's translation as "the constitution is in fact the government"—is of importance for early modern Aristotelian political science. A German scholar, Horst Dreitzel, some time ago quite aptly spoke about Aristotle's "original fall" (*der Sündenfall des Aristoteles)* in having reduced the meaning of *politeia*, in a definition so much commented upon by early modern scholars, to *politeuma*.[13] It is of great interest, I think, that the narrowing of *politeia* to "rule"—or to "government"—caused uneasiness to one important writer of the Elizabethan age, Richard Hooker. In his work *The Laws of Ecclesiastical Polity*, Hooker felt moved to justify his choice of the word "polity" rather than "government": ". . . because the name of Government, as commonly men understand it in ordinary speech, doth not comprise the largeness of that whereunto in this question it is applied. For when we speak of

Government, what doth the greatest part conceive thereby, but only the exercise of superiority peculiar unto Rulers and Guides of others?"[14]

The evidence presented so far would tend to indicate that the term "constitution" was apparently rather a latecomer in early modern political discourse. English-speaking people began to speak of "constitution" in connection with bodies corporate and the body politic around the turn of the sixteenth to the seventeenth century; yet it should be said at the outset that older forms of speech, particularly those connected with "forms" and also "frames" of government, coexisted or survived a long time, even as people with increasing frequency began to avail themselves of the newer term "constitution." By beginning to speak of the "constitution" of bodies corporate, Englishmen in the early seventeenth century initiated a process of conceptual development that was essentially completed during the great period of constitutional reflection in North America toward the end of the eighteenth century. (By "period of constitutional reflection" I mean the period reaching from the Stamp Act crisis through the making of the state constitutions and the federal Constitution to *Marbury* v. *Madison*.)

There are, I submit, two quite distinct roots of applying the word "constitution" to the sphere of government (in the largest sense). The first, and by far the more important one, is to be found in the application of analogies from nature to politics, or, to be more precise, in the transfer to bodies corporate or political of a term that is usually applied to the physical body. The second root is to be found in the rise in importance, around the middle of the seventeenth century, of the legal term "constitutions" (always used in the plural form), which ultimately can be traced back to the *constitutiones* of Roman and canon law.

Now, in greater detail to the first and, I would stress, more important area of origin of "constitution": In 1602 the jurist William Fulbecke observed, "Corporations in the whole course *and constitution of them* doe verie much resemble the naturall bodie of man."[15] The venerable topic of analogies between medicine and politics, between the medical healer and the statesman, found systematic treatment in Edward Forset's book *A comparative Discourse of the Bodies natural and politique*, in which he stated that as "the bodies constitution is thought perfect and at the height" at a certain time of life, similarly the state also "hath such a time, of his good estate." As in medicine, so it was important in politics "exactly to know the constitution and complexion of the bodie politique" before applying the appropriate remedies.[16] The question arises as to whether the doctrine of the "King's two Bodies" might have given occasion to formulate similar analogies, yet my inspection of Ernst H. Kantorowicz's book has yielded only one text, of 1561, that refers to the body politic as "a Body that cannot be seen or handled, consisting of Policy and Government, and constituted for the Direction of the People, and the Management of the public weal."[17]

The most interesting "discovery," tracing early uses of "constitution" in connection with bodies corporate, concerns the use of "constitution" with reference to the Church of England. First in 1592—and not earlier, as far as I can see, in spite of careful search—Henry Barrow, the separatist who was to be executed in 1593, summed up his critique of the Church of England with the statement that its "constitution" was faulty. One of his chief criticisms was aimed at the unchristian composition of the parishes of the Church of England, and thus he denounced the "antichristian constitution of your churches," the important question being that of "the true constituted church," a frequently recurring expression. Barrow raised the question of "the orderly gathering of those parishes at any time into true constitution." In his denunciation of falsely constituted churches, Barrow included *a fortiori* the Church of Rome, asking whether "the publike constitution of the church of Rome in the people, ministrie, ministration, worship, government, etc. be according to the ordinanse of Christ or of Antichrist."[18]

From then on, the notion of the true or false constitution of the Church of Christ played a considerable role in separatist writings and documents. "This false and Anti-christian constitution" of the Church of England was accused in a separatist document of 1596, "A True Confession of the Faith." Anglican writers, in polemical writings against the separatists, took up the issue of "constitution." In 1608 the Anglican writer Richard Bernard took the separatists to task for paying more attention to the church's constitution than to the word of God. Bernard rather ridiculed that word, which was so important to the separatists. What was "lesse talked on any where," in the New Testament, "then [sic] a constitution?" "Christ never condemned such as spake the truth in his name, for want of a constitution." Bernard reproached the separatists for not having defined "this constitution." He poured further scorn and ridicule on them: "Thus like nimble Squirrels, they skip from one tree to another, to save themselves from being taken: name corruptions, they skippe to constitution: tell them of constitution, they will tell you of corruption." Bernard, countering separatist criticism that the constitution of the Church of England was an idol, now charged the separatists with making "an idoll of their owne Constitution"; sarcastically Bernard reminds his readers of another idol, the goddess Diana at Ephesus; "great is the Goddess Constitution, great is *Diana* of the Brownists."[19]

Bernard was answered by several separatists; one of them was John Smyth, who had just split away in the direction of adult baptism.[20] Another one was John Robinson, the minister of the Leyden congregation and hence of the Pilgrims prior to their departure for America.[21] The most interesting separatist writer, however, was Henry Ainsworth, a minister in Amsterdam, who did indeed meet Bernard's challenge by giving a definition of "constitution," thus demonstrating, incidentally, that he knew his Aristotle well:

> But as the constitution of a commonwealth or of a citie is a gathering and uniting of people togither [sic] into a civill politie: so the Constitution of the commonwealth of Israel (as the church is called) and of the citie of God the new *Jerusalem,* is a gathering and uniting of people into a divine politie: the form of which politie is Order, as the hethens [sic] acknowledged, calling politie an order of a citie.

In the margin, Ainsworth carefully supplied the reference to book III of the *Politics:* τάξιν τῆς πόλεως.[22] Replying in his turn to Ainsworth, the Anglican writer Bishop Joseph Hall noted that the separatists used a new term: whether "Physicke, or Lawe, or Architecture" had lent it to the separatists, no one had used that term as "scrupulously" as the separatists. "It is no treason to coyne tearmes: What then is Constitution?"[23]

To his reference to the classic passage from the *Politics,* Ainsworth had added that this order (taxis) "is requisite in all actions and administrations of the church, as the Apostle sheweth, and specially in the constitution thereof." The matter of the constitution of a church was its people: the form was the people's "calling, gathering and uniting togither." It is apparent that Ainsworth had some difficulties with his attempt to fit the separatists' conception of constitution, which very much included or stressed the people as its central element, into a definition of polity that stressed the organizational aspect—the aspect of taxis, of offices and magistracies, of "government."

The separatists'—or, rather, Ainsworth's—attempt to integrate the word "constitution" with the discourse on *politeia* anticipated a development that in the realm of political and constitutional discourse, occurred more slowly and haltingly. In political and constitutional discourse during the first half of the seventeenth century, the notion of "constitution" as "disposition," as a "quality" of the body politic in analogy to the body physical, prevails; and it survives well into the eighteenth century. A few telling examples ought to be given.

In 1607 the legal dictionary of John Cowell refers to "the nature and constitution of an absolute monarchy," with "nature" and "constitution" meaning basically the same thing—namely, disposition or quality (the German word *Beschaffenheit* very precisely renders what was meant by constitution in that context).[24] An extraordinary piece of writing appeared in 1643, by an as-yet-unknown author: *Touching the Fundamen-*

tal Laws, or Politique Constitution of this Kingdome. About the author it has been said that he was "one of the half dozen clearest and most profound thinkers supporting the claims of parliament during the civil war."[25] The author argued against contractual models of the fundamental laws of the kingdom. "Fundamentall Laws then are not things of capitulation between King and people, as if they were Forrainers and Strangers one to another"; instead, fundamental laws were *"things of constitution"* (emphasis supplied). Fundamental laws give both king and subjects "existence and being as Head and Members, which constitution in the very being of it is a Law held forth with more evidence, and written in the very heart of the Republique, far firmlier than can be by pen and paper."

An interesting text, for our purposes, is a book published in 1649 by Nathaniel Bacon, an antiroyalist writer, entitled *A Historical and Political Discourse of the Laws and Government of England from the first Times to the End of the Reign of Queen Elizabeth*. Bacon, applying the celebrated topic of return to first principles, quite directly points to the medical analogy of original health: "For as in all other cures, so in that of a distempered Government, the Original Constitution of the Body is not lightly to be regarded." Note that Bacon almost constantly uses the traditional term "government" for what we would today call "constitution," and he uses "constitution" in the sense of "disposition" or "quality." This emerges very clearly when Bacon, toward the end of his work, sets out to contemplate "the natural Constitution of the People of England": northern melancholy and the choleric temper of the southern peoples meet in England, "in their general Constitution," and make the English "ingenious and active."[26]

A marvelous instance of this kind of thinking is found in an essay from Virginia. In *An Essay upon the Government of the English Plantations on the Continent of America* (1701), the author, perhaps Robert Beverly, wrote that the air and the climate of these colonies were most agreeable for "Constitutions of Body"—the most important thing lacking to make the colonists happy was a "good Constitution of Government."[27] Even at a time when the meaning of constitution has arrived at our modern understanding—at the time of the debate on the federal Constitution in 1787/88—the old analogy crops up again, in Madison's *Federalist* number 38, where the prescriptions to improve (or poison) a patient's constitution are compared with the advice on the proposed (political) constitution for the United States.[28]

The application of "constitution" to the body politic of the state without explicit reference to "nature," with the original analogy to the constitution of the body physical receding into the background and finally to be quite forgotten, sets in about 1610. The parliamentary debate on the "Impositions" of James I provided the occasion. William Hakewill warned that impositions that were imposed upon the people without the consent of Parliament would lead to the "utter dissolution and destruction of that politic frame and constitution of this commonwealth." He was soon followed by the famous jurist James Whitelocke, who said that the royal decision on impositions was "against the natural frame and constitution of the policy of this kingdom, which is ius publicum regni, and so subverteth the fundamental law of the realm and induceth a new form of State and government."[29]

Many years ago, Charles Howard McIlwain referred to the just-cited passage by Whitelocke as the first "modern" use of the term "constitution" known to him. After 1610, McIlwain added, the use of the term had become so frequent that additional references were not necessary.[30] Because I do not quite agree, I would like to make two comments.

First, keeping in mind the profoundly "constitutional" character of the conflict between the monarchs and the Commons in the twenties and thirties of the seventeenth century (think of the Shipmoney case), one is rather surprised to see that the notion of "constitution" does not occur so frequently. It does occur on important occasions, however, and in a context that was gaining in political significance—namely, the context of original health and goodness. In 1626, John Pym pointed to "the ancient and fundamental law, issuing from the first frame and constitution of the kingdom." A few weeks later, the Remonstrance of the Commons against tonnage and poundage referred to "the most ancient and original constitution of this kingdom."[31] It was not until the 1640s that the frequency in use increased noticeably, particularly after the publication of the well-known *His Majesties Answer to the XIX Propositions of . . . Parliament.* Here the "ancient, equal, happy, well-poised and never enough commended Constitution of the Government of this Kingdom" was praised; in another passage, more briefly, the "excellent Constitution of this Kingdom."[32] This progress within the same writing to a kind of shorthand expression is of interest, because it indicates the way in which the common usage was to develop. One would speak of the "constitution of government," but time and again, and ultimately more or less regularly, "of government" would be dropped, because everybody knew that "constitution" referred to government.[33]

Second, commenting again on McIlwain, I would like to stress that it was a long time before the term "constitution" emerged in documents of a publicly binding character. We have previously seen how the debates on England's first and only "written constitution," the so-called Instrument of Government, took place in an older and more traditional sphere of speech. Among republican writers during the Interregnum, there was a search for a new "constitution" in the writings of Sir Henry Vane,[34] and James Harrington rather systematically distinguished between the "institution" and the "constitution" of government.[35] During the Restoration, the Tory writer Roger North noted that the word "constitution" was more frequently supplanting older expressions such as "the Laws of this Kingdom, his Majesty's Laws, the Laws of the Land"; North commented that the word "constitution" was usually presented "with a republican face"![36] It was not until the Glorious Revolution that the term "constitution" was used in a fundamental act of state. In the resolution of the convention that declared the "abdication" of James II and the vacancy of the throne, James was charged with having attempted "to subvert the constitution of the kingdom."[37] From then on—that is, from the time of the Glorious Revolution—the golden age of the "British Constitution" must be dated. *The British Constitution: or, the Fundamental Form of Government in Britain* is the title of a book praising that constitution, which appeared in London in 1727. Soon, in 1733, Bolingbroke would explain:

> By constitution we mean, whenever we speak with propriety and exactness, that assemblage of laws, institutions and customs, derived from certain fixed principles of reason, directed to certain fixed objects of public good, that compose the general system, according to which the community hath agreed to be governed. . . . We call this a good government, when . . . the whole administration of public affairs is wisely pursued, and with a strict conformity to the principles and objects of the constitution.[38]

Finally, in 1748, the publication of Montesquieu's *De l'Esprit des Lois* spread the reputation of the constitution of a free state, that of England, to the reading public of the civilized world.

Yet we must go back, once more, to some other beginning, to other rather curious roots. Quite apart from the meaning of constitution as the disposition of the body natural or politic, the legal term *constitutio* had existed and survived from Roman times. That term, in the civil law, had referred to imperial decrees. In canon law, too, it was used in the sense of (fixed) law, or regulations.[39] In medieval and even early modern English law, the term referred to specific written regulations, as opposed to custom or convention. In medieval and early modern times, the term was usually referred to in the plural form, designating a series or collection of regulations passed at a particular time or referring to a particular object. With the rise of the term "statute" to indicate a law that had duly been passed by the king in parliament, the term "constitution(s)" was reduced to refer to regulations of a lower, often local, rank.[40] Yet, during the crisis of the mid-seventeenth century in England, the plural term "constitutions" rose from its inferior position, to which it had sunk in the later Middle Ages, and was wedded to the word "fundamental"—taken from the expression "fundamental laws," which was first documented in England toward the end of the sixteenth century and rose to great significance during the indeed fundamental constitutional crises of the seventeenth century.[41]

The "upgrading" of "constitutions"—plural form—starts in the early seventeenth century. Forset spoke in 1606 about "original constitutions," and in 1625, Sir Robert Phelips said in the Commons: "Wee are the last monarchy in Christendome that retayne our originall rightes and constitutions."[42] In 1640 the expression "fundamental constitutions" emerged in a famous antiroyalist tract, Henry Parker's *The Case of Shipmoney briefly discoursed*. In what I think is a rather magnificent expression, it said that "by the true fundamental constitutions of England, the beame hangs even between the King and the Subject."[43] In the trial of King Charles I for high treason in 1649, Charles was accused of having subverted the "fundamental constitutions" of the kingdom, yet it was not specified what these fundamental constitutions, or any single one of them, actually were.[44]

In North American history, the plural term "constitutions" plays no negligible role during the early colonial period. "Constitutions"—in the generic sense of regulations or rules—are mentioned in several colonial documents and collections or compilations of laws.[45] On the higher level of the "fundamental constitutions," let us look at two well-known documents. John Locke drafted the "Fundamental Constitutions of Carolina," 120 of them. In the last of these constitutions, he said: "These Fundamental Constitutions, in number a hundred and twenty, and every part thereof, shall be and remain the sacred and unalterable form and rule of Carolina forever."[46] A few years later, William Penn drafted twenty-four "Fundamental Constitutions" for Pennsylvania. Penn's Preamble to them is of interest for the history of constitutional terminology, since he uses the term "constitution" in both the singular and the plural forms.[47] The form "fundamental constitutions" was, however, relatively short-lived: one encounters it during about four decades after 1640, yet it did not survive into the eighteenth century.

There is, however, in the eighteenth-century colonies a not-infrequent reference to the "constitution" of a colony—a long time before the constitutional disputes with the mother country of the 1760s and the early 1770s. The meaning on the whole is analogous to that used in Britain—namely, to the complex of government, but not yet to one specific document. There is a text from Virginia from 1736; there is an interesting essay by Cadwallader Colden from 1744/45, dealing with the constitution of the colony of New York; and there are various references in Massachusetts—Thomas Hutchinson says in his *History* that because every year from 1749 to 1766 he had been on the Council of the Province, he had had "sufficient opportunity to acquaint himself with the constitution and publick affairs of the province."[48] No doubt an additional and systematic search through colonial records, notably of the eighteenth century, would reveal further pertinent materials.

What changed and what was new during the American Revolution and as a result of the Revolution? Documents of the "period of constitutional reflection" from the early sixties down to *Marbury* v. *Madison* abound and are well known. I shall only stress the following five points, which I believe to be of particular interest for a history of the changing meanings of our term.

1. A heightened awareness of the differences, or even cleavages, between laws and the underlying constitution developed because of conflicts such as the Writs of Assistance case in Boston and, above all, the Stamp Act crisis. The word "unconstitutional," which was apparently first used by Bolingbroke yet was rarely and uncommonly used for about three decades, suddenly mushroomed as a result of the Stamp Act crisis. I have shown, in an earlier publication in German, how the use of the word "unconstitutional" suddenly spread in North America, once it had first been used in 1764/65 in Rhode Island.[49] Theoretical awareness that the legislators were inferior to the constitution and *not*, as traditional early modern political theory from Jean Bodin to Sir William Blackstone had it, "sovereign" was greatly helped by the clear expression of this relation of subordination by Emmerich de Vattel. Vattel was the first to clarify an ambiguity that had been left by Locke. Locke had variously used the concept of "supreme power"—he preferred these English words to the term "sovereignty"; "supreme power," as used by Locke, applied both to the legislative power and to that power that "remained in the people." Seventy years later, Vattel clearly distinguished between the constitution and the legislative power, which depended on the former and was inferior to it. Vattel wrote—as quoted by James Otis in 1764: "For the constitution of the state ought to be fixed; and since that was first established by the nation, which afterwards trusted certain persons with the legislative power, the fundamental laws are excepted from their commission." Even clearer is the sentence that immediately follows, which I do not quote from Otis, but which I give in the original French: "Enfin, c'est de la constitution que ces législateurs tiennent leur pouvoir, comment pourraient-ils la changer, sans détruire le fondement de leur autorité."[50] Let it be added that there is an extraordinary similarity (which Edward Corwin noted many years ago) between Vattel and the Massachusetts Circular Letter of 1768, which said: "That in all free States the Constitution is fixed; & as the supreme Legislative

derives its Power & Authority from the Constitution, it cannot overleap the Bounds of it, without destroying its own foundation."[51]

2. As a result of the feeling of oppression, the Americans, after independence, were keenly aware that they wanted protection against "encroachments" on the part of the rulers, be they legislative or executive. The most telling expression of this wish, which again is well known but essential to the story that I outline in this paper, is to be found in the resolves of the Concord, Massachusetts, town meeting of 21 October 1776: "We conceive that a Constitution in its proper idea intends a system of principles established to secure the subject in the Possession and enjoyment of their rights and privileges, against any encroachments of the governing part."[52] A result of this feeling has been the entrenchment of individual rights—themselves a heritage of the English tradition, of the rights of freeborn Englishmen!—in the Bills of Rights (first in Virginia), in state constitutions (both in the organizational parts of these constitutions and in their Bills of Rights), and finally in the Bill of Rights of the United States Constitution, as amended by Amendments I through X (and later, above all, XIV). In this chapter, I shall not dwell on this often-commented-upon development, yet it should be stressed that this process of *constitutionalizing* human rights, including what German scholars have called *Positivierung des Naturrechts*, is one of the great innovations of North American constitutionalism; it has had world-wide consequences which have reached far down into the twentieth century and our own days (Canadian constitutional development is a case in point).[53]

3. Briefly I would like to point to the fact, yet to be systematically explored, that not merely the state constitutions, but the Articles of Confederation as well, were considered to be and were called a Constitution. Montesquieu, in his chapter on the federation of republics as a means to provide for external security, spoke about "une manière de constitution qui a tous les avantages intérieurs du gouvernement républicain, et *la force extérieure* du monarchique . . . la république fédérative." In a chapter heading he also spoke about the "constitution fédérale."[54] Thus it may not be too surprising to encounter various references to the Articles of Confederation, such as Madison's letter to Monroe in August 1785 on trying to include the regulation of trade in the "foederal Constitution." George Washington also referred in the same year to "the Constitution."[55] The task of 1787, then, grew out of the efforts to strengthen a "constitution" that already existed, though that effort was very quickly to take on the form of drafting a new federal Constitution.

4. Well known and hardly in need of comment is the growth of "written constitutions" on the state level and subsequently on the

federal level. The wish to assemble in one document the fundamental rules of government, assigning distinct powers and competences to the various organs or "branches," was a result of the conflict with England as well as the tradition of written basic documents from colonial times. The latter is illustrated by the fact that both Rhode Island and Connecticut retained their colonial charters well into the nineteenth century. It might be advisable to refer to constitutions that assemble all important provisions of the powers of government, separation of the branches, and the protection of individual rights in one document as *documentary* constitutions, as James Bryce suggested more than one hundred years ago.[56] That clarification in terminology would be helpful, perhaps, to do away with a confusion that continues to bedevil contemporary discourse on constitutionalism, particularly in the United States but elsewhere as well—a confusion that ascribes to "written constitutions" per se *paramount* validity. This confusion has been magnified and perpetuated by one of the most famous dicta of American constitutional law, John Marshall's pronouncement in *Marbury* v. *Madison:* "Certainly all those who have framed written constitutions contemplate them as forming the fundamental and paramount law of the nation, and consequently the theory of every such government must be that an act of the legislative repugnant to the Constitution is void."[57]

5. This brings me to my fifth and last point. The rise of the constitution as the *paramount law,* reigning supreme and therefore invalidating, if procedurally possible, any law of a lower level in the hierarchy of legal norms, including "ordinary" legislator-made law, is *the* great innovation and achievement of American eighteenth-century constitutionalism. Awareness of *this* innovation, not of constitutions reduced to written documents, was what evoked the proud commentary of eighteenth-century Americans such as Tom Paine, James Iredell, and James Madison. All three of them compared the new American system with that of Great Britain. All three of them—an interesting illustration of historical awareness and its political use—pointed to the same example of legislative omnipotence in Britain: the Septennial Act of 1716, by which a Parliament in session not merely had provided a longer duration for subsequent Parliaments, from three to seven years, but had prolonged *its own duration* from three by another four years. The opposition of the day had considered that measure an infraction of the British constitution, but indeed there was no device that could have arrested the sovereign, constitutional, and legislative power of Parliament from doing what it did. The advancement of American constitutionalism was measured in comparison to Britain's Septennial Act. For Tom Paine, this act was proof that "there is no constitution in England." In 1786, James Iredell of North Carolina denounced the "principle of

unbounded legislative power" in Britain, which "our constitution [meaning the North Carolina State constitution] reprobates." Iredell also pointed to the Septennial Act as proof that "in England, therefore, they are less free than we are." James Madison, in *The Federalist* number 53, also denounced with the same example "dangerous practices," the possibility of changing "by legislative acts, some of the most fundamental articles of the government." In contrast, James Madison extolled a "constitution paramount to the government."[58] And this, indeed, is the most significant innovation of constitutionalism in America.

NOTES

1. Emmerich de Vattel, *Le Droit des gens; ou, Principes de la loi naturelle*, ed. M. P. Pradier-Fodéré, 3 vols. (Paris, 1863), vol. 3, chap. 3, sec. 27, p. 153.

2. An English translation of the above-named work appeared, without a translator's name, under the title *Law of Nations* in London in 1759.

3. This paper is based partly on my essay *Fundamental Laws and Individual Rights in the Eighteenth Century Constitution*, Bicentennial Essay no. 5 (Claremont, Calif.: Claremont Institute, 1984), and it draws also on my more detailed study, available only in German, "Staatsformenlehre und Fundamentalgesetze in England und Nordamerika im 17. und 18. Jahrhundert: Zur Genese des modernen Verfassungsbegriffs," in *Herrschaftsverträge, Wahlkapitulationen, Fundamentalgesetze*, Studies Presented to the International Commission for the History of Representative and Parliamentary Institutions no. 59, ed. R. Vierhaus (Göttingen: Vandenhoeck & Ruprecht, 1977), pp. 294–328.

4. *Aristotle's Politiques, or discourse of government, translated out of the Greek into French, with expositions taken out of the best authors specially out of Aristotle himselfe, and Plato . . . by Loys le Roy called Regius. Translated out of French into English* (London, 1598). The translator's preface is signed I.D.; I have not yet been able to identify the translator's name. On the popularity of Le Roy's edition of the *Politics* in England see J. H. M. Salmon, *The French Religious Wars in English Political Thought* (Oxford, Eng.: Clarendon Press, 1959), pp. 24, 167.

5. Aristotle, *A Treatise of Government*, ed. A. D. Lindsay (London: Everyman Library, n.d.), p. 76.

6. Aristotle, *Politics*, trans. B. Jowett, ed. M. Lerner (New York: Modern Library, 1943), p. 136.

7. Letter dated 6 Apr. 1565, cited in Sir Thomas Smith, *De republica Anglorum: A Discourse on the Commonwealth of England*, ed. L. Alston (Cambridge, Eng.: Cambridge University Press, 1906), pp. xiiif.

8. Jean Bodin, *The Six Bookes of a Commonweale* (1606), new print, with an introduction by K. D. McRae (Cambridge, Mass.: Harvard University Press, 1962), pp. 406ff.

9. "Declaration of the Parliament of England, expressing the Grounds of their late Proceedings, and of settling the present Government in the way of a free State," dated 21 Mar. 1649, in *Parliamentary History of England*, ed. W. Cobbett (London, 1806–20), vol. 3, cols. 1292–1303. Of great interest as an illustration of "constitutional" discourse without (and before the general acceptance of) the term "constitution" is John Pym's speech at the impeach-

ment of Manwaring (4 June 1628), which is extensively quoted by J. G. A. Pocock in *The Machiavellian Moment: Florentine Political Thought and the Atlantic Republican Tradition* (Princeton, N.J.: Princeton University Press, 1975), p. 358. Pym speaks about forms of government and their "alterations," every "alteration" being a "step and degree towards a dissolution," very much in the tradition of the *metabole politeion*.

10. S. R. Gardiner, *History of the Commonwealth and Protectorate*, vol. 2 (London, 1897), p. 291 n. 1.

11. Of great terminological interest are contemporary references to the parliamentary debates in 1654/55 on the subject of transforming the "Instrument of Government" into an act of Parliament, jointly agreed upon by Parliament and the Lord Protector. If anything the bill under debate was a "constitutional bill," and Gardiner uses this expression (*The Constitutional Documents of the Puritan Revolution, 1625–1660*, ed. S. R. Gardiner [Oxford, Eng.: Clarendon Press, 1906; reprinted in 1968], pp. iii, 427); yet this was emphatically not a contemporary expression, which Gardiner knew. Contemporaries often simply spoke about the "Government" being debated or about the "Articles of Government." Cf. the following significant examples: Bulstrode Whitelocke, one of the eminent jurists of the Interregnum, noted in Sept. 1654 that a certain vote in Parliament had not concerned "the whole Government, consisting of Forty two Articles" (!), but only certain parts of it (*Memorials of English Affairs . . .* [London, 1682], p. 588; also ibid., p. 591); the expression, "Articles of Government" (ibid., pp. 587, 590). A member of Parliament, Guibon Goddard, noted on one occasion that "the Government, or Instrument of Government, might be speedily taken into consideration," and on another that "the House was free to debate the Government" (for this see *The Diary of Thomas Burton*, ed. J. T. Rutt, vol. 1 [London, 1828], pp. xxi, xxiii). Edmund Ludlow also on one occasion spoke about "the whole Government contained in the forty two Articles of the Instrument" (*Memoirs*, vol. 2 [Vevey, 1698], pp. 501f.). The bill itself, which caused these comments, was entitled "An Act declaring *and settling* the government of the Commonwealth of England, Scotland, and Ireland, and the dominions thereto belonging" (emphasis supplied; *Constitutional Documents*, pp. 427–47); of interest is the term "settling" or (as in the Act of 1701) "settlement," meaning a basic "constitutional," as one would say later, regulation of public authority. It should be added—although this anticipates the question of the emergence and the earlier uses of the word "constitution," to be sketched in the pages to follow—that the bill of 1654 on one occasion referred to "the foundation and constitution of the government of this Commonwealth" (ibid., p. 428).

12. *The Acts of the Parliaments of Scotland*, vol. 9 (n.p., 1822), pp. 40–41; also *An Account of the Proceedings of the Estates in Scotland*, ed. E. W. M. Balfour-Melville, Publications of the Scottish History Society, 3d ser., vol. 46 (Edinburgh: Scottish History Society, 1954), pp. 38–39.

13. Horst Dreitzel, *Protestantischer Aristotelismus und absoluter Staat* (Wiesbaden: Steiner, 1970), p. 344. This is a book about the German scholar Arnisaeus. Dreitzel correctly points out that Otto von Gierke had already drawn attention to the fact that early modern (Aristotelian) political science understood *res publica* primarily to mean the relation between offices and competences (*Ordnungsverhältnisse*); thus the character of *politeia* as taxis, true to the famous passage in *Politics* 1278 b, was one-sidedly stressed (ibid., pp. 338f. n. 10, refers to Otto von Gierke, *Das deutsche Genossenschaftsrecht*, vol. 4: *Die Staats- und*

Korporationslehre der Neuzeit [1913; reprint, Graz: Akademische Druck- und Verlagsanstalt, 1954], p. 286).

14. Richard Hooker, *Of the Laws of Ecclesiastical Polity*, Everyman ed., vol. 1 (London, 1907; reprint, London, 1969), p. 297.

15. William Fulbecke, *The Pandectes of the law of Nations: contayning severall discourses of the questions, points and matters of Law, wherein the Nations of the world doe consent and accord* (London, 1602), p. 52 (emphasis supplied).

16. Edward Forset, *A comparative Discourse of the Bodies natural and politique* (London, 1606), pp. 60, 78.

17. Ernst H. Kantorowicz, *The King's Two Bodies* (Princeton, N.J.: Princeton University Press, 1957), p. 7, citing the case of the duchy of Lancaster from Edmund Plowden's *Commentaries or Reports* (London, 1816), p. 212 a.

18. The references cited occur in Barrow's comments on an Anglican tract by H. Gifford, *A Short Reply unto the Last Printed Books of Henry Barrow and John Greenwood . . .* , published December 1591. One exemplar of this book, with Barrow's handwritten marginal notes containing most of his references to "constitution," is in the University Library, Cambridge, England, sign Bb.11.29, where I inspected it. These marginal notes have also been edited in *The Writings of John Greenwood and Henry Barrow, 1591–1593*, ed. Leland H. Carlson (London: Allen & Unwin, 1970), pp. 127ff.; for the passages quoted here see pp. 145, 162, 168, 172; see also pp. 129, 134, 137, 173, 176, 177, 182, 191, 192. Cf. also, apparently in time somewhat preceding these marginal notes, Barrow's "A Few Observations to the Reader of Mr. Giffard [sic] his last *Replie*," ibid., pp. 93ff., here p. 126. Barrow's use of "true constitution" aims at the rightly composed church; his new term "true constitution" is close to meaning true composition. It is of interest that in Barrow's voluminous main work, *A Brief Discoverie of the False Church* (1590), the term "constitution" is not yet applied; there is a long disquisition on the church as the body of Christ, yet no use of the term "constitution," although in another part of that book there is a reference to "cunning physicians" who "wil verie soone espie the constitution and inclination of their patientes" (see *The Writings of Henry Barrow, 1587–1590*, ed. Leland H. Carlson [London: Allen & Unwin, 1967], pp. 586–90: "his church compared to an humane body"; p. 492: "cunning physicians").

19. *A True Confession of the Faith . . .* (facsimile reprint, Amsterdam: Da Capo Press, 1969), p. C 1 verso; Richard Bernard, *Christian advertisements and counsels of peace; also dissuasions from the Separatists schisme, commonly called Brownisme . . .* (London, 1608), exemplar inspected in the library of Emmanuel College, Cambridge, sign 9.5.92, passages quoted on pp. 54, 62, 69, 79–80.

20. *The Works of John Smyth*, ed. W. T. Whitley, 2 vols. (Cambridge, Eng.: Cambridge University Press, 1915), vol. 1, p. xcvii, and esp. vol. 2, "Parallels, Censures, Observations . . . ," pp. 338–53, 375, 376, 377, 464, 476f.; "The Character of the Beast, or The False Constitution of the Church" (also 1609), esp. pp. 565f.

21. *The Works of John Robinson*, ed. Robert Ashton, 3 vols. (London, 1851), esp. "Mr. Bernard's Reasons against Separation discussed," vol. 2, pp. 120, 355; also of interest p. 140: "the visible church being a polity ecclesiastical, and the perfection of all polities"; also vol. 3, p. 407: Robinson's "Answer to 'a Censorious Epistle,' " a letter by Joseph Hall.

22. H. A. [Henry Ainsworth], *Counterpoyson* (n.p., 1608), pp. 169–70.

23. J. H. [Joseph Hall], *A Common Apology of the Church of England against the unjust challenges of the over-just sect, commonly called Brownists . . .* (n.p., 1610), p.

21 (in sec. viii, entitled "Constitution of a Church," he comments that "Constitution is the very state of Brownisme"). It is in this work that the *Oxford English Dictionary* thinks it finds the earliest use of "constitution" as "mode in which state is constituted," citing the "constitution of the Commonwealth of Israel"; yet Hall was using this expression by merely quoting it from Ainsworth's preceding "Counterpoyson."

24. John Cowell, *The Interpreter: or Booke containing the Signification of Words* . . . (Cambridge, Eng., 1607; no pagination); the words cited occur in the entry on "Parliament."

25. Margaret A. Judson, *The Crisis of the Constitution* (New Brunswick, N .J.: Rutgers University Press, 1949; reprint, New York: Octagon Press, 1964), p. 413. The pamphlet *Touching the Fundamental Lawes, or Politique Constitution of this Kingdome* . . . (London, 1643; exemplar inspected in the British Library, London, E.90 [21]), passages cited are on pp. 3–4; anticipating Jowett's terminology: "The outward constitution or polity of a Republick," ibid., p. 5. The thinker that comes closest to the thoughts expressed in this piece seems to me to be Henry Parker, yet this would need further investigation.

26. I used the fourth edition, London, 1739; the passages cited are on pp. iii and 174.

27. *An Essay upon the Government of the English Plantations on the Continent of America*, ed. Louis B. Wright (San Marino, Calif.: Huntington Library, 1945), p. 16.

28. *The Federalist*, ed. Jacob E. Cooke (Middletown, Conn.: Wesleyan University Press, 1961), no. 38, p. 243.

29. J. R. Tanner, *Constitutional Documents of the Reign of James I* (1930; reprint, Cambridge, Eng.: Cambridge University Press, 1961), pp. 253, 260.

30. Charles H. McIlwain, "Some Illustrations of the Influence of Unchanged Names for Changing Institutions," in *Interpretations of Modern Legal Philosophies: Essays in Honor of Roscoe Pound*, ed. P. Sayre (New York: Oxford University Press, 1947), pp. 484–97.

31. Pym's speech, which is referred to by J. G. A. Pocock (see above, n. 9), is in *The Stuart Constitution*, ed. J. P. Kenyon (Cambridge, Eng.: Cambridge University Press, 1966), pp. 16–17. The remonstrance is in Gardiner, *Constitutional Documents*, p. 71. The passage quoted from the remonstrance is an early example of referring to the ancient constitution, a term of rarer occurrence than might be supposed in view of J. G. A. Pocock's book on the ancient constitution and the feudal law. In the reissue of this work, Pocock concedes in his "Retrospect from 1986" that the term "constitution" as used in his book had not been systematically cleared of anachronism and that there was a time when it was more usual to speak of "the laws" as "ancient" (*The Ancient Constitution and the Feudal Law: A Study of English Historical Thought in the Seventeenth Century: A Reissue with a Retrospect* [Cambridge, Eng.: Cambridge University Press, 1987], p. 261).

32. *His Majesties Answer* is republished as an appendix in Corinne C. Weston, *English Constitutional Theory and the House of Lords, 1556–1832* (London: Routledge & Kegan Paul, 1965), pp. 263ff., here pp. 270–71; see also Michael Mendle, *Mixed Government, the Estates of the Realm, and the "Answer to the XIX propositions"* (University: University of Alabama Press, 1985).

33. There are queries about "a new constitution" or "this constitution," quite "modern" sounding, in the Putney and Whitehall debates of 1647 and 1648/49 respectively (see *Puritanism and Liberty*, ed. A. S. P. Woodhouse

[Chicago: University of Chicago Press, 1951], esp. pp. 128, 136, and [chiefly Ireton in Putney] pp. 70f., 78f., 80, 88f., 91, 110f., 120f.).

34. On him and other writers see Michael Weinzierl, "Republikanische Politik und republikanische politische Theorie in England, 1658–1660" (Doctoral diss., University of Vienna, 1974), esp. pp. 43f.

35. *The Political Works of James Harrington,* ed. J. G. A. Pocock (Cambridge, Eng.: Cambridge University Press, 1977), p. 230; cf. also ibid., p. 179, when Harrington, comparing the monarchical and popular forms of government, adds, referring to the latter: "for which kind of constitution I have something more to say than Leviathan hath said or ever will be able to say for monarchy."

36. Quoted by Weston, *English Constitutional Theory,* pp. 99–100.

37. Quoted in William Blackstone, *Commentaries on the Laws of England,* vol. 1 (Oxford, 1765), p. 204.

38. *A Dissertation upon Parties,* in *The Works of Lord Bolingbroke,* vol. 2 (1851), p. 88.

39. E.g., William of Lyndwood's collection of the *constitutiones* of the ecclesiastical province of Canterbury: *Constitutiones provinciales,* or *Provinciale, seu Constitutiones Angliae,* in many editions (I inspected the edition of Oxford, 1679); in 1604 there appeared the collection of post-Reformation English ecclesiastical law under the title "Constitutions and Canons Ecclesiastical."

40. Examples: a statute of the first years of Elizabeth I was entitled "An Acte towching certayne Politique Constitutions made for the maintenance of the Navye," in *Statutes of the Realm,* ed. A. Luders (London, 1810–28), vol. 4, pt. 1, pp. 422–28. In 1601, Thomas Wilson wrote that in cities and boroughs it was the task of the mayor "to make a lawe and constitutions for the benefit of the Citty, which must be confirmed by Common Counsell" (*The State of England unno Domini 1600,* ed. F. J. Fisher, Camden Miscellany no. 16 [London: Camden Society, 1936], p. 21). In 1610 a member of Parliament said that the king, by his letters patent, may incorporate a town, city, or company of merchants, *"and give them power to make constitutions and by-laws for the better order and government of the same"* (emphasis supplied; in *Proceedings in Parliament 1610,* ed. E. R. Foster, vol. 2 [New Haven, Conn.: Yale University Press, 1966], p. 193).

41. The expression "fundamental laws," which apparently originated in France in the 1570s, is first documented in England in Francis Bacon's Epistle Dedicatory to his "Maxims of the Law" (8 Jan. 1596 old style; see J. W. Gough, *Fundamental Law in English Constitutional History* [Oxford, Eng.: Clarendon Press, 1955], p. 51).

42. Forset, *Comparative discourse,* p. 63. Phelips is quoted by G. A. Ritter in "Divine Right und Prärogative der englischen Könige 1603–1640," *Historische Zeitschrift* 196 (1963): 613.

43. Published in London in 1640, p. 7.

44. Gardiner, *Constitutional Documents,* p. 372.

45. These are only a few of several illustrations available: reference to "the framing of their Politique Constitutions" is in *Records of the Colony of New Plymouth in New England,* ed. D. Pulsifier, vol. 11 (Boston, 1861), p. 21; ". . . the said Laws, Constitutions and Punishments . . ." is in *Records of the Colony of Rhode Island and Providence Plantations, in New England,* vol. 1 (Providence, R.I., 1856), p. 145.

46. *The Works of John Locke,* 8th ed. (London, 1777), vol. 4, pp. 519–37.

47. *The Papers of William Penn,* ed. Richard S. Dunn and Mary Maples Dunn, vol. 2 (Philadelphia: University of Pennsylvania Press, 1982), p. 142.

48. For Virginia see a speech by Sir John Randolph after his reelection as Speaker of the House of Burgesses in 1736, which already seems to include a reference to a written document with the meaning of "constitution," to what he calls the "charter" of 1621, officially entitled "An Ordinance and Constitution of the Treasurer, Council and Company" in England; Randolph also still used the older plural form "constitutions," meaning a plurality of rules (see *American Colonial Documents to 1776*, ed. Merrill Jensen [London: Oxford University Press, 1955], pp. 268–71); for New York see Cadwallader Colden's essay "Observations on the Balance of Power in Government" (1744/45), in which he argues that "Our Constitution of Government" was nearly the "same with that which the People of England value so much" and proceeds to give a description of the "proper Ballance" of that constitution (see Jack P. Greene, ed., *Great Britain and the American Colonies, 1606–1763* [New York: Harper & Row, 1970], pp. 252ff.). For Massachusetts see Thomas Hutchinson, *The History of the Colony and Province of Massachusetts Bay*, ed. L. S. Mayo, vol. 3 (Cambridge, Mass.: Harvard University Press, 1936; reprint, Kraus, 1970), p. 184 and passim.

49. For details see Gerald Stourzh, *Vom Widerstandsrecht zur Verfassungsgerichtsbarkeit: Das Problem der Verfassungswidrigkeit im 18. Jahrhundert*, Collection of the Institute for European and Comparative Legal History of the Law Faculty of the University of Graz no. 6, ed. B. Sutter (Graz: Institut fuer Europaeische und Vergleichende Rechtsgeschichte d.Universität, 1974), p. 37.

50. Cf. Stourzh, *Fundamental Laws*, p. 33n.79.

51. Ibid., p. 34n.85.

52. Oscar Handlin and Mary F. Handlin, eds., *The Popular Sources of Political Authority* (Cambridge, Mass.: Belknap Press of Harvard University Press, 1966), pp. 152–53.

53. Cf. Stourzh, *Fundamental Laws*, pp. 11–12.

54. *De l'Esprit de Lois*, bk. 9, chaps. 1 and 2.

55. As early as 2 Jan. 1775, Silas Deane wrote that if one general Congress had caused the colonies to be associated with each other, "another one may effect a lasting Confederation which will need nothing, perhaps, but time, *to mature it into a complete & perfect American Constitution*, the only proper one for Us, whether connected with Great Britain or not" (emphasis supplied); cited by Jack N. Rakove in *The Beginnings of National Politics* (New York: Knopf, 1979), pp. 141ff. Madison to Monroe, 7 Aug. 1785, in *The Papers of James Madison*, ed. R. A. Rutland, vol. 8 (Charlottesville: University of Virginia Press, 1973), p. 333; Washington to McHenry, Aug. 1785, in *The Writings of George Washington*, ed. J. C. Fitzpatrick, vol. 28 (Washington, D.C.: U.S. Government Printing Office, 1938), pp. 228f. Of great conceptual interest in this context is Madison's usage of the term "constitution" both in his "Notes on Ancient and Modern Confederacies" and in his "Vices of the Political System of the United States." In the former piece, Madison noted explicitly the "Vices of the Constitution" of the Amphyctionic Confederacy, of the Achaean Confederacy, of the Helvetic Confederacy, of the Belgic Confederacy, and of the Germanic Confederacy. Cf. *The Papers of James Madison*, ed. W. T. Hutchinson, Robert A. Rutland, et al., vol. 9 (Chicago: University of Chicago Press, 1975), pp. 6, 8, 11, 16, 22. In the "Vices of the Political System of the United States" (Apr. 1787), point 7, Madison noted: "A sanction is essential to the idea of law, as coercion is to that of Government. The federal system being destitute of both, wants the great vital principles of a *Political Constitution. Under the form of such a constitution*, it is in fact nothing more than a treaty of amity of commerce and of alliance, between independent and Sovereign States" (emphasis added), ibid., p. 351.

56. James Bryce, *Studies in History and Jurisprudence,* vol. 1 (Oxford, Eng.: Clarendon Press, 1901), p. 205.

57. 1 Cranch 137.

58. Paine, in *The Rights of Man,* as quoted by Charles H. McIlwain, *Constitutionalism, Ancient and Modern* (Ithaca, N.Y.: Cornell University Press, 1947; paperback, 1958), p. 2; *Life and Correspondence of James Iredell,* ed. G. J. McRee (New York, 1858), vol. 2, p. 148; *The Federalist* no. 53, p. 361. On the "paramount" character of a constitution vis-à-vis the legislative, cf. the interesting texts by Noah Webster (1790) and by Thomas Tudor Tucker (1786) referred to by Gordon S. Wood, *The Creation of the American Republic* (Chapel Hill: University of North Carolina Press, 1969), pp. 278, 280–81. To Wood's contention that no other piece of writing prior to 1787 revealed as clearly and cogently as Tucker's pamphlet *Conciliatory Hints* . . . (published on 21 Sept. 1786 in Charleston, S.C.) how far Americans had departed from the English conception of politics, I would submit that James Iredell's article, to which reference has been made in this note, published in Newbern, N.C., on 17 Aug. 1786, is at least as important a document on the "newness" of the Americans' concept of a constitution as is Tucker's; Iredell's text is referred to by Wood, *Creation of the American Republic,* pp. 461–62. On an earlier statement by Iredell in 1783 that the Constitution was "superior even to the Legislature" see *The Papers of James Iredell,* ed. Don Higginbotham, vol. 2 (Raleigh: North Carolina Division of Archives and History, 1976), p. 449. The idea of a constitution as fundamental and paramount law beyond the reach of normal legislative enactment and alteration was central to Thomas Jefferson's criticism of the political system of Virginia. For this see, first, Query XIII "Constitution" of his *Notes on the State of Virginia,* which shows that Jefferson was aware of older legal usages of the term "constitution" as well as of "the magic supposed to be in the word *constitution*" (see point 5 of his list of the defects of the constitution); second, his "Draught of a Fundamental Constitution for the Commonwealth of Virginia" of 1783; and third, the last paragraph of Jefferson's bill (and act) for establishing Religious Freedom (1786). These three pertinent texts are conveniently found in Thomas Jefferson, *Notes on the State of Virginia,* ed. William Peden (New York: W. W. Norton & Co. for the Institute of Early American History and Culture, 1972), pp. 121–25 (especially 123–24), 209–22, 224–25. For details on the bill on Religious Freedom and its enactment see *The Papers of Thomas Jefferson,* ed. Julian P. Boyd et al., vol. 2 (Princeton, N.J.: Princeton University Press, 1950), pp. 547–53; on its last paragraph see most recently the reflections in Ralph Lerner's essay "Jefferson's Pulse of Republican Reformation," in *The Thinking Revolutionary: Principle and Practice in the New Republic* (Ithaca, N.Y.: Cornell University Press, 1987), pp. 87–88.

4

States, Republics, and Empires: The American Founding in Early Modern Perspective

J. G. A. Pocock

CONSTITUTION, TRADITION, AND THE HISTORY OF DISCOURSE

I have no interpretive program for providing the American Founding with a new face, other than that which may emerge from the program of historical enquiry that I am accustomed to conduct. I am a resident who is well disposed to the republic but am not a citizen of it; and I am therefore aware that enquiry may seem to become, or may actually become, not unlike subversion. Does a guest in the house write the history of the house? He may, if the house shares a history with other houses and if his invitation includes an invitation to write that history. Those who were born in the house, however, may display an acute awareness that it is built apart from other houses, and this awareness may be part of the identity they have acquired by living there: an identity that the guest does not fully share.

To abandon the metaphor: as a historian, I am interested in the face that the Founding acquires when viewed in the context that it shared with other political cultures of the late eighteenth century, especially those which formed a number of kingdoms and colonies (sometimes imprecisely called an "empire") subject to the British Crown. The American colonies had been part of this "empire" before they became "states," and they continued to employ its discourse in the process both of making themselves "states" and of making themselves "united." I therefore am interested in their employment of a "traditional" (i.e., inherited) discourse for "revolutionary" (i.e., self-transformative) purposes. My program emphasizes continuity, in the sense that it situates the Revolution and the Founding in a context that antedates them; but of course, this is in no sense to deny that there was a revolution or that the polity and nation it created were unique. Traditions convey means of rebelling against and transforming tradition itself; what these means are in a particular case determines both what kind of tradition it is and what kind of revolutions have occurred against it.

Because the Revolution led to a Constitution, the Revolution was a Founding, and among other things it founded a "tradition," or a transmissible "style" of politics, which owes much to its founding documents (the Declaration, the Constitution, and others associated with them). It was indeed a "founding," in the neoclassical sense still current in eighteenth-century politics: that the Founders consciously grouped themselves with Theseus and Moses, Lycurgus and Romulus, as founders of a "new order of the ages," differentiates them somewhat from revolutionaries who came after them and saw man's life in history as less the foundation of stable orders than the incessant transformation of the self. The latter element can be found in American revolutionary consciousness, but its coexistence with the consciousness of the neoclassical kind means that the Revolution was a revolution in the early modern, rather than the modern, sense of the term.

Traditions convey assumptions about themselves; and to the extent that they are successful as traditions, these assumptions are self-validating. The historian need not wish to challenge the validity of tradition—indeed, among the processes that he studies is that by which tradition has become established and has validated itself—but into the narrative he will constantly be introducing information other than that which the tradition's assumptions about itself convey. This happens because the historian, and in particular the historian of discourse, is committed by his vocation to operating in an open context; it is, in other words, hard to find any theoretical limit to the number and variety of contexts in which a past historical action may be situated for purposes of interpretation. There must, for this very reason, be rules and disciplinary procedures for admitting new contexts of interpretation and for demonstrating their relevance and validity; but these rules must themselves be constantly open to discussion. The historian may therefore find himself looking at a tradition, especially the founding of a tradition, in contexts other than those which the tradition's assumptions about itself indicate, and making statements that are at variance with those which the tradition makes about itself.

The historian of discourse therefore, operating within these guidelines, may review certain key words and concepts in the political vocabulary of the Founders, situating them in contexts supplied by the mainly Anglophone discourse of the late eighteenth century. His aim may be to bring to light meanings that they derived from these contexts and carried with them as they became involved in the actions and processes of Founding; and he will certainly find that some of these meanings were more or less drastically altered as this happened. He hopes, by doing this, to intensify his understanding of the Founding as a linguistic and political process carried out in the contexts supplied by the times in which it took place; but at the same time he knows that he is dealing with a Founding and that some of these derived and changing words became part of the political structure of the United States. The problem of tradition now surfaces: will he present a reading of the Founding that is at variance with traditional interpretation, and if so, what will be the nature and consequence of the variation? On the plain understanding that this sort of thing can happen, the historian proceeds.

THE DECLARATION OF INDEPENDENCE
AND THE PROBLEM OF THE WORD "STATE"

As long ago as 1976 I found myself wondering how the republic I found myself living in came to be called the United States. It should be explained that in the last quarter of the eighteenth century, the word "state" was not yet—though it was on the way to becoming—the normal term for political associations of all kinds or for political association in the abstract. The idea that "political science" is the study of "the state" is, at least in English, on the whole a nineteenth-century invention, and the Founders were not familiar with it. The most common generic term for "political association(s)" was "commonwealth(s)," and although "commonwealth" was the English form of the Latin *res publica*, either could still be used neutrally to describe political systems either with monarchs or without them. The English regicide Commonwealth of 1649–60 had pushed the word in the direction of kinglessness, but Thomas Hobbes, who was certainly no republican, had written about "the commonwealth," not "the state." Allowing "commonwealth" its "republican" associations, however, it seemed noteworthy that three of the original Thirteen Colonies—Massachusetts, Pennsylvania, and Virginia—were and still are capable of describing themselves as "commonwealths" and that a fourth, Kentucky, had joined them in doing so not long after Independence. A colony that set itself up in independence from the Crown might therefore describe itself as a "commonwealth," and it was linguistically conceivable that the political system brought into being by the Revolution and the Founding might have been called the "United Commonwealths," or even the "United Republics," instead of the "United States."

The initial answer to my problem lay in the Declaration of Independence itself, where it is declared that what were formerly "colonies now are, and of right ought to be, free and independent states." A "state," therefore, is what a colony becomes when it is recognized as "free and independent," and the Declaration contains argument as to the right of a "people" to assert that status and to call on others to recognize it, under the appropriate conditions. In the Declaration we therefore perceive evidence for the presence of the Lockean doctrines that a "people" may of right (1) enter into a "state" of civil society and (2) dissolve its former government and institute a new one; and both of these doctrines are being decisively invoked by the drafting committee and the Congress. But it is not clear that the Lockean process fully accounts for the process by which "colonies" become "states," because the Lockean process culminates in a "state of civil society" but not in "states" as the Declaration employs the word in its plural form. The colonies that become "states" certainly claim to be exercising Lockean rights which obtain in both the "state of nature" and the "state of civil society," but they do not assert that they are "states" solely because they are putting those rights into effect. We need to look a little further.

The primary intention of the Declaration of Independence is not to assert—although it does assert—that a "people" may organize itself into a state, but to effect the separation of one people from another people. Its opening sentence pronounces that "in the course of human events" it may become necessary to do this, and it seems to indicate that the necessity arises from time to time, although it cites no precedent, and we may find it hard to think of one to which its framers may have been referring. The separation of a people from another people was not a process of which Locke had furnished a description, and the Declaration's claim that all men enjoy equal rights, including the right to institute governments to protect them, does not explain how this is to be done. It is necessary to go roundabout, and assert that a government (the Crown) which continues to enjoy legitimate authority over one people (the British) has by misrule forfeited the right to enjoy it over another people (the American). In consequence, the Lockean mechanisms of dissolution and institution have come into play in the latter case but not in the former, and there now exist two peoples, each under its own legitimate government, at war with one another. All the indictments of George III's personal role and actions, which introduce the claim that his authority over the colonies is dissolved by reason of his misgovernment, serve to introduce the Declaration's chief verbal performance, which is a declaration of war, in the name of the American "people," upon the "people" and "state" of Great Britain. The proposition that all men and all peoples are created equal introduces one "people's" right and power to declare itself independent of and at war with another. The Declaration is not a wholly benign document.

The state of war that it declares is temporary, but it introduces a more lasting separation. The "we" in whose name the Congress issues the Declaration—namely, "the representatives of the United States of America in Congress assembled"—are said to hold the British people "as we hold the rest of mankind, enemies in war, in peace friends." These words plainly characterize the "state of nature": not, however, as it obtains prior to the establishment of the "state of civil government" in Locke so much as it obtains between the sovereign actors in the systems of *jus gentium*, or international law, expounded by Grotius, Pufendorf, or Vattel—names that came as trippingly off the tongue of any Founding Father as did those of John Locke, Algernon Sidney and Benjamin Hoadly. The "states" that colonies now become, like the "state" that Great Britain is now externally regarded as being, are "states" in the sense in which the word is used in the discourse of *jus gentium*. Here, indeed, the Latin *status* is perhaps less usual than *civitas*; but the French *états* is used by Barbeyrac, in his translation of Pufendorf, and by Vattel, from which it may be seen rendered as "states" in English. And in the less formal and juristic discourse of "reason of state" or *ratio status*, the French, Italian, English, and other vernacular equivalents of *status* are regularly employed to denote the independent actors—kingdoms, republics, or self-governing "estates"—who pursue their interests in the morally indeterminate universe of "reason of state" or the "state of nature." The power to do this was one of the attributes of sovereignty, but instead of conducting the sovereign's relationships with his (or their, or its) subjects, it conducted relationships between the sovereign and other sovereigns.

This is the power that is claimed for the former British colonies of the Atlantic seaboard by the verbal action that the Declaration of Independence performs in declaring them "states." There are now thirteen "states" in a "state of nature" with respect to the "state" (and people) of Great Britain; and the question must necessarily arise whether these thirteen are in a state of nature respecting one another— as they certainly are with respect to the rest of mankind—and what it is that keeps them from being so if they in fact are not. It is pronounced that "these united colonies" are now and ought to be "united states," but there is no definition of the sense in which they are "united." They are of course united by a common cause and common grievances, but to say this gives no juristic or political form to the relationship that exists between them. The strongly Lockean language used and presupposed by the Declaration encourages the reader to think that "a people" is competent, and may be expected, to embody itself in a "state of civil government"; but how one "people" comes to embody itself in thirteen "free and independent states" neither Locke , Jefferson, nor any other theorist anywhere makes much attempt to explain.

There is, however, the most emphatic language supposing the existence of a single "American people." It is "a people," a singular entity, which now dissolves the bonds connecting it with another; and this use of "a people" in the singular is both striking and momentous. We may and we should account for it by tracing the growth of an American nationalism; but we may also ask whether the term "people" can be used otherwise than in the singular, by the conventions and usage of the language in which the Declaration is framed. It is noteworthy that in one of Jefferson's drafts, which Congress did not adopt, the enslaved Africans are spoken of as "a people." What would be the case if an African "people," on either shore of the Atlantic, should claim its station among the "free and independent states" recognized by the "opinions of mankind" neither Jefferson nor the Congress can be said to envisage; but Jefferson's use of the singular seems to imply the question. Did he use it advisedly or because it was unavoidable?

We may think of a "state" as a civil society, generated by a "people," and find support from the Declaration's language for doing so; but this will not help us much in solving the problem of "states" in the plural: that is, of what happens when thirteen "states" are made to claim that they are "free and independent" and that they are "united." We may pursue this problem by supposing them to be "united" by some pact or confederacy, in virtue of which the Congress is empowered to speak for all; as soon as we suppose this, we see that we are concerned less with "states" as sovereign over their subjects or citizens than with "states" as sovereigns acting with respect to each other. The word "state" now recovers the meaning that it bore in the seventeenth-century discourse of "reason of state": namely, that of a sovereign exercising the power to conclude peace and war by means of treaties or *foedera*. This is the power that Locke termed "federative," and it need not be exercised for the purpose of constituting confederacies or federations: these are relationships between states, of a special (indeed, an enigmatic) sort, and the attribute of sovereignty that we are examining is not necessarily committed to entering upon them. It need only conclude or terminate *foedera*; it need only perform those actions which are entailed by considering other sovereign entities "enemies in war, in peace friends." We have come upon the origins of that discourse of "federalism" which is essential to the making of the Constitution of the United States; and we have found the "federal" power to be, in its simplest and most basic meaning, nothing more than the power by which one "state" acts in respect to others with which it shares a "state of nature." Whatever "unites" thirteen "free and independent states" must be a *foedus*, arrived at by the exercise of the "federative" or "federal" power of each, whether it be transitory or permanent, a treaty, a confederacy, or something more. We have a long way to go before arriving at the extraordinary conclusion by which a "federal government" was vested with some at least of the powers of civil sovereignty over individuals in a "state of civil society": something that, on a strict use of language, the "federal" power could never exercise, because it was charged with acting towards other sovereigns in the "state of nature" that must necessarily exist between them.

THE PROBLEM OF "REPUBLICANISM"
YET AGAIN REVISITED

The historian may now be thought of as having completed his enquiry as to how there came to be United "States," though not as to how they came to be "united." The enquiry has entailed a shift of emphasis from "state" meaning "commonwealth" or "civil society" to "state" meaning the sovereign exerciser of the "federative power" (to employ a Lockean expression). But in the process of becoming "free and independent states," the former "colonies" set about providing themselves with "constitutions" of their own. In so doing, they certainly acquired new governmental structures—exercising civil authority and perhaps sovereignty—in which the "federative power" was less conspicuous than the powers of civil government; and these new governments could be and very soon were termed "republican" in a variety of senses borne by that word in eighteenth-century political discourse. Because the meaning of "republicanism" has been and continues to be crucial in American self-understanding and because it has recently become the matter of debate among historians, I have reason to proceed with an enquiry into how and in what sense the political system in which I live has come to be known by that epithet.

The new "state governments" of the Revolutionary period were early seen to be "republican" in a variety of senses. In the first place, they all repudiated the authority of the Crown, and in that sense they were (and might remain) kingless. There was current a violent invective against kingship, of which Thomas Paine's *Common Sense* is the most famous instance; and "kingship" meant the hereditary exercise of sovereignty by a single person. Since the English regicide of 1649, the word "republic"—which we have seen could mean any kind of *res publica,* political society, or "state" whatever—had acquired the meaning of a political form that explicitly or violently rejected kingship in this sense. When the English temporarily abolished kingship, they became a "republic," "commonwealth," "free state," or "state" *simpliciter;* it was sometimes said that the monarchy had been replaced by "the government of a state." When a Lockean or pre-Lockean language was used and it was said that power had reverted to the people from whom it originated and that they had chosen not to reconstitute it in a monarchical form, the "populist" implications of this language became merged with and even tended to dominate the implications of the word "republic." But it was not necessary to hold a "popular" theory of sovereignty in order to be a "republican"; a republic need not rest on any theory of how sovereignty originated, and it might stress that sovereignty was shared between a number of essentially distinct agencies, instead of originating in a unitary "people."

The new state constitutions repudiated the authority of the Crown, but in most cases they retained the exercise of executive authority by a single person. They differed as to the extent and limits of executive authority, and in no case did they make it hereditary in the single person who exercised it. There were to be no kings in the United States, and no hereditary aristocracies either. But we are at a point where the meaning of the word "kingship" can draw apart from that of the word "monarchy," meaning the exercise of certain functional powers by a single person. In the latter sense, "monarchy" was perfectly compatible with the most advanced theoretical usage of the word "republic"; for this term could, and commonly did, denote a union of some kind between "monarchy," "aristocracy," and "democracy," a single person, an elite council, and a popular assembly. It is further very important to remember that the three Greek-derived words just mentioned might be used either functionally, to denote a number of persons (one, few, many) exercising the powers (executive, judicial, legislative) proper to them; or—simultaneously but not inseparably—they might be used socially, to denote hereditary orders or estates exercising these several powers, as when a family inherited monarchy; a nobility, aristocracy; a property-owning commonalty, democracy. These usages were and still are very often confused.

Since the English civil wars of the seventeenth century, it had been possible to distinguish between these usages. By a paradox of history, the first authoritative account of England as a balance of separated powers had been issued in the king's name, as a vindication of his preeminence: *His Majesty's Answer to the Nineteen Propositions of Parliament* in the summer of 1642. This had contended that monarchy, aristocracy, and democracy—in England, the king, the lords, and the commons—each possessed characteristic virtues and vices and that the latter would corrupt the former when any one of the three existed by itself. In England, however, the wisdom of the ancestors—which was not quite the same as the original decision of the people—had established, as far as was possible to "human prudence," a mixed government consisting of all three, so balanced that each checked the unlimited exercise of power which would cause the corruption of virtue by vice in the other two. It should be noted that this balance obtained both between hereditary estates—of which the monarchy now, rather momentously, became one—and between functioning powers. The *Answer to the Nineteen Propositions* attempts to enumerate what authority, as well as what virtue, each of the three possesses. After the revolution of 1649, when both monarchy and the peerage in Parliament seemed to have disappeared, the first English republican theorists, Marchamont Needham and James Harrington, set about redesigning the balance "without a king or house of lords," as the phrase then ran. They supposed both democracy and aristocracy to be natural to man but held them to be separable from the existence of estates. In Harrington's system there is to be a "natural aristocracy," constituted by the people themselves in the act of recognizing and deferring to those of superior talent; it will possess its own "virtue," the capacity to reflect, and will exercise its own function, that of proposing alternatives between which the many's "virtue," the capacity to decide, entitles them to choose. The difference between aristocracy and democracy is moral, numerical, and functional but has no necessary connection with the existence of estates, orders, or classes. It is therefore an error for historians to treat classical republican theory as if it necessarily entailed a society structured into orders and estates. It could, and it often did; but it did not have to. The American Founders knew this, because they had learned it from Machiavelli, Harrington, and Montesquieu, who knew it also. The theory could presuppose a natural, as well as a hereditary or otherwise constituted, aristocracy; what it must presuppose was a division of human political capacity into various aptitudes or virtues, variously distributed, which could be in some degree assigned to the exercise of functions or powers.

With the restoration of royal parliamentary government in England, this theory of "mixed government" became a doctrine of sovereignty lodged in a trinity of distinct but inseparably coordinated powers. This theory encountered implacable opposition from those who denied that the king was an estate of his own realm and insisted that he retained unmixed sovereignty in his own person, although he himself was bound to exercise it in parliament and in consultation with the lords and commons. As against this, "mixed government" could become a doctrine of "separation of powers"; that is, it could assert that the "balance" between the three components was maintained by distinguishing the powers that each exercised—namely, the executive, judicial, and legislative functions. It could further assert that for any one of the three to encroach upon the other two, to the point of rendering them dependent rather than independent, was to "corrupt" the balance and bring about the decay of its "virtues"; and for a medley of historical reasons, the crown and its ministers were regularly suspected of doing this, less through the exercise of the executive's formal power or "prerogative" than through that of its informal power or "influence," by whose means it pursued despotism by corrupting the people's representatives in the legislature.

A rhetoric of the "separation of powers" therefore arose in Britain, but it was held in check by the evident fact that the legislative power resided, not in either house of Parliament, but in the Crown, which was united with both. Fully to separate the executive from the legislative power and to lodge it in a single person, whether hereditary or elective, would entail the establishment of a republic like that of Venice; and it is hard to find anyone in eighteenth-century Britain who had a program for doing that. Britain was not a republic, and no Lockean dissolution of government had occurred in 1688 or at any other time. The theory of undivided sovereignty in the Crown is probably necessary in order to explain the workings of parliamentary democracy in the present. Insofar as we can trace any response to the American crisis in British political discourse—there is surprisingly little—it therefore takes the form of a turning away from "mixed government" and towards affirming the unity of the legislative sovereignty of king in Parliament. This, in the last analysis, was what the British proposed to retain and what they saw the Americans as having challenged; if the British could not keep it by subjugating the colonies, they could keep it by letting them go.

The Americans may therefore be said to have taken seriously and applied in practice two doctrines—the dissolution of government and the separation of powers—which had been developed in England but which the British had never seriously applied to themselves. To be "republican," however, was not merely to take up a posture on the left wing of mixed-government doctrine; it was also to commit oneself to engaging, one way or another, in a discourse about "virtue," which bulks very large indeed in the discourse of the eighteenth century and has proved deeply confusing to historians during the last twenty years. The notion of civic "virtue" was liable to surface wherever were being felt the effects of the ancient commitment to the proposition that man was by nature a political animal; it is surfacing still. The proposition had been challenged by Christians, who had long held that the city of God was more than the city of man and who were still arguing that it was an error to identify civil with moral personality; but an important part of the eighteenth-century program of reducing Christianity to a civil religion was the reassertion of the Greco-Roman doctrine that man was a political animal and every citizen (or every magistrate) his own priest. But this rebirth of ancient paganism was no sooner attempted than it was challenged by modernity: namely, by the perception that under the conditions imposed by the territorial and commercial state, it was no longer possible for the individual to be the autonomous proprietor, arms-bearer, and direct participant in self-government, as presupposed by antiquity. Great benefits to human life were seen as accruing from this profound change, and to dismiss all discussion of it as "nostalgic" and "reactionary," on the one hand, or "progressive" and "bourgeois," on the other, is proof of an incessant desire to misunderstand. The reflective discourse of the eighteenth century was deeply concerned with the problematic nature of virtue; with the difficulty of maintaining it and the difficulty of moving away from it; with the gains to human culture that came from specialization, politeness, and enlightenment; with the losses to human culture that came from abandoning the belief that the moral personality expressed itself directly in political activity. What was under discussion was not a simple choice between opposed ideals but a painful and complicated process. To write about it as if one set of values could be made rigid and relegated to a past and as if all historical movement could be made to consist of the progress away from it is to give proof of an astonishingly limited understanding of what historical processes are like. I am more than tired of a debate conducted in these primitive terms. If I had wanted to write a book called *The Catonian Moment*, I would have done so. I chose, however, to begin with Machiavelli, the better to make the point that "virtue" in early modern times was invariably regarded as ambiguous and fragile, dynamic and problematic, and will probably continue to be so regarded until Western man gives up the belief that he/she is naturally a political animal. The belief is constantly being assailed and is very hard to kill.

Americans rejected the sovereignty of the Crown in Parliament over the colonies; they rejected it as a model to be adopted by the new states, in the belief that it was corrupt. They therefore found themselves committed to the model of a republic of separated powers, in the belief that this would check the executive's tendency to corrupt the legislature, the aristocracy's tendency to corrupt the democracy, and other tendencies of the same kind. But if it was the function of the republic to prevent corruption, it was therefore its function to preserve virtue, because virtue was the antithesis of corruption; and the American debate must to that extent become a debate as to how far the republic must and could rely upon the virtue of its citizens, how far it might remedy existing defects in that virtue, and how far it could maintain itself in the face of the defects or even the absence of virtue. Americans debated the effects of the transition from a world of agriculture to a world of commerce, from a world of militias to a world of standing armies, from a world of hereditary estates to a world of natural elites (they were not quite ready for the democratic intellect's rejection of any elites at all), and from a world of virtue itself to one of passions, interests, and rights. It is the historicity—if "historicism" is too strong a word—of the American debate that I, as the author of *The Machiavellian Moment*, have been trying to establish; and I have been astonished by the determination of some of my colleagues to treat me as if I were seeking to entrap American culture in its past. All I have claimed is that American culture was sophisticated enough to know that it had a history and that it shared its problems with other cultures. It is strange that this has proved so difficult for some to accept or understand.

REPRESENTATION, EMPIRE,
AND THE PROBLEM OF FEDERATIVE POWER

In the American debate we find formulated a conception of the republic which enters into a complex relationship with the idea of representation, itself one of the modernizing concepts—"modern" in the sense that its invention was medieval and therefore not "ancient"—which challenged and sought to transform the idea of virtue. The tension between the two culminated in Madison's drastic revision of accepted language in the tenth of the *Federalist Papers*, where he announces that a polity in which the citizens govern themselves directly is a democracy; one in which they are ruled by their own elected representatives, a republic. This was a new use for the last-named term, and Madison had not separated himself from the belief that the elected representatives would constitute a species of natural aristocracy, a few whose relation with the many who had chosen them would be what rendered the polity a republic. His dictum could well have collided—although there is interestingly little indication that it did—with Rousseau's thesis that such people were free only when electing their representatives, subject to them only while they were in session. But Madison laid down his revision of accepted definitions with a view, as we all know, to overcoming Montesquieu's pronouncement that a republic was possible only in a territory of limited extent. There was much more to this than the simple distinction between an immediate assembly of directly participant citizens and the gathering of representatives from electorates at a distance; but at this point we have arrived at the fundamental problem of any American union—that of extent. How was the "state of nature" in which the thirteen "free and independent states" might find themselves in respect to one another to be converted into a political space and occupied by a "state of civil society?" The paradox is that the word "republic" and the word "representation" both came forward as possible solutions to the problem of extent: that of "uniting" or associating "states" that jointly occupied a vast area and whose relationship was as yet undefined.

Montesquieu made two frequently cited contributions to the debate in which the Americans found themselves involved on this question. The first was to lay down the dictum that a republic was possible only in a limited territory; the second, immediately following the first, was to point out that it could in certain cases be overcome by establishing what he called a *république fédérative*. This was a league or association of republics, in which each member entrusted its power to conduct external relations—its "federative power"—to an authority that would act for all members (and in that sense represent them). It may be seen that Montesquieu had taken an important step in transferring the meaning of "federative" power from that of an attribute of sovereignty, essential to the being of a "state," to that of an authority common to an association of "states," but that he left it unclear whether the common authority of the *république fédérative* owed its existence to anything more than a pact or *foedus* between states, which would retain the sovereignty of which the "federative power" was an attribute.

Montesquieu gives three modern examples of the *république fédérative:* "la Hollande, l'Allemagne, les Ligues suisses, sont regardées en Europe comme des républiques éternelles." Again, it is not easy to tell from his text what sort of *foedus* or exercise of the "federative" power has made them *républiques éternelles* (which they are by repute rather than formally); but the Dutch and Swiss "confederations" (the former of which called itself a *republiek*) possessed a permanent structure that regulated relations between the member provinces or cantons, and it would be hard for one of these to quit the *foedus* without provoking war with its fellows. Nevertheless, by many criteria these confederations were not states but leagues of states. The second case that Montesquieu gives is more striking. By "l'Allemagne" he must have meant "the Germanic body" of "the Holy Roman Empire of the German Nation," which was an "empire" in the sense that it possessed a head claiming the name and authority of the Caesars but whose members possessed such a variety of independent powers and were bound by so incoherent a collection of shared arrangements that it had been described by the jurist Pufendorf as a "monster, shapeless, huge, and horrifying." That might be going too far, even as a statement of the fact that it displayed the name but not the substance of imperial majesty; but Montesquieu's language reveals to us the linguistic fact that what was called an "empire" could at the same time be called a "republic" and a "confederacy." If these terms approached interchangeability, we need to review our understanding of their meanings.

It seems that all three terms could be used to denote political systems of indefinite extent and multiple structure, but to denote very little more: that is, to denote a plurality of political entities, held together by a *confederatio*, which is no more than the sum of the arrangements, or *foedera*, which exist between them and to which each entity, if it is sovereign, stands committed by the exercise of its sovereign power. All three cases that Montesquieu cited are republics and confederacies; the Dutch and the Swiss are not termed "empires" merely because they lack great extent and symbolic monarchy. The German political system alone could be described by all three terms: a linguistic and political fact that was not as monstrous to Montesquieu as it appears to us.

The British case, which was of deeper concern to Americans, was more elusive. We are accustomed to speak of there having existed a "first British empire," which "fell" or otherwise disintegrated during the War of American Independence; but in doing so we risk reading eighteenth-century events through nineteenth-century eyes. The word "empire," as used by English speakers in the eighteenth century, did not primarily denote a hegemonic central power and its dependent colonies. Its original use had been to declare that the realm of England was "an empire entire of itself," in other words, that the king of England was *imperator in regno suo* and that within his kingdom he possessed an absolute sovereign authority which he shared with no foreign prince or spiritual ruler. The Union of England and Scotland in 1707 had been an "incorporating," not a "federative union," and had therefore set up no "confederacy" or "republic." Whether Scotland had been annexed to England or the two "states" had merged into one that was altogether new, the Crown of Great Britain was as "imperial" as that of England had been before it, and this imperial sovereignty, exercised in Parliament, had resisted American attempts to modify its structure. But the Crown possessed (and retained after 1783) dominion over territorial and other entities outside the realm: over the Isle of Man and the Channel Islands, over Ireland (a subordinate kingdom till 1801), and over various colonies and corporations that had been planted and were trading beyond seas. These were not "realms" or "dominions," and their political status was not clear. The term "empire" therefore came to denote the extension of the king's authority beyond the *regnum* in which *rex* was *imperator*; it acquired the opposite meaning: of an open, not a closed, system—not a "state," but an extended system the terms of whose association were not permanently established. When it was debated, during the 1770s or 1780s, how or whether Ireland or the American colonies might remain within "the empire," it is in this inexact sense, not unlike the Roman-Germanic, that the word is being used. The imperial sovereignty of the Crown, however, as well as the unity that it had imposed on England and the Kingdom of Great Britain, absolutely prohibited any description of this "empire" as a "republic" or "confederacy." Neither meaning of "empire," we should last note, carried many of the meanings of "imperialism" in the modern sense; the phenomenon may have been there, but it was not denoted by this use of language.

There was, finally, a sense in which Europe itself might be described as both "republic" and "confederacy." In contradistinction to the "universal empire" of the Romans, which Charles V had sought and Louis XIV could be accused of having sought to revive, it was said that Europe consisted of a number of independent "states," held together by treaties, commerce, and a shared religion and culture. There are cases in which this is called a "republic," even a "federal republic." The adjective would have meant that it was held together by the great *foedera* or treaties—Westphalia, Utrecht, Paris, later Vienna—which constituted the European "system" or "balance of power." If the relations between "states" constituted a "state of nature," it was not an anarchy; it was capable of being regulated by sovereigns exercising their "federative" power. The debate between Federalists and Antifederalists was a debate over whether the American states should retain their "federative" capacity or should yield it up to a government that would be "federal" in an utterly new sense of the word. Only in this sense were the Antifederalists antifederal at all.

At the end of the second sentence of the first number of *The Federalist*, Publius (that is, Hamilton) declares that the debate over the ratification of the United States Constitution will determine "the fate of an empire in many respects the most interesting in the world." He does not propose to abolish this "empire" and replace it by a "republic," and the continental "republic" went on unembarrassedly terming itself an "empire" far into the nineteenth century. What we are learning from this linguistic investigation is that "empire," "republic," and "confederacy" were in use before and after 1787 to denote political systems that were more extensive than organized and that therefore Montesquieu's dictum that a "republic" was possible only within a limited space ought not to be overinterpreted. Montesquieu himself undermined it by raising the case of the *république fédérative*. In laying it down, he had in mind the polis, ruled by its own citizens meeting together, and the fate of Rome, which conquered the world by means of the virtue of such citizens and failed to remain such a polis in the attempt to govern the world. He was not thinking about a self-abnegating Catonian virtue so much as of a dynamic Machiavellian *virtù*, democratic and expansive; republics that were "commonwealths for expansion" expanded beyond narrow limits and destroyed their virtue, but "commonwealths for preservation," such as Venice and Genoa, stayed within their limits and fossilized it. Adam Smith expounded the same view.

Theorists had asked whether Rome could have expanded without setting up a military structure too great for the republic to bear; they had thought that this might have been achieved by a better association of the provinces within the self-governing activity of the Roman people. The extension of limited rights to the Italian subject cities had led to the social war of the first century B.C., in which the latter had demanded full Roman citizenship and in the end had obtained it; but it was held that this had destroyed the *populus Romanus* by rendering it too huge to meet together. But both David Hume and Smith, who were acquainted with the history of the English monarchy, had pointed out that this need not have happened if they had been able to send representatives or if the Roman people had been capable of electing an assembly to represent themselves. A body of directly participating citizens could not be extended over a vast territory; but representation, the one great invention in politics that had been made since antiquity, had rendered possible the consultative government of extensive realms and had at the same time moderated the violence of democracy by rendering it indirect. But the history of England had shown that it was in the first place the Crown which represented the realm as a whole and that the king had summoned representatives of the commons to join him in ruling it; representation had been a device for the extension of sovereignty and for permitting the executive power to surround itself with a legislative assembly. Nothing that had happened in the seventeenth century had altered that fact; and the case against the doctrine of mixed government was that it tended to obscure the truth of that doctrine.

The United States had not only rejected the sovereignty of the Crown in Parliament; they had also rejected the model of government that it offered, partly on the grounds that the executive possessed too much power to corrupt the people's representatives in Parliament. They were not in a position to solve the problem of extensive power by the quasi-Hobbesian device of investing a single person with the capacity to represent the whole American union and requiring him to summon representatives of the states to join him in exercising that capacity. States that were free and independent could not be represented by a single sovereign; the most they could do was to constitute a central authority by exercising their federative powers. It was possible to imagine that such a central authority might consist of an executive single person and his council, who should balance one another's powers; but among the dangers to be averted was that of investing him with enough power to permit him to corrupt the representatives of the states or of the people and render them his creatures.

Madison's solutions to these problems are well known. He proposed redefining the "republic" as a representative rather than a participatory community; and he proposed that a political community of great extent would display such a multiplication of local and particular interests that there would be little danger that any combination of them would overbalance and dominate the others. If the people of such an extensive "empire" (the word is applicable) were to elect both their legislative representatives and their executive magistrates so that the latter too were representatives, and so that there was space for the rhetoric of democracy, there would be little danger that the legislature would be divided into factions or corrupted by the executive. A widely extended people might therefore exert itself in constituting and regularly electing a government, or a series of governing authorities, which would be the expression of its sovereignty, even though the latter remained dispersed and was expressed rather in the processes of election than in the exercise of authority. The government so constituted would be popular in the sense that the people would have elected and authorized it, and it would be republican both in Madison's new sense of the term and in the sense that the principles of mixed government and separation of powers operated among its agencies.

It remained to be shown how such a "national" government (the adjective is a favorite one with Publius) was to coexist with those of "free and independent states" and how the latter were to be anything more than *municipia* of the people's empire—that is, local governments constituted by the sections into which the "people" were locally divided. The authors of *The Federalist*, the Founders, and the Ratifiers concurred in solving the problem by giving the states a variety of roles in the formation and the conduct of the national government. This was less a solution to the problems of "republic," "representation," and "virtue" than to the problem of "uniting" "states." It was a crucial stage in the very remarkable process by which the adjective "federal" and (in political theory) the noun "federation" came to denote a political system that continued to be a *république fédérative* but was more highly unified than a "confederation" or a "confederacy," because it possesssed a national government exercising sovereignty over individuals, rather than authority over sovereigns. The conversion of the word "federal" to mean government in this sense is no less a transformation than is the conversion of the word "republic" to mean "government through representatives,'' for the reason that "federal,'' so used, is largely divorced from "federative." A government elected by the people to represent themselves in their sovereign capacity cannot possibly be constituted by any exercise of the "federative" power possessed only by sovereign "states"; a government exercising sovereignty over the individuals composing a civil society cannot possibly do so by any exercise of the "federative" power, which exists only to conduct relations with other sovereigns. The transformation of the word "federal" till it comes to denote precisely such a government is a remarkable process in the history of political language, which seems to have been little studied in recent years.

It is well known that the United States Constitution, as well as Madison's arguments in support of it, failed to satisfy those whom we collectively if incorrectly term Antifederalists, although they did not reject the Constitution when they saw that it had been ratified. They may be said both to have accepted the necessity of some kind of federation and to have endorsed Franklin's formulation, "a republic if you can keep it," but to have doubted gravely whether it could be kept on the terms the Constitution offered. Very noticeably, they contended that neither the Constitution nor the arguments of *The Federalist* made adequate provision for saving the virtue of either the citizens or their representatives from corruption; and indeed, there are clear and unmistakable signs among Federalists of a tendency to separate the maintenance of a republican balance from the operations of any moral principle within the personality of the individual as citizen. These signs have been gleefully seized on by those historians who are anxious—for reasons that I find hard to understand—to relegate anything "republican" to a pre-American past, by depicting it as something archaic and impossible, the rule of a Catonic or Platonic agrarian estate, exercising virtue in the shape of a complete denial of self. These historians are saying the thing that is not, or at least was never said by anybody. In no case were the Antifederalists seeking to return the American states to the condition of immediate participatory democracies; they were advocates of the extended republic and of representative government. What they doubted was whether representative institutions, exercised over a vast territory under unified government, could prevent the representatives from being corrupted, either by special interests or by involvement in executive government, or could maintain a citizenry that cared enough to see that their own integrity was the precondition of integrity in their representatives.

It may fairly be said that the debate continues. The Constitution of 1787 established a republic, built on representative institutions, which continues to this day to be concerned with the corruption of government, whether by venality, by the abuse of power, or by the combination of both. It was the function of republics to resist corruption, and this is a reason why one was set up. At the same time, it is the destiny of republics to be assailed by corruption and to be aware of it as an ever-present danger. This one is no exception. The philosophical problem entailed by Madison's redefinition of republic as representation is that which had already been raised by Rousseau (though few Founders seem to have been aware of this): Is representation compatible with virtue, and if not, can it be preserved against corruption? If my moral personality is identical with my civil personality, can it be exercised for me by another person acting in my name? If the two are not identical, what moral relation is there between me and my representatives or rulers? Do they need to be honest? Do I care whether they are honest or not? Is there anything honest in me which must operate to keep them honest, and if not, what becomes of honesty anywhere? These problems continue to torment the civic conscience in the United States, and they keep it prophesying the downfall of the republic (and its empire). These problems have not caused that downfall yet and seem most unlikely to do so; but they keep Americans laudably unhappy, loudly confessing the sins with which the rest of mankind delights to tax them. There is something existential about all this; it is part of the liberal determination to indict liberalism.

PRESIDENCY AND MONARCHY:
COUNSEL, COURT, AND PALACE

The president of the United States is neither an emperor nor a king; he does not in his own person exercise or embody sovereignty. But he is a monarch, in the sense in which that term was used in the old vocabulary of mixed government: a single person who is ultimately responsible for the exercise of executive authority in a republic of separated powers. He therefore has the capacity, by mishandling either his formal or his informal authority, to disturb the relations between the separated powers that compose the republic, and thus to induce corruption in any of its eighteenth-century senses. This was a familiar problem in early-modern politics, and the Founders employed a wealth of early-modern resources in erecting barriers against it.

There was one idiom of early-modern politics with which the Founders—an unusually literate generation—seem to have been less well acquainted than they were with others. This was the idiom of court and counsel, which had produced a substantial literature for the use of those who wished to seek intimacy with princes and to give them advice. It dealt with important moral and political problems: how the prince was to be informed about the state of his realm; how he was to communicate with those who could serve or impede him best; how his personality was to be calmed and moderated by relations with friends at the heart of the awful isolation of power. Ideally, the counsellor should be something between moral tutor and spiritual physician, and there was a literature about his high calling and its spiritual and physical dangers. But it was also well understood that power was to be had by gaining the prince's ear and giving him advice, that the prince would be surrounded by aspiring counsellors seeking access to his person, and that much power was to be had by controlling the channels through which they sought to reach him and he sought to communicate his will. Those who both gave advice and determined who should have opportunity to give it were variously known as *amici,* favorites, *privados,* or ministers; but "counsellor" and "courtier" were close to being interchangeable terms, and from Castiglione's *Book of the Courtier* to St-Simon's *Memoirs of the Court of Louis XIV,* the literature viewed counsel, courts, and palaces in lights ranging from the ideal to the cynical.

In shaping the office of the president of the United States, the Founders were either unaware of this literature or did not consider it relevant. In a republic, all political relationships are in theory public, not private; the Senate was expected to give the president counsel and advice by the exercise of its separate power, and the executive officers whom he appointed were excluded from sitting in Congress. By such devices it was hoped to prevent the appearance of the sinister ministers who had supposedly misled George III, just as the abolition of hereditary monarchy would eliminate the minions, mistresses, and eunuchs who populated the folklore of despotism. It came to be assumed that the president would maintain a homespun and open style, so that access to his person would be republican and democratic and need not be gained through the rings of intermediaries who guarded the outer chambers of princes. The Founders were instituting a monarchical office among the institutions of their republic, but they did not study the literature of court and counsel or include it in the education of their citizens. Their chief magistrate was not to inhabit a court or a palace.

This is not the place to trace the steps by which he has come to do so. The enormous growth in the internal and external activities of the twentieth-century state has much to do with this, and so has the process by which major elected officials—the president especially, but by no means uniquely—have come to be attended by large staffs, who in supplying them with information, determine what information they shall receive and who shall have the power to give it. When the people elect a president, they must wait to discover what train of Georgians or Californians he will bring with him and into what power structures surrounding (but acted on by) his person they will resolve themselves. These structures may as well be called courts, because there is no other word for them in our vocabulary. What we call staffers our predecessors called courtiers, and their business was to advise the prince and determine who was to gain access to his person. The White House has become a palace; the historian knows this when he hears discussion about "the basement of the West Wing," indicating that one's physical location in the architecture of power determines one's access to and exercise of it. The president's wife has become a monogamous and respectable *maîtresse en titre;* under the unofficial but prescriptive title of First Lady, she has a (doubtless increasing) staff of her own, who by their mere existence and location play a part in the politics of access, while her own access to the president becomes on occasion the subject of embarrassed but legitimate concern. Some day perhaps there will be a First Gentleman, and then the conjunction of monarchy and monogamy will really come under democratic scrutiny. Meanwhile, president and spouse inhabit a palace and are surrounded by courtiers; it has taken two hundred years for the norms of early-modern monarchy to reassert themselves at the heart of the modern democracy which has grown out of the early-modern republic that thought it had eliminated them. But a single person exercising executive responsibility does not have to be a king in order for court and palace to take shape around him.

The historian finds all this ironic, but not too deeply disturbing. The phenomena that have been enumerated are not so alien to republicanism or democracy that they cannot be regulated. The Tower Report appears to mark a historic moment, because it proclaims to the Republic that its president is indeed the center of a court; that his efficiency and legitimacy as chief executive depend on his ability to handle not only those who act in his name but also those who inform him about what is being done in it; and that he cannot handle these matters simply by selecting a favorite adviser and then relying on him. Senators and congressmen who are driven to concern themselves with the politics of the White House remind the historian of medieval barons or early-modern parliamentarians, reluctantly intervening to remove obstructive favorites and to assume the supervision of powers that did not properly belong to them, but to the prince. The least modern (but still early-modern) component of the picture is the existence in the world of a great many governments that are so far from being legitimized that you cannot make *foedera* with them or rely on the sedate exercise of the federative power from Foggy Bottom (as the place is so happily named).

The president must take responsibility for so many covert operations that it is becoming hard for him to get through his term without some crippling scandal.

Under these conditions it is possible to imagine, though it would be the height of folly to predict, that the presidency might evolve along lines followed by other modern monarchies. The dignified and effective parts of the office might become separated; the president might become a constitutional monarch, who incarnates and articulates the national dignity and is formally incapable of doing wrong, while the responsibilities of executive office and liaison with the legislative assembly might be discharged in his name by the chief of staff, in the role of prime minister or grand vizier. From Bute, North, and Pitt to Haldeman, Regan, and Baker, it would have taken two centuries for the presidency to revert to the eighteenth-century model from which it began in separation. I do not suppose that this going to happen. American politics are resourceful, and something will be done about these problems. The Constitution of the United States was a great achievement of early-modern politics, and a great deal may be learned by viewing it in the early-modern terms that it perpetuated to the point where they have remained effective means of dealing with late-twentieth-century realities.

BIBLIOGRAPHICAL NOTE

This essay is reprinted, with minor amendments, from *Social Science Quarterly* 68 (Dec. 1987); it appears here by the kind permission of the editor.

It seemed better to leave the essay unfootnoted, but it is greatly indebted to several people. In particular, I wish to thank Professors Gerald Stourzh, Peter Onuf, and Lance Banning; also Professor Robert Ginsberg, for a valuable paper read at the Folger Center for the History of British Political Thought on the concept of an African "people." The essay also interacts closely, in various ways, with the following:

Banning, Lance. *The Jeffersonian Persuasion.* Ithaca, N.Y.: Cornell University Press, 1978.
Diggins, John P. *The Lost Soul of American Politics.* New York: Basic Books, 1985.
Pocock, J. G. A. *The Ancient Constitution and the Feudal Law.* Cambridge, Eng.: Cambridge University Press, 1957; rev. ed., 1987.
———. *The Machiavellian Moment.* Princeton, N.J.: Princeton University Press, 1975.
———. *Virtue, Commerce, and History.* Cambridge, Eng.: Cambridge University Press, 1986.
Pole, J. R. *Political Representation in England and the Origins of the American Republic.* New York: St. Martin's Press, 1966.

Robbins, Caroline. *The Eighteenth-Century Commonwealthman.* Cambridge, Mass.: Harvard University Press, 1958.
Stourzh, Gerald. *Alexander Hamilton and the Idea of Republican Government.* Stanford, Calif.: Stanford University Press, 1968.
Tucker, Robert W., and David C. Hendrickson. *The Fall of the First British Empire.* Baltimore, Md.: Johns Hopkins University Press, 1982.
Weston, Corinne C., and Janelle R. Greenberg. *Subjects and Sovereigns.* Cambridge, Eng.: Cambridge University Press, 1981.
Wood, Gordon S. *The Creation of the American Republic.* Chapel Hill: University of North Carolina Press, 1969.

5

State Sovereignty and
the Making of the Constitution

Peter S. Onuf

Controversy over the ratification of the new federal Constitution revolved around the future place of distinct "sovereign" states in the
American union. The Federalist proponents of the new system and their
Antifederalist opponents offered radically different visions of the new
nation's prospects with or without a more powerful central government.
The Federalists equated the rejection of the proposed system with the
collapse of the union, the onset of anarchy and interstate warfare, and
the ultimate loss of American independence. The Antifederalists countered that the pretended "cure" was far more dangerous than the
symptoms it was supposed to alleviate: the creation of a national
sovereignty meant "consolidation," the obliteration of the states and
the loss of individual liberties.

The Federalists warned that disunion would unleash forces of state
particularism: divided among conflicting sovereignties that acknowledged no binding law or common interest, America would become the
image of Europe. If the states could not be abolished altogether—as
many nationalists would have wished—they should at least be made
subordinate to the national government. The Federalists charged that
disunion was implicit in their opponents' broad definition of state
sovereignty. In response, the Antifederalists rose up in defense of local
liberty and republican self-government, thus forcing the advocates of
the Constitution to disavow any intention of subverting the states'
legitimate rights. In order to disarm their critics, the Federalists had to
argue that their goal was to preserve and strengthen the states, not to
destroy them.

The ratification debate revealed profound disagreement about the proper limits of state power in republican America and about the character and conditions of continental "union." For the first time, Americans systematically explored the implications of these key concepts, thus initiating a transformation in political thought on the national level that drew on a rich legacy of changes in the states over the prior decade.[1] Debate over the meaning of "state sovereignty" in the Founding Era reflected a convergence of local and national perspectives: the sovereign people created state governments to guarantee their rights and promote their common welfare; at the same time, however, the existence of the separate states depended on their membership in a larger community of states.

STATE SOVEREIGNTY

The Federalists eventually realized that bold assertions of federal supremacy at the expense of the states would guarantee the rejection of the Constitution. Yet the nationalist reformers had long been convinced that state sovereignty was the fundamental problem of American politics and that federal supremacy was the only solution. In late 1786, for instance, a Connecticut writer asserted that Americans faced a clear choice: "We must have one *sovereignty,* or *Thirteen,* each supported by an army."[2] A few months later, another essayist agreed that although the states coexisted "under the appearance of friendship," they "secretly hate and envy, and endeavour to thwart the interest of each other."[3] Domestic disorders compounded anxieties about interstate conflict. The notorious Shaysite uprising in western Massachusetts even led politicians such as Stephen Higginson, who had previously resisted challenges to states' rights, to conclude that "the powers of the Union must be increased, and those of the States individually must be abridged."[4]

Convinced that a decisive change in public sentiment had prepared the way for the institution of a strong national government, the reformers anticipated that the Constitutional Convention would administer the death blow to state sovereignty. In a widely reprinted newspaper essay, "Harrington"—probably Benjamin Rush—called on the states to "come forward, and first throw their sovereignty at the feet of the convention."[5] Several delegates endorsed this solution to the nation's woes. George Read of Delaware thus was in favor of "doing away [with the] States altogether and uniting them all into one great Society."[6] Delegates from the large states recoiled at such assaults on their territorial integrity but wanted to achieve the same end by circumscribing state powers: according to Hamilton, the states "*as States* . . . ought to be abolished."[7] Under the new regime they should be considered as subordinate "corporations," occupying a position in the union analogous to that of cities and counties in the respective states.[8]

Many constitutional reformers agreed with Gouverneur Morris that "State attachments, and State importance have been the bane of this Country."[9] Rufus King told the Constitutional Convention he was "astonished" that "we should be ready to sacrifice this substantial good"—the security of individual rights—"to the phantom of *State* sovereignty."[10] The advocates of states' rights and interests were "intoxicated with the idea of their *sovereignty*," commented the future Antifederalist Elbridge Gerry, even though "we never were independent States."[11]

If state sovereignty was insubstantial and illusory, however, the states themselves were durable fixtures on the political scene. In secret deliberations at Philadelphia the ultranationalists such as Morris could fantasize about obliterating the states: "What would it be to the happiness of America . . . if all the Charters & Constitutions of the States were thrown into the fire, and all their demagogues into the ocean"?[12] But the delegates understood that the states would have to play a major role in any broadly acceptable federal regime.[13] Forthright rhetorical assaults on state sovereignty were clearly ill advised. Recognizing this, the authors of the *Federalist* series conceded that popular attachment to the states was a fact of American political life, invoking it—in one of their more ingenious formulations—as a leading justification for a more energetic national regime.[14] The Federalists could hardly expect the voters to leave their darling states without adequate constitutional protection against federal encroachments; language that too clearly suggested the states' subordinate and dependent place in the new scheme seemed to substantiate the Antifederalist warnings about the dangers of "consolidation." The advocates of ratification sought to neutralize such concerns by showing that the states would retain an integral role in the new federal government and would exercise a continuing "sovereignty" where powers were not expressly delegated.[15]

The challenge for the reformers was to show that the proposed Constitution "supports and adds a dignity to every government in the United States."[16] The "great end" of the new regime, proclaimed Roger Sherman, was "to protect the several states" against "foreign invasion" and domestic disorder and to facilitate "a beneficial intercourse" among them. Hoping to counter conventional libertarian warnings about the dangers of a more powerful and distant national government, Sherman and his fellow Federalists insisted that the Constitution was "well framed to secure the rights and liberties of the people and for preserving the governments of the individual states."[17]

The necessity of compromising the wide array of interests represented at Philadelphia gave the constitutional reformers a foretaste of political reality. The delegates promoted their constituents' interests shamelessly, threatening to bolt the convention and, presumably, to sacrifice the union if they were not satisfied. Not surprisingly, the resulting concessions to specific interests tended to exaggerate the role of the states generally. Discrepancies in the size of states thus worked to bolster the "federal principle," regardless of the delegates' real preferences. Connecticut's Oliver Ellsworth insisted that "an equality of voices" in Congress was the only means "to secure the Small States ag[ain]st. the large."[18] By preserving the equal voting principle in one branch, the delegates of small states—who, with few exceptions, were enthusiastic nationalists—guaranteed that the states as corporate entities would play an integral part in the new system. Solicitude for sectional interests also led the delegates to qualify their commitment to a consolidated continental government and to concede a larger role to the states. While Morris thought that equal state voting was a "vicious principle," he admitted that it might provide "some defence for the N[orthern]. States" against a combination of southern and new western states.[19]

When negotiating terms of union with each other, the nationalist-minded reformers thus had to acknowledge the practical necessity—and even the desirability—of preserving the states. The Federalists subsequently portrayed these prudent concessions as leading principles of the new order, casting themselves as defenders of the states' essential rights and interests. The Federalists turned the actual process of constitution making on its head; in fact, most of the delegates had come to Philadelphia intending to create a powerful, fully sovereign national government. Many reformers, the Antifederalists correctly noted, would happily have dispensed with the states altogether.

During the ratification controversy, the Federalists repeatedly linked equal representation in the Senate with the preservation of state sovereignty.[20] Making the best of what he privately considered a bad arrangement, James Madison assured his fellow delegates at the Virginia convention that the apparent capitulation to the small states on the representation question would in fact preserve the rights of all the states. State governments would be able to check federal encroachments: the election of the Senate by the state legislatures, Madison explained, "secures an absolute dependence of the former on the latter."[21] Other proponents of the Constitution were more comfortable in acknowledging the legitimacy of state claims. In Pennsylvania,

"Democratic-Federalist" wrote that the principle of proportional representation did not apply to the upper house, because senators would be *"representatives of the sovereignties of their respective states."*[22] The North Carolinian James Iredell further suggested that the Senate, by "protecting the sovereignty of the states," would serve "as a guard against any attempt of consolidation."[23]

If many reformers remained convinced that state sovereignty was the "bane" of American politics, the process of drafting and defending a national constitution converted them into self-proclaimed proponents of states' rights. But they had to define states' rights in a way that could accommodate the radical expansion of federal power. Robert R. Livingston captured the magnitude of this task at the New York convention, asserting that "we are attempting to build one government out of thirteen; preserving, however, the states, as part of the system."[24] Clearly, the states would have to be in some sense taken apart if they were to provide materials for building a single continental government. But how, then, could they be "preserved"?

REPUBLICAN STATES

The Federalists could not deny that the states would have to sacrifice some of their powers. One solution was to assert that the sovereign people retained an undivided, undiminished authority that was delegated to governmental officials for specific purposes.[25] By invoking this idea of "popular sovereignty," the defenders of the new scheme could evade the troublesome question of supremacy and subordination in the distribution of powers. The Federalists also justified this reallocation of authority by arguing that the exercise of sovereign powers by the states was ultimately incompatible with their republican character. In securing the authority of the national government over all general concerns, most notably over foreign policy, the new Constitution would promote the rule of law over and among the states; the states would only give up the power to do themselves—and each other—harm.

Pelatiah Webster argued that a strong national government would best support republican government in the states. He contrasted the likelihood of violent conflict between disunited states with the adjudication of disputes in which states acknowledged "a supreme power, *superior to and able to controul* each and all of its parts." Even "a *wrongful decision*" by a recognized tribunal was "preferable to the continuance of such destructive controversies" between "strong contending bodies." Recognizing no authoritative means of rendering justice, the states inevitably would resort to force in upholding what they judged to be their "rights." Yet, everyone agreed, no man or state was qualified to be the judge in his own case: "rights" defined in such partial fashion were indistinguishable from "interests." Reduced to their "natural," disunited condition, the American states would not survive long as republics. In the event of disunion, both the ends of state policy—the pursuit of interest masquerading as rights—and the means for implementing it—warfare—would subvert and ultimately destroy republican liberty.

Webster argued that the states could be saved from themselves by being barred from exercising sovereign powers and by submitting to the federal government's superintending authority. "The new Constitution leaves all the Thirteen States, complete republics, as it found them," he wrote; indeed, it "gives an establishment, support, and protection to the internal and separate police of each State, under the superintendency of the federal powers, which it could not possibly enjoy in an independent state."[26]

Webster touched on several of the Federalists' most important themes. Their basic premise was that the states were interdependent: the union was like a building, with each state playing a crucial structural role. If the state pillars were withdrawn, the whole edifice would collapse.[27] The states would not survive the general calamity: "The strongest-nerved state, even the right arm, if separated from the body, must wither."[28] It was clear to Livingston, for instance, that New York's very "existence, as a state, depends on a strong and efficient federal government."[29] The states would become progressively weaker and more vulnerable as the bonds of union weakened; by the same logic, James Wilson added, their "respectability and power will increase with that of the general government."[30]

The argument for interdependence was an argument against a broad definition of state sovereignty. Invoking their "realistic" assessment of international politics, the Federalists advanced the paradoxical argument that the complete independence of the separate states would make them dependent on foreign powers and thus would destroy American independence. "Once we were dependent only on Great Britain," wrote Oliver Ellsworth. Because the union was already virtually dissolved, however, "now we are dependent on every petty state in the world."[31] We may be "independent of each other," Thomas Dawes exclaimed in the Massachusetts debates, "but we are slaves to Europe."[32] Only by presenting a united front could the new nation vindicate its rights and promote its interests. Yet if the conduct of foreign policy were to devolve on the states, the Americans' effective power would diminish even while the occasions for its use—against each other as well as foreigners—would multiply.

By emphasizing the "duty" of the national government "to protect and secure the states," the Federalists were able to make a critical rhetorical move.[33] Nationalist reformers had traditionally inveighed against the states as the root of all evil; the Federalists now portrayed them as the *victims* of an imperfect union. Edmund Randolph revealed the development of this position in a speech to the Virginia convention. Because of the defective organization of the union under the Articles, he asserted, Congress had not been "able to cherish and protect the states." Indeed, the central government "has been unable to defend itself against the encroachments made upon it *by* the states. . . . every one of them [Virginia included] has conspired against it."[34] Randolph thus endorsed the states' claims to protection, while condemning independent efforts to vindicate those claims as being dangerous threats to the peace and welfare of the entire union. The states were equally victims and villains; their character depended ultimately on the effectiveness of the union.

The Federalists insisted that only a strong union could guarantee the survival of the states. Outside the union, the states would be vulnerable to internal and external assaults; even if they successfully resisted division, annexation, or recolonization, their republican governments would be imperiled. Without an "effective superintending control," Randolph warned, thirteen distinct states would be unable to "avoid a hatred to each other deep and deadly."[35] Ellsworth explained that the states would then be subject to the same "ambition," "avarice," and "jarring passions" that actuated individuals in a state of nature.[36] Unrestrained by law and unable to look beyond the immediate gratification of selfish interest, the American states would soon degenerate to the moral level of Old World sovereignties—even if their republican forms were temporarily to survive.

The tenuous and deteriorating condition of the present union provided a frightening glimpse of the future: the states had already betrayed republican principles by refusing to acknowledge one another's rights and by selfishly promoting their interests at one another's expense. The apparent premise of interstate relations was that one state's gain was the others' loss. As a result, "the breath of jealousy has blown the cobweb of our confederacy asunder."[37] "Instead of supporting or assisting" one another, complained Hugh Williamson of North Carolina, "we are uniformly taking the advantage of one another."[38] Because of this destructive competition, Noah Webster wrote, the "present situation of our American states is very little better than a state of nature." Under these conditions, he concluded, "our boasted state sovereignties are so far from securing our liberty and property, that they, every moment, expose us to the loss of both."[39]

When states acted "naturally," without restraint of law or respect for the general welfare, they ceased to be republics. Before the convention met, a Philadelphia writer warned that "anarchy" would be the certain result "unless some rule is prescribed, [and] some motive introduced" to "enforce a regard to the general interest."[40] This unwillingness to acknowledge a superior authority would subvert common loyalties; respect for rights and a rule of law would give way to a vicious struggle for relative advantage. A truly republican state, the Federalists suggested, did not pretend to be fully "sovereign." Americans had established state governments on the solid foundation of popular consent, recognizing the necessity of limiting the power of the states in order to guarantee general interests as well as individual rights. Joined in union to secure themselves from the dangers of international power politics, the American states disavowed the conventional prerogatives of sovereignties.

The Federalists suggested that the willingness of the states to submit to the legitimate authority of the general government was the best test of the states' republican character. Would the American states be as rational as those proverbial enlightened men who emerged from their natural condition to enter into social contracts? The individual who joined society renounced the "natural right of being the judge of his wrongs and the executioner of the punishment he might think they deserved." "Plain Truth" insisted that states would have to make analogous sacrifices to enjoy the benefits of union: "state sovereignty . . . is as incompatible with the federal Union, as the natural rights of human vengeance is with the peace of society."[41] The Federalists invoked this argument repeatedly, justifying a reallocation of power in the federal system by pointing to the dangerous tendencies of state politics under the Articles. Clearly, they insisted, "States in confederacy, like individuals in society, must part with some of their privileges for the preservation of the rest."[42] But the progressive deterioration of Congress's authority had obscured this vital principle, encouraging the states to reclaim these "natural privileges" and thus accelerating the collapse of the union.

The sacrifice of states' rights that was entailed by union, the Federalists emphasized, was more apparent than real. After all, states, like individuals in their natural condition, were at best unreliable judges of their own rights and interests. The cool, rational, and impartial deliberations of an effective national government would be a valuable corrective to the passionate excesses of unchecked state power. David Ramsay showed how the restraints on states would work to their ultimate advantage:

When several parishes, counties, or districts, form a state, the separate interests of each must yield to the collective interest of the whole. When several states combine in one government, the same principles must be observed. These relinquishments of natural rights, are not real sacrifices: each person, county, or state, gains more than it loses, for *it only gives up a right of injuring others,* and obtains in return aid and strength to secure itself in the peaceable enjoyment of all remaining rights.[43]

By identifying the advantages of civilized society with the renunciation of the natural rights that are "enjoyed" in a condition of lawless anarchy, Federalists such as Ramsay suggested that the American states would fulfill their republican destiny by perfecting their union.

Who would oppose this evidently irresistible logic? The Federalists had no doubt that if efforts to reform the union were to fail, "it will be owing to the narrow minds, or selfish views of little politicians" in the states.[44] In order to preempt this predictable opposition, the convention appealed directly to the sovereign people in each state to approve the Constitution. The "demagogues" who had gained power so easily in the states had the most to lose if the union were revitalized; they gratified their "ambition" and "avarice" by catering to the whims of the mob and by promoting their states' immediate interests, whatever the ultimate cost.[45] Should the union collapse, state leaders would be well situated to seize unlimited power—perhaps under the plausible pretext of military emergency—and to extinguish civil liberty.

Attacks on state officeholders followed logically from the redefinition of statehood and state sovereignty in Federalist polemics. The proponents of the new Constitution contrasted the state republics, which were properly secured in their legitimate rights and interests, with incipient state despotisms, preparing—consciously or not—for the inevitable war of all against all. The preservation of republican liberty therefore depended on a stronger union. But if Americans were to reject the Constitution and thus chose disunion, the states would come to resemble the dangerously independent sovereignties that perpetuated a state of war and destroyed liberty in Europe. Demagogues would exploit interstate rivalries and popular discontent until a new regime of tyranny would be instituted.

THE ANTIFEDERALIST RESPONSE

How could the Federalists be so confident that war would break out among the disunited states? Challenging the Federalist analysis at every point, the Antifederalists asserted that there was no "crisis" in American politics. They concluded that disunion would be preferable to the loss of republican liberty under a "consolidated" national government.

The Antifederalists exploited many of the same fears and anxieties that figured prominently in their opponents' rhetoric. Federalists and Antifederalists alike warned against the loss of republican liberty and the dangers of "despotism" and counterrevolution. Each party predicted that the other's victory would lead to a bloody denouement: civil war would lead to despotism; or despotism, to civil war. They differed, of course, on key premises. The Federalists were convinced that the new nation was already in the throes of a crisis that required appropriately heroic remedies; the Antifederalists countered that the "crisis" had been brought on by the reformers themselves. The Federalists traced America's many troubles to the rapid deterioration of the union, which was apparent in discordant state commercial policies, frontier separatism, and Congress's notorious "imbecility." The Antifederalists dismissed all these pretexts for reform, asserting that a "consolidated" national government represented the gravest possible threat to American freedom.

James Winthrop of Massachusetts developed the Antifederalist argument most fully in his "Agrippa" series. Because "Europe is engaged, and we are tranquil," there was no need for precipitate action.[46] After due deliberation, good republicans would realize that "the powers of Congress over the citizens should be small in proportion as the empire is extended."[47] Everyone knew that "no extensive empire can be governed upon republican principles."[48] If the central government were not carefully limited, it would soon exercise despotic authority and destroy the states. Winthrop was convinced that "the authority of Congress to decide disputes between states is sufficient to prevent their recurring to hostility."[49] Meanwhile, mutually beneficial commerce would be "a bond of union"; the "different situation, wants and produce" of the respective states "is a sufficient foundation for the most friendly intercourse."[50]

Winthrop implied that the union would perfect itself—unless consolidationists should succeed in imposing a strong government over the states. Under such a despotic regime, Winthrop and his Antifederalist allies explained, the interests of the remote, less favored parts of the empire would be sacrificed. This meant that "the extremes of the empire"—including New England—will "be drained to fatten an overgrown capital."[51] Under free governments, however, different sections of the continent would meet each other on an equal footing; reciprocal needs would draw the states closer together.

Although many opponents of constitutional reform can be called "men of little faith" who were primarily dedicated to protecting local liberties and to preserving their own power, Winthrop was not alone in articulating a broader, optimistic vision of America's future prospects.[52]

In contrasting a consolidated union based on force with a voluntary, harmonious union of states, these polemicists expressed their faith in the transformative powers of republicanism. Under the new republican dispensation, commercial exchange and the pursuit of common interests would supersede the recourse to threats and coercion that traditionally "governed" relations among states. From this rhetorical high ground, the Federalists' insistence on a more "respectable" nation that would be capable of holding its own against supposedly hostile European powers seemed tantamount to a disavowal of republicanism itself. The citizens of the separate, independent American republics were being asked to sacrifice their rights and liberties to a distant, irresponsible central government. And whatever constitutional limitations the Federalists promised, the Antifederalists were convinced that the new government would soon take on the characteristics of the despotic regimes that it was supposed to protect the continent against.

The Antifederalists charged that constitutional reformers had little faith in republican government. To promote their own narrow interests, the Federalists intended to make America over in Europe's image. The Federalists' argument that the putative tendency toward disunion would Europeanize American politics was a calumny on the states. "The state governments answer the purposes of preserving the peace," Melancton Smith told his fellow New Yorkers. It was ridiculous to predict that the states would ever go to war with each other: "The idea of a civil war among the states is abhorrent to the principles and feelings of almost every man of every rank in the union." Anyone who thought differently was only "fit to be shut up in Bedlam."[53]

Republics would never have a plausible incentive to destroy one another. "The citizens of republican borders are only terrible to tyrants," Patrick Henry explained; "Instead of being dangerous to one another, they mutually support one another's liberties." It therefore followed that the true "union" of republics—their mutual forbearance and support—did not depend on formal political or constitutional arrangements.[54] The Antifederalists insisted that the division of the continent among sovereign states would guarantee liberty. George Mason opposed the Constitution because he believed "popular governments can only exist in small territories."[55] Invoking the authority of "celebrated writers" such as Montesquieu, the Antifederalists unanimously agreed with Brutus (probably Melancton Smith) that "a free republic cannot succeed over a country of such immense extent." "In a large extended country," Brutus explained, "it is impossible to have a representation, possessing the sentiments, and of integrity, to declare the minds of the people."[56] In the words of the Antifederalist dissenters at the Pennsylvania convention, "nothing short of the supremacy of despotic sway could connect and govern these United States under one government."[57]

If the movement for a stronger union endangered liberty and threatened to reestablish monarchical rule in America, it followed that efforts to divide overlarge states would advance the republican cause.[58] Only "Cato" and a few similarly bold polemicists were willing to carry their argument this far. Cato told New York readers that "the extent of many states . . . is at this time almost too great for . . . a republican form of government." The choice therefore had to be made between forming larger, "more vigorous," and "despotic" governments or dividing the states "into smaller and more useful, as well as moderate ones." The Vermonters' successful rebellion against New York showed how precarious state authority could be over distant frontier regions. Of course, if New York had had a proper army at its disposal, it "never would have lost Vermont." But New Yorkers would have paid a high price to keep up a "standing army" and hold on to Vermont: "If we may believe the experience of ages," Cato concluded, it would have meant "the destruction of their liberties."[59] It was much more doubtful that a continental government—while it retained the semblance of a republican form—could uphold its extended jurisdiction.

Most Antifederalists agreed that the nationalists who sought to "melt" the states "into one empire" were enemies of republican liberty. But young Samuel Bryan of Pennsylvania, calling himself Centinel, went one step further, contrasting the invidious designs of constitutional reformers with the efforts of freedom-loving separatists who rose up against the "inconveniencies and disadvantages" of "remote," unresponsive, and unrepresentative state governments.[60] In Maryland, "A Farmer" (probably John Francis Mercer, a recent arrival from Virginia) developed the most forthright Antifederalist endorsement of separatism. As long as we remain *"in a confederacy,"* he wrote, "our state disputes . . . would subside before injury": the people of the different states would never lose control of their governments. But "in a *national* government," disputes among states would reflect "the deeprooted differences of interest." Inevitably, "part of the empire must be injured"—while the other would gain—"by the operation of general law." "Should the sword of government be once drawn" under such circumstances, he continued,

> I fear it will not be sheathed, until we have waded through that series of desolation, which France, Spain, and the other great kingdoms of the world have suffered, in order to bring so many separate States into uniformity, of government and law; in which event the legislative power can only be entrusted to one man (as it is with them) who can have no *local attachments, partial interests,* or *private views* to gratify.

But the genius of republican government, in which the people were "free, government having no right to them, but they to government," was to protect private interests and nourish "local attachments." This freedom constituted the foundation of social happiness; it included not only the right to self-government but also the right to "separate and divide as interest or inclination prompted."[61]

Antifederalists such as "A Farmer" discounted the seriousness of interstate conflict under the Confederation. Some even agreed that disunion would be no catastrophe: the American republics would offer no ready target for foreign invaders, and citizen-soldiers would always be vigilant and valiant in defense of local liberties. In the Virginia convention, James Monroe pointed to the successful resolution of the controversy over western lands through the large cessions of land by the states. "Nor," he added "is there an existing controversy between any of the states at present." "This great source of public calamity" had been eliminated *without* benefit of a strong central government.[62]

The tendency of American politics was toward an increasingly stable balance of power among the states, which had resulted from the adjustment of state boundaries and the spread of more effective and responsive local governments. The Federalists were misled by the apparent discord unleashed by popular partisanship. But because of the "natural moderation of the American character," such disputatiousness had never amounted to more than "a warfare of argument and reason." After all, differences of interest and sentiment over such an extensive continent were natural and inevitable. As long as the United States remained a true confederation of independent republics, these differences would never lead to violence. Because the people were always ready to flee from anything approaching despotism, "moderation" must always be the first "law of self-preservation" for the American states.[63]

The Antifederalists countered Federalist warnings about approaching anarchy by predicting the outbreak of "a civil war with all its dreadful train of evils" as the states sought to defend the tattered remnants of their sovereignty and independence against consolidation.[64] The resulting "violent dissensions between the state governments and the Congress" would inevitably "terminate in the ruin of the one or the other."[65] The opponents of the Constitution dwelled as much on the horrors of civil discord that would accompany efforts to establish the new order as on the despotic rule "consolidation" necessarily entailed. Luther Martin thought that the Federalists' insidious plan to by-pass the state legislatures and to gain endorsement for the new Constitution through state ratifying conventions would "introduce *anarchy* and *confusion*, and . . . *light* the *torch of discord and civil war* throughout this continent."[66] Consolidationists ultimately would fail, George Mason said, but not before "the People of these united States [would become] involved in all the Evils of Civil War."[67] Others feared that credulous voters would be all too willing to endorse the new system; for them, "the seeds of civil discord" had been "plentifully sown" in the Constitution itself.[68] The constant struggle for control of the powerful national executive ("an *Elective King*") would "lay the foundation of clamors, broils, and contentions that will end in *blood*."[69]

The common theme in all these predictions was that the campaign to strengthen the union would destabilize American politics. The Americans' love of liberty and their patriotic attachment to their states would provoke resistance to consolidation: by their own strenuous efforts to block ratification, the Antifederalists anticipated a much broader—and much more violent—popular reaction. If dissenters exaggerated the dangers of the new order and the malign intentions of its sponsors, they were only giving fair warning of the depth and the scope of the controversy that such concentrated power inevitably would promote. Americans would be compelled to reenact the classic struggle between power and liberty that had driven the Revolutionaries to declare their independence. But now, with the avatars of power so effectively disguised as republicans, liberty lovers were facing an even more deadly and insidious challenge.

Denying the authenticity of their opponents' "crisis," the Antifederalists counseled patience. Although most of them acknowledged the need to revitalize Congress, their emphasis on the dangers of consolidation led them to take a relatively benign view of the consequences of disunion. By emphasizing specific burdens that the new regime would probably impose on their states or regions, the dissenters implied that no union at all might be preferable. That conclusion flowed logically from the conventional assumptions that "mankind are governed by interest"[70] and that "interest is the bond of social union." The apparently irreconcilable, "jarring interests" of the different parts of the country (so "different in soil, climate, customs, produce, and every thing") argued against their continuing union.[71] Coercion, the reliance on military force to enforce national authority, was no substitute for a voluntary union of free republics.

The Antifederalists tailored their warnings to their local audiences and thus seemed to offer contradictory arguments against the Constitution: but they all agreed on the basic principle that it should never be in the power of one section to legislate for the others. According to the Antifederalist view, the Articles of Confederation, for all of their obvious defects, had given the states adequate security against each other and thus had enabled them to preserve a union that a strong central government certainly would long since have destroyed. "The southern parts of America have been protected by that weakness so much execrated," Patrick Henry told the Virginia convention.[72] Because the interests of the different parts of the continent were so diverse and their natural connections so tenuous, a *weak* central government, carefully confined to the few common concerns of all the states, was the best guarantor of union. *"From the weakness of all,"* the Maryland Farmer added, *"you may be governed by the moderation of the combined judgments of the whole, not tyranized ever by the blind passions of a few individuals."*[73] Under a confederation with "limited powers," wrote James Winthrop, a natural harmony and balance would be established among the states. Instead of violent contests for relative advantage, an "enlarged intercourse" among the states would draw them into closer interdependence. As a result, he concluded, "our union shall outlast time itself."[74]

But what sort of "union" did Antifederalists such as Winthrop have in mind? If the Confederation was their model, nationalist reformers charged, the opponents of the Constitution were really advocating disunion. As critics had been saying for years, the "confederacy" was no more than a "cobweb"; "it is not a union of sentiment;—it is not a union of interest;—it is not a union to be seen—or felt—or in any manner perceived."[75] Some Antifederalists were so wary of the Federalists' consolidated regime that they appeared to be willing to concede the point; their "union" was purely voluntary and uncoerced—it had no political existence at all.

The Maryland Farmer pushed this logic to the extreme, boldly confronting the Federalists' leading justification for a stronger union. Just as he endorsed separatism within the states, he was willing to risk the supposed dangers of disunion. If this meant that American politics would become more like Europe's, the Farmer welcomed the change. Europeans had made great progress toward a more enlightened and rational system, precisely because their division "into small independant States" had preserved "a degree of social happiness very different from what exists in other parts of the world." The European state system thus constituted a plausible model for the American union:

> Those States who admit the sanction of the laws of nature and nations form as it were a *great federal republic*, and the balance of power, even under an imperfect system, has prevented those great revolutions and shocks which sweeping myriads of mortals at a blow, degrade mankind in the eye of philosophy, to a level with the ants and other insects of the earth.[76]

The Farmer told the Federalists that they had everything backwards. The proliferation of small, independent states did not reduce the United

States to a state of anarchy, thus multiplying occasions for war and violence. It was, instead, the efforts of nationalist reformers to extend and consolidate the authority of the central government that threatened a continental blood bath.

CONCEPTS OF STATEHOOD

The Antifederalists believed that the survival of the American union ultimately depended on the voluntary affinities and harmonious interests of the new American republics. "Union" grew out of and expressed an *existing* general interest that optimists such as James Winthrop saw growing stronger over time. The supposed "crisis" in American politics, the Antifederalists averred, was being blown all out of proportion by cryptonationalists who aimed to abolish the states and destroy individual liberties. In fact, the Confederation of sovereign states had worked remarkably well in maintaining peace among its members and in allowing them to achieve common goals.

The course of the ratification debate worked against the Antifederalists, however; it exposed contradictory elements in their logic and opened up new polemical opportunities for the defenders of the proposed Constitution. On the level of theory, the Antifederalist brief for states' rights was not clearly distinguishable from the outright assertion of state sovereignty and the negation of national authority. And in light of their minimalist conception of voluntary union, the Antifederalists' warnings about the liabilities of the new system for the peculiar interests of particular states seemed to point directly toward disunion. Given the conflicting state and sectional interests that provided the Antifederalists with so many arguments against "consolidation," it was hard to imagine that the present Confederation could long survive or that its successors—thirteen distinct sovereignties or a smaller number of regional confederations—would be able to coexist peacefully.

The Federalists benefited from the discrepancy between the idea of distinct, self-sufficient state sovereignties, which they imputed to their adversaries, and the conventional perception that the states were interdependent and that their governments exercised only limited powers. The key premise in the Federalist argument was that the status quo was inherently unstable: the unmistakable decline in congressional authority had created a vacuum of power that "demagogues" in the states had already moved to fill. This same inexorable redistribution of power would fragment interests, weaken the bonds of union, and threaten to inaugurate an anarchic reign of selfishness and party politics. The Federalists thus rejected the Antifederalist argument that union naturally grew out of common interests: the Federalists were convinced that the true interests of the American people would remain unrecognized and unfulfilled until a strong national government, capable of restraining and directing narrow local interests, was instituted.

By depicting the Antifederalists as disunionists and by aiming Federalist rhetoric at the pernicious effects of unbounded state sovereignty, the Federalists could portray themselves as the true conservators of an original federal compact that was being jeopardized by the centrifugal tendencies of recent American politics. Wittingly or not, the opponents of reform reinforced these tendencies, aiding and abetting the demagogic leaders who stood to benefit most from the collapse of the union. The Federalists claimed that the real interests of the continent were being disguised and distorted by the ascendancy of state interest. But the American voters—once they had been enlightened by Federalist rhetoric—would come to see that the success of petty politicians in promoting their states' pretensions to unlimited sovereign power would be disastrous for civil liberty and republican government—and ultimately for the states themselves. State governments ceased to be truly republican when they overstepped the boundaries of their legitimate authority: they became artificial, despotic excrescences that thwarted the genuine will and interests of the American people.

Constitutional reform was directed less at resolving an existing crisis than at preventing the ultimate Europeanization of American politics. The Antifederalists were on strong ground in questioning the extent of the present crisis, and they had ample grounds for arguing that the states had *not* behaved in the dangerously destructive ways that the Federalists had predicted they would in the future. But the Federalists succeeded in shifting debate forward in time, exploiting recent developments—unrest in Massachusetts, potentially divisive state policies in commercial regulation and in handling the national debt, the increasingly apparent "imbecility" of Congress—to project the inevitable transformation of the American states into hostile sovereignties. The states could only preserve their republican character by remaining within their proper sphere and eschewing the perilous temptations of sovereign power.

NOTES

1. On the absence of theorizing about national government in the Confederation period see Jack N. Rakove, *The Beginnings of National Politics: An Interpretive History of the Continental Congress* (New York: Knopf, 1979), pp. 183–91. Gordon S. Wood, in *The Creation of the American Republic, 1776–1787* (Chapel Hill: University of North Carolina Press, 1969), provides a comprehensive treatment of developing political ideas.

2. Item in *New-Haven* (Conn.) *Gazette*, 7 Dec. 1786.

3. Item in *Massachusetts Sentinel* (Boston), 11 Apr. 1787; Merrill Jensen et al., eds., *The Documentary History of the Ratification of the Constitution*, 7 vols. to date (Madison: State Historical Society of Wisconsin, 1976–   ), 13:79; this piece had been reprinted fifteen times throughout the country by Sept. 1.

4. Stephen Higginson to Henry Knox, 8 Feb. 1787, Henry Knox Papers, Massachusetts Historical Society, Boston, vol. 19.

5. "Harrington" [Benjamin Rush?], "To the Freemen of Pennsylvania," *Pennsylvania Gazette* (Philadelphia), in *Documentary History of Ratification*, 13:116–20, at 118–19; reprinted thirty times by Aug. 11.

6. George Read's speech, June 11, in Max Farrand, ed., *The Records of the Federal Convention of 1787*, 4 vols. (New Haven, Conn.: Yale University Press, 1911–37), 1:202. All citations are to Madison's notes.

7. Alexander Hamilton's speech, 19 June, ibid., 1:323. For further discussion of this point see Peter S. Onuf, "State Equality and a More Perfect Union: Maryland and the Ratification of the Constitution," unpublished manuscript.

8. Rufus King's speech, 19 June; James Madison's speech, 28 June; Gouverneur Morris's speech, 7 July—all in *Records of the Federal Convention*, 1:323–24, 447, 552.

9. Morris's speech, 5 July, ibid., p. 530.

10. King's speech, 30 June, ibid., p. 489.

11. Elbridge Gerry's speech, 29 June, ibid., p. 467.

12. Morris's speech, 7 July, ibid., p. 553.

13. On the pragmatism of the framers, see John P. Roche, "The Founding Fathers: A Reform Caucus in Action," *American Political Science Review* 55 (1961): 799–816.

14. This point is well developed by Edward Millican in "One United People: The Federalist Papers and the National Idea," unpublished manuscript.

15. Peter S. Onuf, *The Origins of the Federal Republic: Jurisdictional Controversies in the United States, 1775–1787* (Philadelphia: University of Pennsylvania Press, 1983), pp. 198–209.

16. "One of the People," *Pennsylvania Gazette*, 17 Oct. 1787, in *Documentary History of Ratification*, 2:186–92, at 190.

17. "A Citizen of New Haven" [Roger Sherman], *Connecticut Courant* (Hartford), 7 Jan. 1788, in *Documentary History of Ratification*, 3:524–27, at 524, 527.

18. Oliver Ellsworth's speech, 29 June, in *Records of the Federal Convention*, 1:468.

19. Morris's speech, 13 July, ibid., p. 604.

20. See, for instance, Sherman and Ellsworth to Gov. Samuel Huntington, 26 Sept. 1787 in *Documentary History of Ratification*, 3:351–53; "Aristides" [Alexander Contee Hanson], "Remarks on the Proposed Plan of a Federal Government" (Annapolis, Md., 1788), in *Pamphlets on the Constitution of the United States*, ed. Paul Leicester Ford (Brooklyn, N.Y., 1888), pp. 217–57, at 223–24.

21. Madison's speech at the Virginia convention, 6 (?) June 1788, *The Debates in the Several State Conventions on the Adoption of the Federal Constitution*, ed. Jonathan Elliot, 5 vols. (Philadelphia, 1876), 3:97.

22. "Democratic Federalist," *Independent Gazetteer* (Philadelphia), 26 Nov. 1787, in *Documentary History of Ratification*, 2:294–98, at 296; see also William R.

Davie's speech at the North Carolina convention, 24 July 1788, in *Debates in the Several State Conventions*, 4:21.

23. James Iredell's speech at the North Carolina convention, 28 July 1788, in *Debates in the Several State Conventions*, 4:133.

24. R. R. Livingston's speech at the New York convention, 1 July 1788, ibid., 2:385.

25. The idea of "popular sovereignty" is elaborated in Wood, *Creation of the American Republic*, pp. 524–36.

26. Pelatiah Webster, "The Weakness of Brutus Exposed: or, Some Remarks in Vindication of the Constitution" (Philadelphia, 1787), *Pamphlets on the Constitution*, pp. 117–31, at 119, 120, 128.

27. Oliver Wolcott's and Richard Law's speeches at the Connecticut convention, 9 Jan. 1788, in *Documentary History of Ratification*, 3:557, 559. See the discussion in Onuf, *Origins of the Federal Republic*, pp. 201–4.

28. Gen. William Heath's speech at the Massachusetts convention, 30 Jan. 1788, in *Debates in the Several State Conventions*, 2:121.

29. Livingston's speech at the New York convention, 19 June 1788, ibid., p. 211.

30. James Wilson's speech at the Pennsylvania convention, 4 Dec. 1787, in *Documentary History of Ratification*, 2:469–85, at 477.

31. "Landholder" [Ellsworth], II, *Connecticut Courant*, 12 Nov. 1787, in *Documentary History of Ratification*, 3:400–403, at 401.

32. Thomas Dawes's speech at the Massachusetts convention, 21 Jan. 1788, in *Debates in the Several State Conventions*, 2:58.

33. Samuel Holden Parsons to William Cushing, 11 Jan. 1788, in *Documentary History of Ratification*, 3:569–73, at 570.

34. Edmund Randolph's speech at the Virginia convention, 6 June 1788, in *Debates in the Several State Conventions*, 3:82, my emphasis.

35. Randolph, "Letter on the Federal Constitution" (Richmond, Va., 1787), in *Pamphlets on the Constitution*, pp. 259–76, at 264.

36. Ellsworth's speech at the Connecticut convention, 4 Jan. 1788, in *Documentary History of Ratification*, 3:541–45, at 542.

37. *Massachusetts Sentinel*, 11 Apr. 1787, ibid., 13:79.

38. Hugh Williamson, "Remarks on the New Plan of Government," *State Gazette of North Carolina*, [1788], in *Essays on the Constitution of the United States*, ed. Paul Leicester Ford (Brooklyn, N.Y.: Historical Printing Club, 1892), pp. 393–406, at 403.

39. [Noah Webster], "An Examination into the leading principles of the Federal Constitution" (Philadelphia, 1787), in *Pamphlets on the Constitution*, pp. 25–65, at 55.

40. Item in *Pennsylvania Herald*, 9 May 1787, in *Documentary History of Ratification*, 13:97.

41. "Plain Truth," "Reply to An Officer of the Late Continental Army," *Independent Gazetteer*, 10 Nov. 1787, ibid., 2:216–23, at 218.

42. James White to Gov. Richard Caswell, 13 Nov. 1787, in *Letters of the Members of the Continental Congress*, ed. Edmund Cody Burnett, 8 vols. (Washington, D.C.: Carnegie Institution, 1921–36), 8:681–82.

43. David Ramsay, "An Address to the Freemen of South Carolina, on the subject of the Federal Constitution" (Charleston, [1788]), in *Pamphlets on the Constitution*, pp. 371–80, at 373, my emphasis.

44. "Extract of a letter from a gentleman in Virginia," *Independent Gazetteer,* 26 June 1787, in *Documentary History of Ratification,* 13:145–47, at 145–46.

45. "Harrington" [Rush], *Pennsylvania Gazette,* 30 May 1787, ibid., 13:116–20, at 118; Henry Knox to ?, [Sept. 1787], ibid., 13:279–80; George Nicholas, draft of speech, 16 Feb. 1788, Durrett Collection, University of Chicago, fol. 4.

46. "Agrippa" [James Winthrop], III, *Massachusetts Gazette,* 30 Nov. 1787, in *Essays on the Constitution,* pp. 59–62, at 62.

47. "Agrippa," IX, *Massachusetts Gazette,* 28 Dec. 1787, ibid., pp. 79–81, at 80.

48. "Agrippa," IV, *Massachusetts Gazette,* 3 Dec. 1787, ibid., pp. 63–65, at 64.

49. "Agrippa," XIII, *Massachusetts Gazette,* 14 Jan. 1788, ibid., pp. 93–101, at 100.

50. "Agrippa," VIII, *Massachusetts Gazette,* 25 Dec. 1787, ibid., pp. 76–78, at 77, and XIII, 14 Jan. 1788, ibid., pp. 93–101, at 100.

51. Ibid., p. 98. See Onuf, *Origins of the Federal Republic,* pp. 192–93, for further discussion of this point.

52. The famous characterization of the Antifederalists is from Cecelia Kenyon's influential essay "Men of Little Faith: The Anti-Federalists on the Nature of Representative Government," *William and Mary Quarterly,* 3d ser., 12 (1955): 3–43; see also Herbert J. Storing, *The Complete Anti-Federalist,* vol. 1: *What the Anti-Federalists Were "For"* (Chicago: University of Chicago Press, 1981); and James H. Hutson, "Country, Court, and Constitution: Antifederalism and the Historians," *William and Mary Quarterly* 38 (1981): 337–68.

53. "A Plebeian" [Melancton Smith], "An Address to the People of the State of New-York: Showing the necessity of making Amendments to the Constitution" (New York, 1788), in *Pamphlets on the Constitution,* pp. 87–115, at 95–96, 97; see also Smith's speech at the New York convention, 20 June 1788, in *Debates in the Several State Conventions,* 2:223–24.

54. Patrick Henry's speech at the Virginia convention, 7 June 1788, *Debates in the Several State Conventions,* 3:145.

55. George Mason's speech at the Virginia convention, 4 June 1788, ibid., 3:30.

56. "Brutus" [Melancton Smith?], 18 Oct. 1787, in *Documentary History of Ratification,* 13:411–21, at 418.

57. "The Dissent of the Minority," *Pennsylvania Packet,* 18 Dec. 1787, ibid., 2:617–40, at 626; see also Samuel Chase, "Notes of Speeches Delivered to the Maryland Ratifying Convention," Apr. 1788, in *The Complete Anti-Federalist,* ed. Herbert J. Storing, 7 vols. (Chicago: University of Chicago Press, 1981), 5:79–91, at 81.

58. "Old Whig," IV, *Independent Gazetteer,* 27 Oct. 1787, in *Documentary History of Ratification,* 13:497–502, at 499; Monroe's speech at the Virginia convention, 10 June 1788, in *Debates in the Several State Conventions,* 3:215.

59. "Cato," III, *New York Journal,* 25 Oct. 1787, in *Essays on the Constitution,* pp. 255–59, at 257, 258.

60. "Centinel" [Samuel Bryan], I, *Independent Gazetteer,* 5 Oct. 1787, in *Documentary History of Ratification,* 2:158–67, at 164.

61. "A Farmer" [John Francis Mercer], III, *Maryland Gazette* (Baltimore), 7 Mar. 1788, in *Complete Anti-Federalist,* 5:29–32, at 30–31.

62. Monroe's speech at the Virginia convention, 10 June 1788, in *Debates in the Several State Conventions,* 3:212.

63. "Farmer," III, *Maryland Gazette* (Baltimore), in *Complete Anti-Federalist,* 5:29–32, at 32.

64. Item in *Independent Gazetteer,* 22 Jan. 1788, in *Documentary History of Ratification,* 2:657.

65. "An Officer of the Late Continental Army," *Independent Gazetteer,* 6 Nov. 1787, ibid., 2:210–16, at 211.

66. Luther Martin, "The Genuine Information, Delivered to the Legislature of the State of Maryland, Relative to the Proceedings of the General Convention, Held at Philadelphia, in 1787," *Maryland Gazette* (Annapolis), 28 Dec. 1787–8 Feb. 1788, in *Records of the Federal Convention,* 3:172–232, at 230.

67. Mason to Gerry, 20 Oct. 1787, in *The Papers of George Mason,* ed. Robert A. Rutland, 3 vols. (Chapel Hill: University of North Carolina Press, 1970), 3:1005–7, at 1006.

68. Benjamin Harrison to Washington, 4 Oct. 1787, in *Documentary History of the Constitution of the United States of America,* 5 vols. (Washington, D.C.: Department of State, 1905), 4:312–13.

69. Benjamin Gale's speech at the Connecticut convention, 12 Nov. 1787, in *Documentary History of Ratification,* 3:420–29, at 426.

70. William Grayson's speech at the Virginia convention, 11 June 1788, in *Debates in the Several State Conventions,* 3:282.

71. Timothy Bloodworth's speech at the North Carolina convention, 28 July 1788, ibid., 4:135.

72. Henry's speech at the Virginia convention, 9 June 1788, ibid., 3:151–52.

73. "Farmer," III, *Maryland Gazette* (Baltimore), 18 Mar. 1788, in *Complete Anti-Federalist,* 5:32–36, at 36.

74. "Agrippa" [Winthrop], XIV, *Massachusetts Gazette,* 18 Jan. 1788, in *Essays on the Constitution,* pp. 102–4, at 103.

75. Item d., New York, 23 Apr. 1787, rpt. from *Massachusetts Sentinel* (Boston), in *Carlisle* (Pa.) *Gazette,* 9 May 1787; "Lycurgus," II, *New-Haven Gazette and Connecticut Magazine,* 23 Feb. 1786. See the discussion in Cathy Matson and Peter Onuf, "Toward a Republican Empire: Interest and Ideology in Revolutionary America," *American Quarterly* 37 (1985): 496–531, at 526–27.

76. "Farmer," VII, *Maryland Gazette* (Baltimore), 15 Apr. 1788, in *Complete Anti-Federalist,* 5:64–66, at 65.

6

James Wilson's
New Meaning for Sovereignty

Garry Wills

The doctrine of sovereignty was an extremely clever explanation of an anomaly—how one man could speak for all men. As Judith N. Shklar has written, "The word sovereignty has scarcely any meaning at all apart from absolute monarchy."[1] According to theories of sovereignty, the people will the monarch into being. Bodin and Althusius, Hobbes and Locke, each in his own way, argues that the people are a body crying for a head.

An age that toppled monarchs would not, one might suppose, treat the doctrine of sovereignty any more tenderly. The theory of capitation would not have survived decapitations. But the republics of the eighteenth century—America first, then France—showed a strange fondness for the idea of sovereignty. They were determined to keep it, even to exalt it, after purging it of any association with the single royal person.

In France, this exalting was mainly the work of Jean Jacques Rousseau, who (as Shklar has noted) turned the doctrine on its head.[2] But what can explain the love for sovereignty in America? Americans should have had greater difficulty with the doctrine than did Rousseau, who at least kept the "single" and "inalienable" notes from prior versions of the doctrine. Some Americans spoke about multiple, even competing, sovereignties within the larger framework of confederacy. Each state was anxious, in drawing up its first constitution, to affirm that it had no superior, that it was equal to each other state in police power over its own affairs (though this proved to be a simulacrum of traditional sovereignty in the important areas of diplomacy and war making).

Then, when some individuals tried to forge a stronger central government, men such as James Wilson found a return to the idea of inalienable sovereignty useful. It let them say that the sovereign people could not be bound by earlier contracts, specifically the Articles of Confederation. Further, in defending the new central government's separated powers, despite America's lack of separate social orders, it was useful to posit a unitary popular sovereignty exerted through all departments of the government—one and the same power exercised either directly or through representatives. Wilson was the principal spokesman for this popular-representation defense of apparently privileged bodies such as the Senate and the executive office.[3]

There would be further claims made for divided or rival sovereignties in America's future. But the single inalienable sovereignty of the people was needed and was ready to hand when the Constitution had to be ratified. One reason for its being so ready to hand is that Wilson had Rousseau's *Social Contract* at his elbow during the ratifying period.

It is not even radical enough to say, with Shklar, that Rousseau turned sovereignty on its head, making the people at the bottom become the top of government. For him, the people were the bottom and the top simultaneously. Rousseau's principal innovation was not in making the people sovereign but in saying that they must *always* remain the *only* and active sovereign—a concept for which he had only a partial precedent (and an undeveloped one) in Althusius.[4] Most of what we call government was for Rousseau only the executive (*Social Contract*, 3.1, 3.11), with the legislative power being retained in the body of citizens, who meet in almost continual legislative assembly. He rejected the normal tripartite division of government into legislative, executive, and judiciary.

Thus it may come as a surprise that Rousseau kept an even older division of government—into the one, the few, and the many. That Polybian theory was derived from musical concepts of harmony; but Rousseau—despite his interest in musical theory, or perhaps because of it—substituted a mathematical formula for the musical analogy. The one is to the few as the few are to the many, in a continuous proportion (*Social Contract*, 3.1). Rousseau's immediate aim in this chapter was to address the question that Montesquieu had made unavoidable—namely, the fixing of a government's size to correspond with its esprit. But Rousseau's truly revolutionary act of thought lay in his definition of the terms for this proportion. The one, the few, and the many had been separate orders within Roman society, for Polybius; separate estates within England, for Blackstone; separate departments of government, for some explicators (mainly critics) of the United States Constitution. According to Rousseau's formula, the three elements are not separate, external parts of the society. ''The one'' is the people taken collectively, as sovereign. "The many" is the people once again, but now taken individually, as subjects. Top and bottom are the same, yet different. "The few" is some number of the sovereign subjects, rotating through office, where they mediate between their own sovereign selves and subject selves before performing that service for others.

Rousseau solves the problem of the one and the many by making the people *both* of the extreme terms of his proportion. Every individual, insofar as he or she partakes of the general will, is the single sovereign. Every individual, insofar as he or she obeys the general will, is a subject. Containing the sovereign and the subject in one person is the achievement of the citizen, the self-ruling person.

Other theories had made the division in society external—by birth, class, initiation, ordination, or whatever. For Rousseau, the key division of any legitimate society is *within the individual*. The savage, the sovereign, the subject, the citizen—all play out an internal drama. That is why, in a deeper than the first and obvious meaning of *Social Contract*, 3.2, there are as many forms of government in the state as there are citizens in it—each citizen struggling to subdue the savage, to form the sovereign, and to keep the subject obedient. The famous paradoxes of Rousseau—that the citizen is forced to be free (1.7), that the criminal wills his own death (2.5), that civil order is freer than nature (1.8), that the sovereign needs no protection from itself (1.7)—are totalitarian when read as the imposition of one part of society on another. But Rousseau means for them to be read as part of the *internal* drama of self-rule, in which the particular will is at odds with the general will in each individual. (The official, with his triple will, is the seat of a more complex struggle, and is more likely to lose that struggle [3.2], which is one reason why legitimate governments are so rare [2.10].)

Because Rousseau's one and many are the same, his system can be read as extreme in either of two directions, the authoritarian or the individualist. He meant for it to be read in both directions at once. Paradox and conflict are at the heart of his system. The citizen is a divided self, a *reflective* creature. Rousseau, like Saint Augustine, was a great student of himself; and one must stand over against oneself in order to observe oneself. The great self-studiers, from Plato to Sigmund Freud, are the multipliers of inner selves. Saint Augustine took his doctrine of a trinity of personalities in God from introspection of the different powers in his own soul.

Individual self-rule as an inner discipline, the sovereign's triumph over the subject, is replicated on the social scale by the self-mirroring presence of fellow citizens engaged in the joint labor of self-exposition and mutual education that is the state. Rousseau's public festivals, the designated censors, the civil religion—all these form a politics as pedagogy, the political equivalent of the tutor's work in *Emile*.

Rousseau was the most radical reformulator of the doctrine of sovereignty during the eighteenth century. It should not be surprising that *The Social Contract* had little if any impact on most of the founders of our Constitution. That makes all the more arresting James Wilson's profound understanding and use of Rousseau during the 1780s and 1790s. Wilson had been in advance of Jefferson and others in adopting the concept of America's sister parliaments, which had become the legal basis of the Revolution by the mid 1770s.[5] It is less recognized that he maintained his speculative radicalism into the 1780s. Paul Merrill Spurlin found no reason to make Wilson more than a minor exception to the rule of the *Social Contract*'s lack of importance in America.[6] Wilson cites the *Contract* three times in his *Law Lectures*,[7] but two of the three references are slight and deal with unimportant matters. Robert McCloskey, in republishing the *Lectures*, gives Wilson's three citations in the form that they took in the manuscript, but says he could not trace the edition Wilson was referring to.[8] The quotation of *Social Contract*, 1.5, in Wilson's second lecture (McCloskey, pp. 115–16) proves that it was the London edition of 1764, the English translation by William Kenrick (pp. 17–18)—a very rare book in America, though John Adams had two copies of it, presumably bought on separate trips through England.[9] Wilson may well have brought his copy with him when he came from Scotland in 1765, from an Edinburgh made very much aware of Rousseau by Hume's dealings with him, which were in their early stages in France. At any rate, Wilson had studied the book well and used large excerpts from it *without* citation in the ratifying debates of 1787, as well as in the *Law Lectures* of 1790.[10] Indeed, Wilson's favorite doctrine, which he drilled into his audience from the opening pages of the *Lectures*, is that of an *inalienable* popular sovereignty that is expressed through the general will.

Let me quote first from Wilson's *Lectures*—from a part that makes no direct citation of Rousseau—and then from Kenrick's translation of Rousseau, so that the reader can judge how reliant Wilson was on the book that must have been open before him. This is from the seventh lecture, "Man as a Member of Society" (p. 239 in McCloskey):

> In the social compact, each individual engages with the whole collectively, and the whole collectively with each individual. These engagements are obligatory, because they are mutual.

Here is Kenrick's Rousseau, from book 2, chapter 4:

> The engagements, in which we are bound to the body of society, are obligatory, only because they are mutual . . . engagements with themselves, viz., each individual with all collectively, and all collectively with each individual.

And here is Wilson's version of the general will:

> In order to constitute a state, it is indispensably necessary, that the wills and the power of all members be united in such a manner, that they shall never act nor desire but one and the same thing in whatever relates to the end for which the society is established.

Wilson, in emphasizing that the citizen never ceases to be sovereign, demanded a high and continuing degree of citizen participation in the government. He was the only one at the framing convention who favored the direct election of senators *and* the president; and in framing the Pennsylvania Constitution, he tried to make voting mandatory. In his first law lecture, he wrote: "Every citizen forms a part of the sovereign power: he possesses a vote, or takes a still more active part in the business of the commonwealth. The right and the duty of giving that vote, the right and the duty of taking that share, are necessarily attended with the duty of making that business the object of his study and inquiry" (McCloskey, p. 73). This duty of the citizen to be a student of government is Rousseau's excuse, in his prologue to *The Social Contract*, for writing about politics: "The right of giving that vote is sufficient to impose on me the duty of making those affairs my study, thinking myself happy in discussing the various forms of government, to find every day new reasons for admiring that of my own country" (Kenrick's translation, p. 2). Wilson continues: "In the United States, every citizen is frequently called upon to act in this great public character. He elects the legislature, and he takes a personal share in the executive and judicial departments of the nation" (McCloskey, p. 73). He was not speaking lightly when he said: "The publick duties and the publick rights of every citizen of the United States loudly demand from him all the time which he can prudently spare, and all the means which he can prudently employ, in order to learn that part which it is incumbant on him to act" (ibid.). Wilson, in delivering the first public law lectures that expounded the United States system of government, was performing an act that he put on a par with his work in framing the Constitution of the United States and that of Pennsylvania, so much was his a citizen politics of continual *pedagogy:*

> I have been zealous—I hope I have not been altogether unsuccessful—in contributing the best of my endeavors towards forming a system of government; I shall *rise* in importance, if I can be equally successful—I will not be less zealous—in contributing the best of my endeavors towards forming a system of education likewise in the United States. I shall rise in importance because I shall rise in usefulness. (McCloskey, p. 85, italics added)

Blackstone, in opening his Vinerean lectures, the first to be given on English law in the universities, argued that a knowledge of the law was useful to any educated gentleman. Wilson, who wanted his lectures to be the American Blackstone, although he was *anti*-Blackstone in doctrine, said that in America every *citizen* must know the law over which he is sovereign.

It is true that Rousseau's citizens were to meet in assembly themselves, without the use of delegates, as in America. Wilson, unlike Madison, thought the intermediation of representatives was a regrettable (but necessary) departure from the ideal of direct democracy.[11] But Wilson calls voting for representatives an act of original—originating—sovereignty, constitutive each time of the legitimacy of the government—something that Rousseau also said when he admitted that Englishmen exercised their original sovereignty when voting for representatives (3.14). Englishmen only lost their freedom when their representatives met apart from them. But Rousseau's assembly had to resolve itself into a committee of the whole to perform particular governmental functions (3.17), and Wilson treated government as such a committee for particular functions empowered by the electorate.

We should remember that Wilson's generation in Philadelphia, through the electorate, had overthrown three governments and had framed and passed four constitutions, in addition to forming a Council of Censors to consider constitutional revision at stated intervals. The son of a poor Scots farmer, Wilson himself had been a failure during the first twenty-four years of his life; later he had signed the Declaration of Independence, taken a leading part in framing the second federal constitution, taken the leading role in ratifying that constitution, been the principal author of the second Pennsylvania Constitution, served as a Supreme Court Justice, and become the first public expositor of the Constitution to ordinary citizens as well as to law students. For him, the concept of citizen participation was a matter of continually refashioning the very frame of government. Elections themselves had the potential of asking Rousseau's first questions of any assembly at this gathering: Does the present government please? Should it continue in operation? (*Social Contract*, 3.18)

Wilson, if anything, took Rousseau's idea of the individual citizen as sovereign further than his mentor had. Because of his participation in the Trenton Trial of 1782, in which jurors decided the claims to new territories affecting sovereign powers, Wilson foresaw a continuing role for citizens in their sovereign role as administrators of international law.

> The law of nations respecting agreements and compacts between two or more states, between a state and the citizens of another state; between citizens of different states; and between a state, or the citizens thereof and

foreign states, citizens, or subjects will still be applicable, as before the national constitution was established, to controversies arising in all those different enumerated cases. . . . This deduction, if properly founded, places the government of the United States in an aspect, new indeed, but very conspicuous. It is vested with the exalted power of administering judicially the law of nations, which we have formerly seen to be the law of sovereigns. . . . To every citizen of the United States, this law is not only a rule of conduct, but may be a rule of decision. As judges and jurors, the administration of the law is, in many important instances, committed to their care. (McCloskey, pp. 281–82)

Again, Wilson was thinking largely of territorial disputes to be settled by citizen jurors, but his own experience and the theory that he had developed from Rousseau made each electoral situation potentially revolutionary, because the primary mark of a self-ruling citizenry is what Wilson calls, in his first lecture, "the revolution principle" on which America is founded.

Permit me to mention one great principle, the *vital* principle I may well call it, which diffuses animation and vigor thru all the others. The principle I mean is this, that the supreme or sovereign power resides in the citizens at large; and that, therefore, they always retain the right of abolishing, altering or amending this constitution, at whatever time and in whatever manner they shall deem it expedient. (McCloskey, p. 77)

As he said at the ratifying convention in November 1787: "The people possess, over our constitutions, control in *act*, as well as in right. The consequence is, that the people may change the constitutions whenever and however they please. This is a right, of which no positive institution can ever deprive them." This was the teaching of Rousseau, who said the people could not alienate their sovereignty even to the social contract itself (*Social Contract*, 1.7).

For Wilson, no less than for Rousseau, the only legitimate government was a continuing revolution. This, the most radical view of sovereignty, was at the heart of the most profound analysis of the Constitution in the 1780s.

NOTES

1. Judith N. Shklar, *Men and Citizens: A Study of Rousseau's Social Theory* (Cambridge, Eng.: Cambridge University Press, 1969), p. 168.
2. Ibid.
3. For Wilson's crucial role on this point see Gordon S. Wood, *The Creation of the American Republic, 1776–1787* (Chapel Hill: University of North Carolina Press, 1969), pp. 603–4.

4. Cf. Ronald Grimsley, *Jean-Jacques Rousseau: Du Contrat Social* (Oxford, Eng.: Oxford University Press, 1972), pp. 56–57.

5. *Considerations on the Nature and Extent of the Legislative Authority of the British Parliament* (1774).

6. Paul Merrill Spurlin, *Rousseau in America, 1760–1809* (University: University of Alabama Press, 1969), pp. 35, 61.

7. The passages in the *Law Lectures* (as edited by Robert Green McCloskey [Cambridge, Mass.: Harvard University Press, 1967]), are pp. 70 (= *Social Contract*, 4.4), 115–16 (= 1.5), and 442 (= 2.5). Only the second citation quotes Rousseau's own words (in translation).

8. Robert Green McCloskey, *The Works of James Wilson* (Cambridge, Mass.: Harvard University Press, 1967), pp. 854–55.

9. Information from the archives of the Boston Public Library.

10. Wilson's lectures were published posthumously by his son, without having been prepared for the press by their author. They are full of unacknowledged quotations. Some of these, especially to Reid and Kames, have been recognized by Morton White and others. The extent and centrality of Wilson's use of Rousseau has not hitherto been recognized.

11. Max Farrand, *The Records of the Federal Convention of 1787* (New Haven, Conn.: Yale University Press, 1966), vol. 1, pp. 132–33; *The Documentary History of the Ratification of the Constitution by the States: Pennsylvania,* ed. Merrill Jensen (Madison: State Historical Society of Wisconsin, 1976), p. 564.

7

The Language
of Faculty Psychology
in *The Federalist Papers*

Daniel Walker Howe

The *Federalist Papers* are often treated as a kind of secular scripture, an authoritative statement of how American political institutions work or should work. Even assuming that the authors—Alexander Hamilton, James Madison, and John Jay—shared the passion for fame which they understood so well, they must have succeeded here beyond their wildest dreams. Today, lawyers cite *The Federalist* in their briefs. Conservatives have treated it as the embodiment of traditional wisdom; liberals have found in it the origins of broker-state pluralism. Most of the scholarship dealing with *The Federalist* has been written by political scientists, theorists, or commentators whose concerns have led them to inquire into the enduring validity of the papers. Sometimes their judgments have been critical, but even then, they have been based on the assumption that the papers should be evaluated by the standard of their present relevance.[1] I have written this essay from the standpoint of intellectual history. It does not seek an accurate description of the American polity or a normative statement of values that we should try to live up to, but rather an understanding of a document in the context of its age. To extend the metaphor of secular scripture, I propose to locate *The Federalist* in what biblical scholars call its *Sitz im Leben*, its original setting in life. As Rudolf Bultmann showed in his great works on the New Testament, scriptures need to be related to their own world view before we can accurately assess what timeless truths they may convey to us.

Recent scholarship has demonstrated the importance of the intellectual conventions of an age in defining an author's intentions. In this essay, I address what J. G. A. Pocock terms "the politics of language"—

that is, the study of how the vocabulary and assumptions of an intellectual paradigm can be put to political use.[2] The conventional paradigm that did the most to shape the argument of *The Federalist* was eighteenth-century faculty psychology. By examining the authors' use of the language of faculty psychology we can discover what they meant by such crucial terms as "interest," "balance," "reason," "passion," and "virtue" in *The Federalist*. Only then can we appreciate how they were adapting conventional conceptions to the needs of a new nation and a new political order.

The authors of *The Federalist* were practical men, writing under intense pressures, with a strong sense of the campaign strategy they were pursuing. They submerged their individual differences in the collective *persona* of Publius, who for our purposes may be treated as a single author.[3] Since faculty psychology was a widely shared set of assumptions, it was natural for Publius to employ it. We may infer that Publius advocated the adoption of the Constitution in the terms he did not only because he believed in a certain model of human nature but also because he expected that that model would make for an effective presentation. The particular version of faculty psychology that Publius employed influenced both his substantive arguments (his political science) and his techniques of persuasion (his rhetoric).[4] Indeed, the political science and the rhetoric of *The Federalist* are intimately related to each other through their common dependence on this psychological vocabulary.

FACULTY PSYCHOLOGY

Probably every reader of *The Federalist* has noticed that its arguments are based on ideas about universal human nature. These ideas form a coherent model. But no one has identified the sources of this model or analyzed how Publius used it in defining his audience and constructing his case. Most interpreters of Publius have presented only a partial picture of his model of human nature. Some have considered him a pessimist, in the tradition of Thomas Hobbes and John Calvin, emphasizing the need to impose control on the evil passions of man.[5] More often, Publius has been treated as a protoliberal, concerned with men who are pursuing their own interests, sometimes rationally calculated, in a system that is more amoral than immoral.[6] Most recently, some scholars have treated Publius as a classical republican who believed in the possibility of virtue in human affairs.[7] All of these interpretations can be synthesized within the paradigm of the faculty psychology that Publius employed, which found places in human nature for passion, interest, and virtue.

The word "faculty," like the word "facility," is derived from the Latin for "power."* "What is a power but the ability or faculty of doing a thing?" asks Publius rhetorically (33:3).[8] Faculty psychology, in ancient, medieval, or modern times, is the study of the human powers. From Pythagoras, Plato, Aristotle, and the Stoics onward, human nature has been sorted out into different powers, some shared with plants, some with animals, and some—the rational and moral powers—with God. The medieval scholastics elaborated the system, and the Protestant reformers retained it. John Locke and other philosophers of the Enlightenment modified the tradition but nevertheless carried it on. In the form that Publius inherited, faculty psychology was hierarchical. It treated human nature as including all the components of "the great chain of being," from mere existence to animation, sensation, and rationality. Mankind lived in a "middle state," part of nature yet above it—both body and spirit, animal and divine, neither all good nor all evil.[9]

All systems of faculty psychology are essentially teleological, because the faculties are defined in terms of their purpose. As the moral philosopher Francis Hutcheson explained it, divine providence so designed the human faculties that "they form a machine, most accurately subservient to the necessities, convenience, and happiness of a rational system."[10] When a person allowed certain faculties to get out of control, he was perverting the divinely intended harmony of the system. Earlier generations had synthesized faculty psychology with Christianity, identifying the perverse misuse of God-given faculties with sin. Human passions (or affections, as they were also termed) were legitimate faculties in their place, but there was a standing danger that they might be indulged or followed inordinately. Archbishop Thomas Cranmer had expressed it in his litany: "From all inordinate and sinful affections, . . . Good Lord, deliver us." The conventional theological formulation held that the proper supremacy of reason among the faculties had been jeopardized by the corruption of human nature in the fall of mankind. As John Milton wrote in *Paradise Lost,*

> Reason in man obscured, or not obeyed,
> Immediately inordinate desires
> And upstart passions catch the government
> From reason, and to servitude reduce
> Man till then free. . . .[11]

---

* I have modernized spelling and punctuation in passages cited from *The Federalist.*

In his studies at Princeton, Madison had been exposed to the same Calvinist tradition as had Milton, in which both freedom and virtue were equated with the supremacy of rationality.

The influence of psychology on political theory and rhetoric was facilitated in the eighteenth century because all three subjects were often treated at the time in connection with the enormous intellectual structure called moral philosophy, the ancestor of all the modern social sciences as well as of ethical theory and epistemology as we know them.[12] This philosophical connection gave to eighteenth-century psychology and political economy their strongly normative coloration. The interlocking relationships among various disciplines within moral philosophy made it all the easier for Publius to use his concepts of applied psychology as a basis both for his ideas about good government and for his techniques for persuading men to adopt it.

Eighteenth-century science was taxonomic in its preoccupations, so the faculty psychologists of the time struggled toward greater precision, and they debated definitions. The powers of man were arranged in a kind of natural history of the mind by a series of Enlightenment moral philosophers, beginning with Anthony Ashley Cooper, the earl of Shaftesbury. In the elaborate system developed by Thomas Reid, the human faculties were classified as "mechanical," "animal" (called "sensitive" by Aristotelians), and "rational." The mechanical powers were involuntary reflexes. The animal, or sensitive, powers were physical appetites (hunger and sex), instinctive desires (such as gregariousness), and—most important for Publius—the "passions" or "affections," which we would call the emotions. The rational powers included both conscience (called the "moral sense" by many writers) and prudence, or self-interest.[13]

Reid's system was followed by a large and distinguished school, including the Scottish evangelical cleric and moral philosopher John Witherspoon, who emigrated to America to become president of Princeton, a signer of the Declaration of Independence, and the teacher of James Madison. Not that the influence of this form of faculty psychology has to be traced through personal connections: it was common intellectual property during the eighteenth century, and both Madison and Hamilton (who had been educated at the Anglican King's College) employed it in *The Federalist*.[14] Madison and Hamilton did not need to confer about whether to accept the conventions of faculty psychology; these were presuppositions of their argument. But it is a mark of their successful collaboration that they both resorted to faculty psychology with such eloquence and power in the construction of their case.

The version of faculty psychology that Reid formulated and Publius adapted to his own purposes had two distinctive characteristics. The first of these was the degree of rationality accorded to self-interest. This contrasted sharply with the faculty psychology of the medieval scholastics and Protestant reformers, who had treated motives of self-regard (or self-love) as "passions." The second distinguishing mark of this school was that the moral sense was considered a rational faculty, in contrast with the opinion of eminent critics such as Hutcheson, David Hume, and Adam Smith (all of whom were Scots, like Reid and Witherspoon), who held that the moral sense was an affection—that is, an emotion.[15] We know that Publius took several of his arguments—notably the one showing the advantages of large republics over small ones—from Hume. But when it came to the fundamentals of human nature, Publius stood by the more conventional outlook typified by Reid. Hume's view of human motivation as entirely passionate, which is exemplified in his dictum that "reason is, and ought only to be the slave of the passions," challenged traditional faculty psychology and did not lend itself to Publius's purposes.[16]

Of central importance to Publius's strategy was his treatment of the motives of self-interest. "Interest" for Publius, as for eighteenth-century writers in general, was not yet simply equated with economic interest but meant self-regarding motivation, broadly understood. At the same time, Publius fully recognized that "it is a general principle of human nature that a man will be interested in whatever he possesses" (71:1), especially his material possessions. Albert O. Hirschman has shown how, in the course of the eighteenth century, certain self-regarding motives such as avarice and ambition, which had previously been classified as "passions," came to be grouped into a new category called "interests" and ranked as rational, rather than sensitive, powers, even though they still retained some of the characteristics associated with passions.[17] Publius knew that eighteenth-century faculty psychology was a discipline in flux (37:6). He took remarkable advantage of this transitional moment in the history of ideas. He treated self-interest as an intermediate motive, sometimes partial, short-term, and passionate (in the derogatory sense of "selfish passions" [20:21]), but capable of being collective, long-range, and rational. Short-term self-interest he identified with the Articles of Confederation and with his adversaries; long-term self-interest he allied with reason, virtue, and the Constitution.

By his use of faculty psychology, Publius placed his arguments in the context of Enlightenment behavioral science. Throughout *The Federalist*, appeal is made to immutable scientific laws of human behavior, as illustrated by historical examples and confirmed by the Americans' own experiment in free government (16:1, 22:13, and passim).[18] But the strategy also connected Publius with an even larger context. This was the classical, medieval, and modern tradition that identified liberty with order. Faculty psychology had always taught that the liberty of the individual's will required preventing any faculty from disturbing the harmony of the mind (especially any passion from usurping the authority of reason). Publius made use of the paradigm to present his case for guarding political liberty with social order. In both systems, parts were subordinated to the welfare of the whole, balances were struck between conflicting motives, and order was based on a rational hierarchy.

THE HIERARCHY OF MOTIVES

The faculty psychology employed by Publius posited a definite sequence of rightful precedence among conscious motives: first, reason; then, prudence (or self-interest); then, passion.[19] The inherent tragedy in the human condition was such, however, that these motives varied inversely in power: passion was the strongest; reason, the weakest. Alexander Pope, who summed up so much of the conventional wisdom of the age, declared, "The ruling passion conquers reason still."[20] Upon this model of human nature Publius based his political philosophy. "Why has government been instituted at all?" asked Hamilton's Publius. "Because the passions of men will not conform to the dictates of reason and justice without constraint" (15:12). Madison's Publius agreed: "What is government itself but the greatest of all reflections on human nature? If men were angels, no government would be necessary" (51:4).

The juxtaposition of "reason and justice" was typical of Publius; sometimes he spoke similarly of wisdom and virtue (for example, 2:10). The rational faculty, for Publius as for Reid, was the one that apprehended objective truth, both descriptive and normative (or as they would have said, "speculative" and "practical"). Yet reason-cum-conscience was but a feeble monarch over the other faculties. If it had might, as it has right, it would rule the world, the great eighteenth-century moralist Joseph Butler had affirmed.[21] Publius put it this way: "There are men who could neither be distressed nor won into a sacrifice of their duty; but this stern virtue is the growth of few soils" (73:1).

Within the category of self-interest, "immediate interests," as Publius called them, "have a more active and imperious control over human conduct than general or remote considerations" (6:9). Consequently, the interests that most resembled passions were stronger than those partaking of the nature of prudential reason. These rules of individual motivation were also applicable to political entities. "The mild voice of reason, pleading the cause of an enlarged and permanent interest, is but too often drowned before public bodies as well as individuals, by the clamors of an impatient avidity for immediate and immoderate gain" (42:9). Distinctions could also be made among the social affections (or passions) in terms of their power. People show less and less emotional attachment to groups as these get progressively larger: "a man is more attached to his family than to his neighborhood, to his neighborhood than to the community at large," et cetera (17:4). More tragically, "to judge from the history of mankind, we shall be compelled to conclude that the fiery and destructive passions of war reign in the human breast with much more powerful sway than the mild and beneficent sentiments of peace" (34:4).

This psychology gave Publius his basis for discrediting the Articles of Confederation: they relied too much on "the weaker springs of the human character" (34:4). "It was presumed that a sense of their true interests, and a regard to the dictates of good faith, would be found sufficient pledges for the punctual performance of the duty of the members to the federal head. The experiment has, however, demonstrated that this expectation was ill-founded and illusory" (23:7–8). As usual, history confirmed the precepts of moral philosophy.

Yet the same psychology that taught the statesman that political institutions must take account of the perversity of human nature posed a great problem for the political advocate. How could one persuade the public to adopt the institutions it so sorely needed? Some eighteenth-century rhetorical theorists, such as the highly regarded Scot Hugh Blair, openly advised the judicious invocation of the passions in persuasive expression.[22] Still, Publius does not invoke them; indeed, he deplores them. "It is the reason of the public alone that ought to control and regulate the government," writes Madison-Publius. "The passions ought to be controlled and regulated by the government" (49:10). His own rhetoric is coldly and carefully rationalistic, as in the famous number 10, in which a sequence of dual alternatives creates an impression of impeccable deductive logic. Sometimes Publius reasons from "axioms," as in number 23; elsewhere he prefers an inductive approach citing the "lessons of history," as in number 20. Throughout, the reader Publius addresses is "an impartial and judicious examiner," one who is "dispassionate and discerning" (61:1).

Norman Fiering has described the eighteenth century as the time of an intellectual revolution in which reason was displaced in supremacy by "the lowly and dangerous passions."[23] The sentimentalist school of moral philosophy, which I have already mentioned, challenged the idea that the moral sense was rational; rhetoricians such as Blair legitimated the passions; religious pietists and evangelicals demanded an awakening of holy affections; the subversive psychology of Hume, like that of Hobbes earlier, attributed all human motivation to passion, denying even the possibility of rational control. This growing acceptance of the affections, or passions, was alien to Publius; if it was a revolution, he was a counterrevolutionary. To him, the passions were dangerous. Like the Old Lights who opposed the Great Awakening, Publius distrusted "enthusiasm" (1:5, 46:3, 83:18). He judged policy questions by whether they conduced to the supremacy of reason; he rejected a proposal to call frequent constitutional conventions because "the *passions*, therefore, not the *reason*, of the public would sit in judgment" (49:10). He deplored the formation of political parties because they appealed to passion rather than reason (50:6).

Although Publius was rather old-fashioned in his distrust of passion, he was quite up to date in his techniques for controlling it. While Christian philosophers of earlier times had typically striven to repress undesirable feelings, the Enlightenment hit upon the technique of balancing them off against each other, "like the antagonist[ic] muscles of the body," in Hutcheson's simile. Even antisocial motives could have their uses in a system that made proper use of the principle of countervailing passions.[24] Madison-Publius heartily endorsed "this policy of supplying, by opposite and rival interests, the defect of better motives" (51:5). He summed up the advantages of the separation of political powers in terms of countervailing psychological passions: "Ambition must be made to counteract ambition" (51:4). Hamilton-Publius applied the same psychology when he urged the wisdom of making the president eligible for reelection: the temptation to abuse power would be counterbalanced by the desire to stay in office, so that "his avarice might be a guard upon his avarice" (72:5). In *The Federalist*, the Constitution is presented as a marvel of social engineering, based on a sound psychology, that will use human nature to control human nature, among both the governors and the governed, without requiring recourse to tyrannical coercion.[25]

Publius's rhetoric, like his political science, sought to turn selfishness to advantage. Publius enlisted prudential motives on the side of reason and virtue, to add "the incitements of self-preservation to the too feeble impulses of duty and sympathy" (29:13). His argument was designed to show that "the safety of the whole is the interest of the whole" (4:11). The crisis of the Revolutionary War had temporarily "repressed the passions most unfriendly to order and concord" (49:7); what was needed now was a new sense of crisis, which would once again ally an enlightened prudence with reason and virtue so as to overcome passion and petty self-seeking.

The rhetorical posture of Publius remains remarkably consistent throughout *The Federalist*. Number 1 begins by asking "whether societies of men are really capable or not of establishing good government from reflection and choice," or whether they must forever be bound by "accident and force" (1:1). "Happy will it be if our choice should be directed by a judicious estimate of our true interests"—but this is unlikely. The proposed plan affects too many "particular interests" not to arouse "views, passions, and prejudices little favorable to the discovery of truth" (1:2). What Publius fears is that "a torrent of angry and malignant passions will be let loose" (1:5), frustrating all attempts at rational discourse. He himself will engage in rational argument, without impugning the motives of individuals. (The motivation of the human race, however, is quite another matter.) Publius makes his own style of rhetoric a pattern for how he hopes the debate as whole can be carried on: he is confident that in elevating it to the general welfare, he will force his adversaries to meet him on his own ground, instead of himself descending to pettiness and passion. However he may feel provoked, Publius will take his stance with Prospero in *The Tempest:* "Though with their high wrongs I am struck to th' quick, / Yet with my nobler reason 'gainst my fury / Do I take part."

While recognizing that it is not easy to know the good, Publius has no doubt that the good does objectively exist (71:2). And for all his disparagement of the strength of rational and virtuous motives, he still assumes that they, too, exist and have a fighting chance to prevail. "As there is a degree of depravity in mankind which requires a certain degree of circumspection and distrust, so there are other qualities in human nature which justify a certain portion of esteem and confidence. Republican government presupposes the existence of these qualities in a higher degree than any other form" (55:9). Publius never goes so far as to embrace utilitarianism; and he never actually defines the moral good in terms of collective benefits; but he does argue that a collective prudence can both assist and foster virtue. The Constitution, Publius is confident, will provide a setting designed to promote the worthy qualities over the unworthy ones—and, as we shall see, the worthy people over the unworthy ones as well.

FACULTY PSYCHOLOGY AND THE POLITICAL ORDER

The analogy between the human mind and the political commonwealth, "in which there are various powers, some that ought to govern and others that ought to be subordinate," is one of the oldest staples of philosophical discourse.[26] It remained as popular with the eighteenth-century "moderns" as it had been with the "ancients"; indeed, the grouping of both psychology and "civil polity" (political theory) under the umbrella of moral philosophy encouraged this. Publius was convinced that groups had dynamics that were analogous to those of individuals, with the same tragically inverse relation between the legitimacy of motives and their power. "In all very numerous assemblies, of whatever characters composed, passion never fails to wrest the scepter from reason" (55:3), and the larger the assembly, "the greater is known to be the ascendancy of passion over reason" (58:14). Once dominated by passion, an assembly became a "mob" (55:3). It was a misfortune that the debate over the Constitution "touches the springs of so many passions and interests" (37:1); therefore it was all the more essential to keep the discourse on a high level and out of the hands of demagogues.

Publius wanted a system of government that would provide scope for the exercise of the faculties, which he called "liberty," and would offer security to retain their fruits, which he called "justice" (for example, 10:6, 8). The faculties of different people were not equally developed; some individuals were more wise and virtuous than others, just as some were more adept at making money. A well-designed system of government should allow men to exercise their political faculties and should favor those whose "fit characters" (10:17) were most politically desirable. "The aim of every political constitution is or ought to be," Publius wrote, "to obtain for rulers, men who possess [the] most wisdom to discern, and [the] most virtue to pursue, the common good of the society," although he was cautious enough to add, "and in the next place to take the most effectual precautions for keeping them virtuous" (57:3). Publius did not envision a free-for-all such as that of the later social Darwinians; he wanted a teleological—that is, a purposeful—system designed to favor wisdom and virtue. Of course there would always be struggles, just as there are within the breast of even the upright citizen; but a good constitution would moderate them and influence their outcome.[27]

The best example that Publius could offer his readers of a wise and virtuous elite was the Constitutional Convention itself. "Without having been awed by power, or influenced by any passions except love for their country, they presented and recommended to the people the plan produced by their joint and very unanimous counsels" (2:10). This is a highly idealized picture of the convention, which he crafted for rhetorical purposes to illustrate a perfect rationality. ("Love of country" as a good passion will be considered below.) The delegates rose above party and faction to achieve "unanimity," Publius claimed (37:9). That the delegates were actually far from unanimous in endorsing the outcome of their deliberations was irrelevant. In Publius's scheme, the Fathers of the convention occupied a place analogous to the semimythic lawgivers of antiquity—Solon, Lycurgus, Romulus (38:1–4)—and required some veneration even before their work was implemented. "Let our gratitude mingle an ejaculation to heaven for the propitious concord which has distinguished the consultations for our political happiness'' (20:21), he wrote in a rare expression of religious devotion. As a benevolent Providence had designed the faculties of (unfallen) man for the welfare of the individual, the wise lawgiver had contrived a complex machinery in harmony with (fallen) human nature for the welfare of the community.

Throughout *The Federalist* there runs an implicit analogy between the human mind and the body politic. Just as the mind has faculties of reason (knowing wisdom and virtue), prudence (knowing self-interest), and the passions, so there are in society a small natural aristocracy of wisdom and virtue, a larger group of prudent men who are capable of understanding their enlightened self-interest, and the turbulent masses, who are typically motivated by passion and immediate advantage. Publius recognized a certain correlation between the development of the faculties and social class. A man whose station in life "leads to extensive inquiry and information" would be able to rise above "the momentary humors or dispositions which may happen to prevail in particular parts of the society" and make a good political leader (35:10). Artisans, on the other hand, "are sensible that their habits in life have not been such as to give them those acquired endowments, without which in a deliberative assembly the greatest natural abilities are for the most part useless," and would tend to elect better-educated merchants and professional men as their political representatives (35:6). This elitism will come as no surprise in the light of what we have learned about patterns of deference in eighteenth-century American political culture.[28] Although Publius was probably not writing for an audience of artisans, he claimed that artisans would agree with him, and he credited them with sense. He noted that "there are strong minds in every walk of life that will rise superior to the disadvantages of situation," but he felt that "occasional instances of this sort" did not invalidate the general rule (36:1).

"The idea of an actual representation of all classes of the people by persons of each class is altogether visionary," Publius insisted. Most political representatives in the new government would and should be large landholders, merchants, or professional men (35:6–11). If a single social group could be identified as impartial, it was the professionals, who were not tied to any particular property interest, as the landowners and merchants were (35:7). The short-sighted masses were not likely to look after the general interests of society as well as these elite groups would. To be sure, "the people commonly *intend* the PUBLIC GOOD," Hamilton-Publius granted. "But their good sense would despise the adulator, who should pretend that they always *reason right* about the *means* of promoting it" (71:2). Madison-Publius, enumerating examples of "wicked" legislation in number 10, cited only instances that, in their eighteenth-century context, favored the have-nots against the haves: paper money, an abolition of debt, an equal division of property (10:22). It was all to the good that only a few far-sighted "speculative" men would pay attention to the affairs of the new national government, while the "feelings" of the average citizens were occupied with the mundane affairs of their particular states (17:8). Federal tax policy was a subject that Publius considered would be particularly well entrusted to a small group of "inquisitive and enlightened statesmen," who would not attempt to mirror the diverse composition of society (36:5; cf. 35:5, 10).

Publius defined his audience as consisting of "the candid and judicious part of the community" (36:17). Yet he was not engaged in an academic inquiry; he was an advocate, a campaigner. He had to combine rationality with motivation in order to persuade effectively. He found the key to his rhetorical problem in eighteenth-century faculty psychology, in the concept of enlightened self-interest. Bishop Butler had taught that the conscience could enlist the aid of prudence to help the former control the passions. By the latter part of the century this had become a standard technique for strengthening the motive to rationality in human behavior.[29] Publius, for all of his pessimism about the weakness of unaided reason, was convinced that a well-designed constitution could make rational and moral use of self-interested motives. Before this constitution could be implemented, however, the public would have to be persuaded that this was not only just but also in their own true interest.

Publius credits his audience with being members of the wise and virtuous elite. But he does not appeal only to disinterested motives. He is eager to demonstrate how the proposed Constitution can be of tangible benefit to various economic interests (see especially numbers 4, 11, 12, and 13) as well as to "the prosperity of commerce" in general (12:2) and, in the largest sense, to all who have an interest in "the effects of good government" (37:5). There are, then, two audiences implied for his presentation: the direct audience of dispassionate inquirers and the larger, indirect audience that is capable of enlightened self-interest. Even if most members of the direct audience were already supporting the Constitution, *The Federalist* serves a campaign function: the indirect audience will be enlisted in the cause (presumably by the readers) in order to help control the passionate multitude. Although Publius does not make it explicit, there is an analogy with the cooperation that he foresees in Congress between the disinterested professional men and the representatives of the great landed and mercantile interests (36:1).

This interpretation, derived from an internal analysis of *The Federalist*, is supported by what we know from other sources about the conduct of eighteenth-century electioneering. Robert H. Wiebe has described it thus: "The gentry addressed their speeches and pamphlets, rich with learned allusions and first principles, to one another, not to the people, who would have to receive their instruction from others closer to them in the hierarchy. The art of persuasion centered around the conversion of a secondary tier of gentlemen."[30]

Against the rationalistic and elitist appeal of *The Federalist*, the Antifederalists seem to have employed a rhetorical strategy of their own. They concurred in the faculty psychology's estimate of the weakness of human nature, perhaps even more consistently than Publius did: they refused to believe in the ability of even an elite few to follow the guidance of wisdom and virtue. If there was any hope of overcoming evil, it lay in the common sense and feeling of the common man, which they addressed.[31] Publius complained that the rhetoric of the Antifederalists suggested "an intention to mislead the people by alarming their passions, rather than to convince them by arguments addressed to their understandings" (24:8). To their distrust of any officeholders, Publius replied that "the supposition of universal venality in human nature is little less an error in political reasoning than the supposition of universal rectitude" (76:10). If supporters of the Constitution were willing to trust the rulers, its opponents, according to Publius, placed too much faith in the masses who were ruled—"but a nation of philosophers is as little to be expected as the philosophical race of kings wished for by Plato" (49:6).

FACULTY PSYCHOLOGY AND
MIXED GOVERNMENT

The Constitution, most recent scholars agree, broke with the venerable tradition of "mixed government" that balanced monarchy, aristocracy, and democracy, by rejecting the European practice of representing different orders of society in the legislative body.[32] Publius indeed boasted that Americans had discovered the secret of "unmixed" republican government (14:4). Yet Madison, Hamilton, and the other framers of the Constitution also respected many of the values of mixed government as these had been passed down from ancient, medieval, and early-modern political writers—such values as stability, balance, and the supremacy of common over partial interests (63:9–12).[33] Could these be salvaged in the new polity? Publius's creative response to this problem was to argue that the proposed Constitution conferred the procedural benefits of mixed government without its social inequities. The elements that it mixed were no longer monarchy, aristocracy, and democracy, but executive, legislative, and judicial. Checks and balances among these branches were "powerful means by which the excellencies of republican government may be retained and its imperfections lessened or avoided" (9:3). Publius provided a kind of mixed government with a psychological rather than a social justification. Through faculty psychology, he described what he saw as the advantages of mixed government that the Constitution would preserve, even for a country without a European social structure.

For Publius, the art of governing was a decision-making process analogous to that of an individual; the institutions of government were analogous to the individual's faculties of mind. In both cases, reaching a correct decision required a careful act of balancing. Precipitate, ill-advised action was to be avoided; long-term prudence and morally right actions were to be desired. An individual would do well to act from more than one motive, because reason was weak and the passions were unreliable. In politics, then, a measure of institutional complexity was advantageous, because "the oftener a measure is brought under examination, the greater the diversity in the situations of those who are to examine it, the less must be the danger of those errors which flow from want of due deliberation, or of those missteps which proceed from the contagion of some common passion or interest" (73:8). The intention was not so much to frustrate particular social groups as to provide the right mix of motives. A well-structured government would resemble the balanced mind of a wise person, while a poorly constructed government, like a weak mind, was prone to fall under the tyranny of some capricious passion (63:7).

In Publius's argument there is a marked, if implicit, tendency for the different branches of government to mirror particular faculties of mind. As we have seen, Publius's rhetoric sorted his potential audience into three horizontally defined, hierarchically ordered groups—rational men, self-interested men, and passionate men; he addressed only the first two. But these groupings would not do for the structure of government, because all of the functions of government should be rational. Therefore Publius invoked a different set of faculties in explaining the structure of government, a grouping that was equally legitimated by psychological tradition but was "vertical" rather than "horizontal" in conception. The psychological faculties to which the branches of government correspond were all aspects of reason: "understanding," "will," and "conscience." These conventional terms of faculty psychology provide the keys to Publius's exposition of the powers of the legislative, executive, and judicial branches of government, respectively. In an individual, the understanding received and processed information, the will took action, and the conscience, or moral sense, judged right from wrong. In the system of faculty psychology that Publius was following, all were supposed to operate rationally and resist the "impulse of passion."[34]

The judiciary, in Publius's scheme, was the conscience of the body politic, interpreting its common moral standards (84:4). Not only did Publius invest this branch with the power of judicial review of legislation (78:10–12); he even asserted that judges had a power to correct the operation of "unjust and partial laws," whether or not these were unconstitutional (78:19). For one who doubted the virtue of mankind in general, Publius placed astonishing confidence in that of judges—but this was because of the faculty they exercised, which was at once the most reliable and the weakest. "The judiciary, from the nature of its functions, will always be the least dangerous" branch of government, he explained; it has "neither force nor will, but merely judgment" (78:7). The executive branch partook of the qualities of the "will," which explains why "energy" and "unity" were so essential to it, even in a republican system (70:1, 7). As the will ought to implement fixed principles and the conclusions of the understanding, according to Reid's psychology, so the executive ought to enforce only the laws enacted by the legislature. In identifying the executive with the will, Publius was not making the presidency supreme but was emphasizing its rationality and subordination to the law.

The understanding was the faculty through which the individual acquired his knowledge of the world, and Publius conceived of the legislative branch as the one through which the government acquired "a due knowledge of the interests of its constituents" (56:1). "Interests," as we know, could be either rational or passionate. The faculty of the understanding included both "rational" and "sensitive" aspects, among the latter being dangerous motives of passions. The legislature likewise had both rational and emotional aspects; indeed, it possessed a weakness for "all the passions which actuate a multitude" (48:5). In traditional faculty psychology the will "had the special task, among others, of controlling the passions lodged in the sensitive appetite."[35] Fortunately, the president, the embodiment of the faculty of the will, had a veto over congressional legislation and thus could prevent "unqualified complaisance to every sudden breeze of passion, or to every transient impulse" (71:2). Within the legislature itself, Publius looked to the Senate to impart more of the rational quality that he feared might be deficient in the House of Representatives (62:9). Due to their longer terms, larger constituencies, and the indirect method of election, senators would be "more out of the reach of those occasional ill humors or temporary prejudices'' to which democratic assemblies are prone (27:2).

Discussions about the ratification of the Constitution usually point out that its proponents wanted a stronger, more energetic government. Yet analyses of *The Federalist* often emphasize the limitations on governmental power that it endorses. An understanding of Publius's faculty psychology helps to resolve this seeming paradox. The branches of government that he wanted to strengthen were the ones that he associated with the greatest rationality: the judiciary, the executive, and the Senate; the elements that he wanted to limit he associated with narrow self-interest and the passions: the state governments and all popular assemblies, including the House of Representatives. While the national government would express the general welfare, Publius identified the states with partial views (15:14); and when the states became subject to "violences" and "passions," he expected that the federal government would be "more temperate and cool" (3:14, 16).

More important even than one-to-one correspondences between governmental institutions and psychological faculties is Publius's pervasive argument that just as a healthy human mind balances short-, intermediate-, and long-term goals, so should a healthy polity. As the individual possesses powers responding to each of these objectives, so should a commonwealth. This carry-over of attitudes derived from faculty psychology into the realm of politics helps to explain Publius's misgivings about majority rule. Hamilton-Publius and Madison-Publius agreed that only the "deliberate sense of the community," not every numerical majority, was entitled to prevail (71:2; 63:7). *The Federalist* quoted Jefferson with approval: "An *elective despotism* was not the government we fought for" (48:8). As Publius presented the matter, it was not so much the people themselves who were being limited as their passions, nor any aristocracy that was being empowered; it was the qualities of virtue and wisdom. From our point of view, of course, there resulted a compromise of majority rule. "The people," Publius warned, "stimulated by some irregular passion, or some illicit advantage, or misled by the artful misrepresentations of interested men, may call for measures which they themselves will afterwards be the most ready to lament and condemn." Enforced delay was the appropriate remedy, "until reason, justice, and truth can regain their authority over the public mind" (63:7). Publius wanted calm and thorough deliberation; if this should occasionally prevent a good law from passing—a possibility he admitted (62:6)—so be it. "Every institution calculated to restrain the excess of law-making, and to keep things in the same state, in which they may happen to be at any given period, [is] much more likely to do good than harm" (73:9).

FACULTIES AND FACTIONS

Publius's analogy between psychology and political science extends to his treatment of factions, which twentieth-century commentators have viewed as the most interesting aspect of *The Federalist.* Madison's Publius defines faction as the collective expression of "some common impulse of passion, or of interest, adverse to the rights of other citizens, or to the permanent and aggregate interests of the community" (10:2). (Hamilton's Publius uses the word in the same sense.) "The latent causes of faction are thus sown in the nature of man" (10:7). "Faction" was not a value-free concept for Publius; a faction was by definition evil. The idea of inevitable evil in human nature did not surprise men who were well acquainted with the Christian doctrine of original sin and its secularized versions in eighteenth-century faculty psychology.

Although Publius mentions only "passion" and "interest" in his initial definition of faction, his discussion also refers to "opinion" as a source of faction. It would appear that even the faculty of reason, being "fallible" and prone to corruption by "self-love," can give rise to factions of a theological or ideological nature (10:6–7).[36] More often, however, factions stem from passions—writ large and inflamed by ambitious demagogues. In this collective form, passions become more dangerous than ever: "a spirit of faction can lead men into improprieties and excesses for which they would blush in a private capacity," pointed out Hamilton's Publius (15:12). "But the most common and durable source of factions," continues number 10, derives from motives of self-interest, specifically, "the various and unequal distribution of property" (10:7)—an inequality that has already been traced to "the diversity in the faculties of men" (10:6).

Most of the modern analyses of what Publius says about faction have focused on property interests rather than on psychological faculties. One consequence of this is that little attention has been devoted to the important connection between faction and passion.[37] All factions, even those that do not originally derive from passion, have the effect of unduly strengthening passion over reason. Partisanship comes to substitute for independent judgment (49:10, 50:6). Publius has a horror of "the arts of men who flatter [the people's] prejudices to betray their interests" (71:2). The demagogue is a sinister figure in *The Federalist:* he lurks, ready to exploit the passions and create a faction. He is the natural enemy of the statesman, who has virtue and the common interest at heart.[38] The Constitution, Publius argues, will provide a context within which the statesman can defeat the demagogue. Fittingly, he both begins and ends his series of letters with warnings against demagogues (1:5, 85:15).

Most factions arise from the class of motives called interests, which are intermediate between passion and reason. There is a legitimate scope for the rational pursuit of one's interest but only in a broad context. Eighteenth-century moral philosophy invariably drew a distinction between benevolent and malevolent passions; implicit in *The Federalist* is an analogous distinction between benevolent and malevolent interests.[39] The Constitution will be in the true common interest. By definition, the interests that produce faction are adverse to the common interest, therefore they are narrow and evil. Publius also condemns motives of short-term interest that are closely akin to passion (for example, 3:15, 42:11). Narrow or short-sighted interests are not ennobled in Publius's presentation; a good government will "break and control" their violence (10:1), not be the vehicle for their expression and rule.[40] Such interests pose a particular problem in the legislative branch. One of the reasons why that branch is so prone to the evils of factionalism, Publius argues, is that legislators are constantly being cast in the dual role of advocates and judges in the causes before them (10:8). Their self-interest corrupts what should ideally be a disinterested pursuit of the common good.

Publius maintains that the Constitution will be able to limit "the violence of faction" (10:1) in three different ways. The first is suppression by military force. This is discussed by Hamilton's Publius in number 9 and by Madison's Publius in number 43; it shows how seriously they took the threat that factions posed to legitimate government. However, there were two alternatives to force in dealing with factions. Both alternatives derived from models developed in faculty psychology; they are described primarily in Madison's number 10. One of these methods was to enlighten the quality of the self-interest involved, in this case by refining it through the medium of representatives who would take broader views than their constituents did and hence would be less susceptible to demagogy and factionalism. The representatives of "enlightened views and virtuous sentiments" would be "superior to local prejudices and to schemes of injustice" (10:21). The other method was to pit factions against each other, so that they would cancel each other out, just as countervailing passions did. Both methods would work better in a large republic than in a small one, Madison points out, since the larger constituency provides a more effective filter for the talents of representatives and also a larger number of "parties and interests," thus reducing the chance that any one of them would be able to oppress the rest (10:20). "In the extent and proper structure of the Union, therefore, we behold a republican remedy for the diseases most incident to republican government," concludes number 10. The Constitution will be beneficial not only because of its carefully designed structure of checks and balances but also because it creates a large, and therefore stable, republic.

To mitigate the evils of faction, Madison-Publius placed less faith in enlightened representatives than in the countervailing effect of other factions (10:20). Hamilton-Publius, although he had much less to say about the principle of countervailing factions, also endorsed it (for example, 26:10). This does not mean that Publius considered factions good, but only that he accepted their inevitability and sought to mitigate their effects. The "policy of supplying, by opposite and rival interests, the defect of better motives, might be traced through the whole system of human affairs, private as well as public," he pointed out, placing his political science in the context of his psychology (51:5). Just as passions such as ambition could be made to counteract the ambition of others, so could factions neutralize each other's evil, especially if there are enough of them that "you make it less probable that a majority of the whole will have a common motive to invade the rights of other citizens" (10:20). "In the extended republic of the United States, and among the great variety of interests, parties, and sects which it embraces, a coalition of a majority of the whole society could seldom take place on any other principles than those of justice and the general good" (51:10). Justice and the general good were the goals. What looks to twentieth-century eyes like broker-state pluralism was, to Publius's contemporaries, subsumed within a familiar scheme of eighteenth-century moral philosophy—namely, the principle of countervailing passions.[41]

Of course, factions could be majorities as well as minorities (10:2). Indeed, the factions that Publius was chiefly worried about were the ones that commanded a majority; minority factions were easily limited. But "when a majority is included in a faction, the form of popular government . . . enables it to sacrifice to its ruling passion or interest both the public good and the rights of other citizens" (10:11). Thus, Publius's desire to limit faction was related to his desire to limit majority rule, as well as to his desire to control passion and to affirm the supremacy of reason and virtue—qualities that Publius assumed were "comprehensible only by a natural elite," as Gordon S. Wood has observed.[42]

POLITICAL REPRESENTATION AND VIRTUE

Now that we have seen how Publius constructed his political science on the model of his faculty psychology, it becomes apparent why political representation should identify an elite of wisdom and virtue. The governors of a polity should be analogous to the higher faculties of an individual. A "republic," which Publius defined as a representative democracy (39:4), was preferable to a direct democracy because of the superior quality of the representatives, as compared with the people as a whole. A system of representation could "refine and enlarge the public views by passing them through the medium of a chosen body of citizens whose wisdom may best discern the true interest of their country and whose patriotism and love of justice will be least likely to sacrifice it to temporary or partial considerations" (10:16).

As means of achieving the proper ends of representation, Publius considered large constituencies superior to small ones. They provided a larger pool of talent from which to recruit "fit characters" (10:17), and those who represented large constituencies would be "less apt to be tainted by the spirit of faction" (27:2), because they would have more varied interests to serve. Publius accordingly argued that the national government would successfully recruit "the best men in the country" for its elective offices (3:8). It has been observed that Publius was adapting what had been considered the traditional advantages of "virtual" representation (the wisdom of the representative) to a political situation wherein only "actual" representation was practiced.[43] This may be compared with his adaptation of the advantages of "mixed government" to a situation in which no legally recognized estates of the realm would exist.

Representation, according to Publius, was a refining process in which higher faculties (that is, motives and abilities) were sorted out, concentrated, and strengthened. Indirect elections performed this function better than direct ones did. This is why he reposed special confidence in senators and presidents, who would be elected indirectly (64:4, 68:8). Repeatedly, we have seen how Publius put his faith in complexity as a means of inhibiting passion, both in individuals and in groups. Government is divided into state and federal authorities, along one axis, and into legislative, executive, and judicial branches, along another. Society itself is beneficially complex, being composed of many interests, as is human nature, with its varied faculties. By the same token, complex elections are safer and more effective than are simple ones. Publius also believed that long terms were better than short ones, because experience is so valuable (53:9); and—within limits—fewer representatives were better than more, because smaller bodies are more selective and partake less of the "infirmities incident to collective meetings of the people." The danger in large assemblies is that "ignorance will be the dupe of cunning; and passion the slave of sophistry" (58:14).

Can one go so far as to argue that Publius believed it was the responsibility of government to promote virtue in general, or that the

Constitution would make Americans a more virtuous people than they already were? Some commentators have thought so, although they have had to draw on evidence outside *The Federalist* to make their case.[44] It is clear that Publius tried to enlighten self-interest and to enlist it on the side of reason, rather than on the side of passion. It is also clear that he wished to reward the qualities of *public* virtue and wisdom with political power. However, he has little to say about the highest faculties of *private* morality and speculative reason, because the specific task before him did not require that he discuss them.[45] No one then felt that the ratification of the Constitution touched upon the educational or religious institutions of the country, for example. Publius's letters are single-minded in their focus on the campaign for ratification. They are masterpieces of special pleading. Accordingly, it is a mistake to try to extract from them a complete political theory or a comprehensive statement of the relation between government and virtue, such as one finds in Aristotle.

In spite of the knowledge and admiration of the ancients that Publius and his generation possessed, the classical conception of civic virtue was alien to *The Federalist*. The ancient philosophers, particularly Aristotle, held that human nature could only be properly fulfilled through political participation; the truly good man had to be politically active.[46] Publius acknowledged no such imperative. In number 10 he defended representation, which the ancient world never developed, as being superior to participatory self-government. Life under the Articles of Confederation had left Publius disillusioned with widespread political participation and American public virtue; that is why American political institutions needed to be restructured to strengthen the hand of virtue. The experience of public service would no doubt benefit the representatives themselves, by broadening their views; therefore, one could argue that Aristotelian virtue was still relevant to them. And after all, Aristotle never expected his standards of civic virtue to apply to any but a small elite. But it would not have served Publius's purposes to pursue this subject explicitly, so he did not. He was more interested in proving the utility of the representatives to the government than in proving the utility of the government to the representatives.

The neoclassical school of Machiavelli, Harrington, and Montesquieu had developed its own elaborate tradition of civic virtue as a precondition for free government.[47] The Antifederalists drew heavily upon these writers, especially Montesquieu, to argue that republican virtue would be corrupted in a large and centralized polity.[48] Publius's relationship to the neoclassical tradition was more ambiguous. What this tradition had to say about balanced government as a safeguard against faction and demagogy was still relevant to him, but its conception of the sentiment of patriotism played only a very small role in *The*

Federalist. "Virtue," as Publius used the word, was not simply equivalent to love of country, as it was for Montesquieu; it was a moral quality that included a sense of honor and justice. Still less did it resemble Machiavelli's *virtù*, the dynamic force of character that can reshape a polity. Publius's "virtue" was a quality of rational insight, not a sentiment or feeling.[49] When Publius had occasion to mention patriotism or love of country, he clearly labeled it a "passion" (2:10; cf. p. 116 above), and he treated it as something quite different from virtue. He assumed that such sentiments of loyalty would attach themselves more firmly to the states than to the new national government (17:4). To the extent that national institutional traditions could be cultivated, thus adding the sentiments of habit to other motives for obedience to government, that would of course be all to the good (27:4; 49:6).

Both the classical and the neoclassical schools had based republican institutions on civic virtue. Publius retained the connection between republicanism and virtue, but he considered civic virtue to be a rarity, and he used the paradigm of faculty psychology to prove this. He went on to justify the Constitution as a system that could enhance the power of public virtue, drawing on principles that moral philosophers had developed for enhancing the power of virtue in the individual.[50]

CONCLUSION

At the end, Publius returns to his rhetorical strategy and points with modest pride to his success. "I have addressed myself purely to your judgments and have studiously avoided those asperities which are too apt to disgrace political disputants" (85:4). He has proved at least some parts of his case with the conclusiveness "of mathematical demonstration" (85:14). The tone has been in keeping with Publius's objectives. He writes on behalf of a small group of lawgivers to a minority audience, through whom he hopes to reach a decisive segment of the political community. He writes to demonstrate that the Constitution will approve itself to the enlightened self-interest of practical men. He writes about society by using psychological metaphors, showing that the Constitution will control the disorders and instabilities that he terms "passion."

The argument itself is at one with the rhetoric in which it is couched. An elite of wise and virtuous lawgivers have constructed a system to pool and maximize society's small store of reason and morality. The system depends on mingling these scarce resources with baser but more plentiful ones in order to achieve a serviceable alloy of mixed motives. Not even the most complex and carefully devised electoral system can guarantee the best rulers; therefore, "enlightened statesmen will not always be at the helm'' (10:9). But if a virtuous person is unavailable, a selfish one may do, provided his self-interest coincides with social utility. Hence the emphasis on broadening and enlightening self-interest. Even some of the passions can be put to work: ''the love of fame,'' for example, ''the ruling passion of the noblest minds'' (72:4), can motivate a statesman to do deeds of public service.[51] Like Jonathan Edwards, Publius considered true virtue a rare and precious metal; unlike Edwards, he would accept counterfeit tender if it could purchase social advantage.

Publius was actually more typical of eighteenth-century writers on moral philosophy than was Edwards. Publius was writing in a tradition that stemmed from Bernard Mandeville's once-startling dictum: ''Private vices by the dextrous management of a skillful politician may be turned into public benefits.''[52] A far-greater moral philosopher, Adam Smith, had applied this principle to the economic realm. A well-designed economic system, Smith taught, would take advantage of the psychological fact that individuals pursue wealth for themselves under the (mistaken) impression that it will bring them happiness. It was a providence of God that men's very selfishness and foolishness could serve society. Like Publius, Smith never confused socially useful behavior with genuine virtue.[53] Another contemporary of Publius's, Benjamin Franklin, also sought to enlist selfishness in the public cause by teaching that honesty was the best policy.

The language of faculty psychology provided Publius with a familiar vocabulary with which to conceptualize an unfamiliar politics. It was a vocabulary that his audience understood and respected. Through it, he could invoke conventional wisdom on behalf of the drastic innovation he was advocating. By analogy to the faculties of the human mind, Publius showed how the balance of powers in the Constitution, like that in a wise individual, would lead to balanced decisions. The new government would affirm reason and justice over passion and partisanship, he argued. A letter from Madison to Washington in 1787 shows how Madison was already starting to think in these terms before composing his share of *The Federalist*: ''The great desideratum which has not yet been found for Republican Governments seems to be some disinterested and dispassionate umpire in disputes between passions and interests.''[54] After the Philadelphia Convention had completed its work, the federal government that it created appeared to answer this need for a dispassionate authority, and faculty psychology provided the language in which to explain it.

The model of faculty psychology that Publius used, emphasizing the supremacy of reason, rather than revelation or tradition or even the will of the majority, enabled Madison and Hamilton to pick and choose widely from the theories and experiences of the past to suit the circumstances of the present. Elements of classical republican theory, such as a concern with "balance" and "virtue," survived in new guises, synthesized with insights from Scottish moral philosophy. Within the overarching frame of reference that faculty psychology provided, Publius found it possible to invoke a variety of political authorities on particular issues, even including one of the leading critics of faculty psychology, David Hume.[55]

Given the task of advocating the Constitution in the America of 1787/88, the way in which Publius made use of faculty psychology was brilliant. It reconciled the old with the new, providing a much more effective vocabulary than the old-fashioned one of "mixed government," which John Adams persisted in using.[56] It put Publius in the mainstream of eighteenth-century educated opinion and spoke directly to the cultural values of the gentry class who constituted his primary audience, while avoiding any direct challenge to more democratic values that would have been tactically unwise. Part of the beauty of the system was that it did not require that passion and partisanship be repressed altogether, but took advantage of them in order to overcome them. The model of "countervailing passions," which had been so carefully constructed by eighteenth-century moral philosophers, offered Publius a means of reconciling political conflict with order.

While working within the intellectual and social conventions of his age, Publius adapted the language of faculty psychology to an original and distinctive message. Despite its pessimism about human nature, his message is ultimately optimistic. Reason can, if aided by wisely contrived institutions, reassert its rightful supremacy. Chaos and coercion are not the only alternatives. *E pluribus unum* was the paradoxical motto of the Union: "Out of many, one." Publius had argued just such a set of paradoxes: out of passion, reason; out of complex procedures, a just result; out of selfishness, the common good.

Publius's use of faculty psychology, which was originally designed for the circumstances of 1787/88, also helps to account for the lasting popularity of *The Federalist* and its conversion into secular scripture. Membership in Publius's audience is not restricted by time and place; it can be achieved by anyone who wants it. Conceptualizing his readers in terms of their faculties, Publius addresses the better nature within each complex person. He wins us over by insisting that he will not (*sic!*) flatter us, that he trusts our judgment because we too understand the weakness of human nature (63:7). Whatever selfishness may characterize most people, "no partial motive, no particular interest, no pride of opinion, no temporary passion or prejudice" must influence us. Each of us can act "according to the best of his conscience and understanding"

(85:5). "What more could be desired by an enlightened and reasonable people?" (77:11).

NOTES

I wish to thank the John Simon Guggenheim Memorial Foundation and the University of California, Los Angeles, for their support during the research and writing of this essay, as well as the following scholars for their helpful comments and criticisms: Joyce Appleby, Terence Ball, Richard Beeman, Ruth Bloch, Norman Fiering, James Moore, J. G. A. Pocock, J. R. Pole, Robert Rutland, and Gordon S. Wood.

An earlier version of this essay appeared under the title "The Political Psychology of *The Federalist*," in the *William and Mary Quarterly*, 3d ser., 44 (July 1987): 485–509 (©1987 by Daniel W. Howe).

1. Canonization of *The Federalist* began early; Thomas Jefferson prescribed it as a required text at the newly founded University of Virginia. What I call the "scriptural" approach to *The Federalist* has produced some superb scholarship: e.g., Martin Diamond, "The Federalist, 1787–1788," in *The History of Political Philosophy*, ed. Leo Strauss and Joseph Cropsey (Chicago: University of Chicago Press, 1972), pp. 631–51; and Gottfried Dietze, *The Federalist: A Classic on Federalism and Free Government* (Baltimore, Md.: Johns Hopkins University Press, 1960). Those who criticize *The Federalist* in terms of its present validity include Robert A. Dahl, in *A Preface to Democratic Theory* (Chicago: University of Chicago Press, 1956); James MacGregor Burns, in *The Deadlock of Democracy: Four-Party Politics in America* (Englewood Cliffs, N.J.: Prentice-Hall, 1963); and Morton White, in *The Philosophy of the American Revolution* (New York: Oxford University Press, 1978) and *Philosophy, "The Federalist," and the Constitution* (New York: Oxford University Press, 1987).

2. J. G. A. Pocock, *Politics, Language, and Time: Essays on Political Thought and History* (New York: Atheneum, 1971), p. 19. For a sophisticated recent application of this approach see Anthony Pagden, ed., *The Languages of Political Theory in Early-Modern Europe* (Cambridge, Eng.: Cambridge University Press, 1987).

3. Even those who have thought they detected differences between Madison's Publius and Hamilton's have not claimed that these extended to his psychology: see Alpheus Thomas Mason, "The Federalist—A Split Personality," *American Historical Review* 57 (1952): 625–43.

4. For more on the rhetoric of Publius see Albert Furtwangler, *The Authority of Publius: A Reading of the "Federalist" Papers* (Ithaca, N.Y.: Cornell University Press, 1984); Forrest McDonald, "The Rhetoric of Alexander Hamilton," *Modern Age* 25 (1981): 114–24; Robert Lee Silvey, "Language, Politics and *The Federalist*: A Linguistic Approach to Interpretation" (Ph.D. diss., City University of New York, 1982); and Donald Rolland Wagner, "The Extended Republic of *The Federalist*: An Examination of Publius' Rhetoric" (Ph.D. diss., University of Georgia, 1979).

5. E.g., Benjamin F. Wright, "*The Federalist* on the Nature of Political Man," *Ethics* 59 (1949): 1–31; and Richard Hofstadter, *The American Political Tradition and the Men Who Made It* (New York: Random House, 1948), pp. 3–17. For recent

arguments that Publius is in the tradition of Hobbes, see George Mace, *Locke, Hobbes, and the Federalist Papers* (Carbondale: Southern Illinois University Press, 1979); or of Calvin see John Patrick Diggins, *The Lost Soul of American Politics: Virtue, Self-Interest, and the Foundations of Liberalism* (New York: Basic Books, 1984).

6. The scholarly literature, stemming from Charles Beard and Harold Laski, that treats Publius as a protoliberal pluralist is so large that it has a historiography of its own: see Paul F. Bourke, "The Pluralist Reading of James Madison's Tenth *Federalist,*" *Perspectives in American History* 9 (1975): 271–95.

7. Gordon S. Wood argues that Publius retained a concern with virtue in government even while he was transcending classical political theory in other ways (*The Creation of the American Republic, 1776–1787* [Chapel Hill: University of North Carolina Press, 1969], pp. 505, 606–15). Garry Wills emphasizes Publius's concern for virtue even more (*Explaining America: The Federalist* [Garden City, N.Y.: Doubleday, 1981]). See also two articles by Jean Yarbrough: "Representation and Republicanism: Two Views," *Publius* 9 (1979): 77–98, and "Republicanism Reconsidered: Some Thoughts on the Foundation and Preservation of the American Republic," *Review of Politics* 41 (1979): 61–95.

8. There are so many editions of *The Federalist* in circulation that I have chosen to cite it by number and paragraph, separated by a colon. I use the edition by Jacob E. Cooke (Middletown, Conn.: Wesleyan University Press, 1961), which has the most complete scholarly apparatus, along with Thomas S. Engeman et al., eds., *The Federalist Concordance* (Middletown, Conn.: Wesleyan University Press, 1980), which is keyed to it.

9. See H. N. Gardiner et al., *Feeling and Emotion: A History of Theories* (New York: American Book Co., 1937), pp. 89–118; Perry Miller, *The New England Mind: The Seventeenth Century* (Cambridge, Mass.: Harvard University Press, 1939), pp. 239–79; William T. Costello, *The Scholastic Curriculum at Early Seventeenth-Century Cambridge* (Cambridge, Mass.: Harvard University Press, 1958), pp. 94–97; and Norman Fiering, *Moral Philosophy at Seventeenth-Century Harvard: A Discipline in Transition* (Chapel Hill: University of North Carolina Press, 1981), chaps. 3 and 4. For the application of faculty psychology to literature and philosophy see Arthur O. Lovejoy, *The Great Chain of Being: A Study of the History of an Idea* (Cambridge, Mass.: Harvard University Press, 1936); and E. M. W. Tillyard, *The Elizabethan World Picture* (New York: Macmillan, 1944). The concept of psychological "faculties" does not lack defenders even today: see Jerry A. Fodor, *The Modularity of Mind: An Essay on Faculty Psychology* (Cambridge, Mass.: MIT Press, 1983).

10. Francis Hutcheson, *An Essay on the Nature and Conduct of the Passions and Affections . . .* (1742), ed. Paul McReynolds (Gainesville: University of Florida Press, 1969), p. 183 (emphasis deleted and capitalization modernized).

11. *The Book of Common Prayer* (1549), "Litany and Suffrages"; John Milton, *Paradise Lost,* bk. 12, lines 86–90. See J. Rodney Fulcher, "Puritans and the Passions: The Faculty Psychology in American Puritanism," *Journal of the Behavioral Sciences* 9 (1973): 123–39.

12. Rhetoric had a history of its own going back to the medieval *trivium*, but during the eighteenth century a "new rhetoric" appeared, which was associated with moral philosophy, particularly in Scotland. Adam Smith lectured on rhetoric while holding the chair of moral philosophy at Glasgow; Hugh Blair, the age's most widely read writer on rhetoric, was strongly influenced by Scottish moral philosophy. Other writers who bridged the two disciplines

included George Campbell and Lord Kames. See Gladys Bryson, *Man and Society: The Scottish Inquiry of the Eighteenth Century* (Princeton, N.J.: Princeton University Press, 1945); Daniel Walker Howe, *The Unitarian Conscience: Harvard Moral Philosophy, 1805–1861* (Cambridge, Mass.: Harvard University Press, 1970); Wilbur Samuel Howell, *Eighteenth-Century British Logic and Rhetoric* (Princeton, N.J.: Princeton University Press, 1971); and Drew R. McCoy, *The Elusive Republic: Political Economy in Jeffersonian America* (Chapel Hill: University of North Carolina Press, 1980).

13. Thomas Reid, "Essays on the Active Powers of Man" (1788), in *The Works of Thomas Reid*, William Hamilton, ed. 6th ed. (Edinburgh, 1863), vol. 2, pp. 543, 551, 572, 579.

14. At the time when Madison and Hamilton were writing *The Federalist*, the last volume of the definitive redaction of Reid's lectures (cited above) was just being published. I have not determined whether either Madison or Hamilton had access to it, but the faculty psychology they drew on was a pattern of thought with which they and their readers were well familiar, not a paraphrase or transcription of any single book.

15. Scholars have rightly emphasized Publius's debt to Scottish writers: see especially Douglass Adair, "That Politics May Be Reduced to a Science: David Hume, James Madison, and the Tenth *Federalist*," *Huntington Library Quarterly* 20 (1957): 343–60; Roy Branson, "James Madison and the Scottish Enlightenment," *Journal of the History of Ideas* 40 (1979): 235–50; and Wills, *Explaining America*. In doing so, however, they have sometimes created the misleading impression that all Scottish philosophers thought alike. For a corrective see Daniel Walker Howe, "European Sources of Political Ideas in Jeffersonian America," *Reviews in American History* 10 (Dec. 1982): 28–44.

16. David Hume, "A Treatise of Human Nature," in *Philosophical Works* (London, 1886), vol. 2, p. 195. Morton White's recent study *Philosophy, "The Federalist," and the Constitution* (cited in n. 1) confirms that Publius did not follow Hume's moral philosophy, despite his other borrowings from Hume. On the latter see also Geoffrey Marshall, "David Hume and Political Skepticism," *Philosophical Quarterly* 4 (1954): 247–57; and Theodore Draper, "Hume and Madison: The Secrets of Federalist Paper No. 10," *Encounter* 58 (Feb. 1982): 34–47. Unlike Madison's Publius, Hamilton's Publius openly acknowledged his use of Hume (*Federalist*, 85:14).

17. Albert O. Hirschman, *The Passions and the Interests: Political Arguments for Capitalism before Its Triumph* (Princeton, N.J.: Princeton University Press, 1977).

18. On this context see Merle Curti, *Human Nature in American Thought: A History* (Madison: University of Wisconsin Press, 1980), esp. pp. 5–7, 88–91, 107–12; as well as H. Trevor Colbourn, *The Lamp of Experience: Whig History and the Intellectual Origins of the American Revolution* (Chapel Hill: University of North Carolina Press, 1965). All in all, *The Federalist* is one of the masterpieces of what Henry F. May has called "The Moderate Enlightenment" in *The Enlightenment in America* (New York: Oxford University Press, 1976).

19. James P. Scanlan first sorted out Publius's treatment of human motives into these three groupings, though he did not connect them with faculty psychology or eighteenth-century rhetorical theory ("*The Federalist* and Human Nature," *Review of Politics* 21 [1959]: 657–77).

20. *Moral Essays*, epistle 3, line 153.

21. Joseph Butler, *Five Sermons Preached at the Rolls Chapel and a Dissertation upon the Nature of Virtue . . .* (1726), ed. Stephen Darwall (Indianapolis, Ind.: Hackett, 1983), p. 40.

22. Hugh Blair, *Lectures on Rhetoric and Belles Lettres* (Philadelphia, 1866), pp. 234–64. First published in 1783, this textbook was reprinted many times in America, beginning in Philadelphia in 1784.

23. Fiering, *Moral Philosophy*, p. 148.

24. Hutcheson, *Essay*, p. 183. There is a perceptive discussion of this in Hirschman, *Passions and Interests*, pp. 20–31.

25. See Maynard Smith, "Reason, Passion and Political Freedom in *The Federalist*," *Journal of Politics* 22 (1960): 525–44.

26. The quotation is from Reid, "Essays," in *Works*, vol. 2, p. 573, discussing Pythagoras. This analogy had also been prominent in Aristotelian, Thomistic, Renaissance, and Reformation thought. For examples of reasoning by analogy in eighteenth-century America see Robert H. Wiebe, *The Opening of American Society: From the Adoption of the Constitution to the Eve of Disunion* (New York: Knopf, 1984), p. 9.

27. By no means would all commentators on *The Federalist* agree with this paragraph, but see David F. Epstein, *The Political Theory of "The Federalist"* (Chicago: University of Chicago Press, 1984); Yarbrough, "Representation and Republicanism," pp. 77–98; and Paul Carson Peterson, "The Political Science of *The Federalist*" (Ph.D. diss., Claremont Graduate School, 1980), pp. 96–99. Wills is inclined to admire Publius's dedication to virtuous leadership (*Explaining America*, pp. 268–70), while Wood detects an element of class hypocrisy in it, even while stressing that the Constitution and the theory of popular sovereignty, which was invented to justify it, were later put to democratic use (*Creation of the Republic*, pp. 471–508).

28. See J. R. Pole, "Historians and the Problem of Early American Democracy," *American Historical Review* 67 (1962): 626–46. Locke, too, believed in the "differential rationality" of the social classes, according to C. B. Macpherson, *The Political Theory of Possessive Individualism: Hobbes to Locke* (Oxford, Eng.: Clarendon Press, 1962), pp. 230–38.

29. *The Works of Joseph Butler*, ed. W. E. Gladstone (Oxford, 1896), vol. 1, pp. 97–98; Hirschman, *Passions and Interests*, p. 43.

30. Wiebe, *Opening of American Society*, p. 40. Clinton Rossiter comments that *The Federalist* served as "a kind of debater's handbook in Virginia and New York" during the ratification campaign (see his "Introduction" to *The Federalist Papers* [New York: New American Library, 1961], p. xi).

31. See Cecelia M. Kenyon, "Men of Little Faith: The Anti-Federalists on the Nature of Representative Government," *William and Mary Quarterly*, 3d ser., 12 (1955): 3–43; Lois J. Einhorn, "Basic Assumptions in the Virginia Ratification Debates: Patrick Henry vs. James Madison on the Nature of Man and Reason," *Southern Speech Communication Journal* 46 (1981): 237–340; and Curti, *Human Nature*, pp. 112–16.

32. For example, Diamond, "Federalist," pp. 642–43; Wood, *Creation of the American Republic*, pp. 553–62, 602–15; Wills, *Explaining America*, pp. 104–7; and George W. Carey, "Separation of Powers and the Madisonian Model: A Reply to the Critics," *American Political Science Review* 72 (1978): 151–64. The European theorists of mixed government who were most relevant to the Americans are described by Zera S. Fink in *The Classical Republicans: An Essay in the Recovery of a Pattern of Thought in Seventeenth-Century England* (Evanston, Ill.: Northwestern University Press, 1945); Caroline Robbins, *The Eighteenth-Century Commonwealthman . . .* (Cambridge, Mass.: Harvard University Press, 1959); and J. G. A. Pocock, *The Machiavellian Moment: Florentine Political Thought and the Atlantic Republican Tradition* (Princeton, N.J.: Princeton University Press, 1975).

33. See Gilbert Chinard, "Polybius and the American Constitution," *Journal of the History of Ideas* 1 (1940): 38–58; Paul Eidelberg, *The Philosophy of the American Constitution: A Reinterpretation of the Intentions of the Founding Fathers* (New York: Free Press, 1968); and Paul Peterson, "The Meaning of Republicanism in *The Federalist*," *Publius* 9 (1979): 43–75.

34. Reid, "Essays," vol. 2, pp. 533–36 (reason vs. passion), 537–41 (understanding and will), 589–92 (conscience).

35. Fiering, *Moral Philosophy*, p. 147.

36. Hume, whom Madison-Publius was following here, made it clearer that factions could derive from "principle"—that is, reason—as well as from "interest" and "affection" (see Adair, "Politics Reduced to a Science," *Huntington Library Quarterly* 20 [1957]: 343–60).

37. Epstein corrects this in *Political Theory of "The Federalist*," pp. 68–72.

38. Madison may well have intended the figure of the demagogue to correspond to his rival Patrick Henry, providing another instance of how Publius used the conventions and vocabulary of the age to his political purposes.

39. Cf. Scanlan's distinctions between "true" and "immediate" interests and between "common" and "personal" interests (*"Federalist* and Human Nature," pp. 663, 664).

40. Wills, for all that his work has been justly criticized, is absolutely right to stress this point (*Explaining America*, pp. 201–7).

41. Thanks to Adair and Wills, Publius's indebtedness to David Hume is well recognized. However, the principle of countervailing passions was widely accepted by eighteenth-century moral philosophers, and its application to factions was not peculiar to Hume; Adam Ferguson, for example, endorsed it in *An Essay on the History of Civil Society* (Edinburgh, 1767). See also Arthur O. Lovejoy, *Reflections on Human Nature* (Baltimore, Md.: Johns Hopkins University Press, 1961), pp. 37–66.

42. Wood, *Creation of the American Republic*, p. 610.

43. See Yarbrough, "Representation and Republicanism," pp. 77–98.

44. E.g., Ralph Ketcham, "Party and Leadership in Madison's Conception of the Presidency," *Quarterly Journal of the Library of Congress* 37 (1980): 258. Martin Diamond addressed this elusive question in a series of articles in which he reached slightly varying conclusions: see, esp., "Ethics and Politics: The American Way," in *The Moral Foundations of the American Republic*, ed. Robert H. Horwitz (Charlottesville: University Press of Virginia, 1977), pp. 39–72.

45. For some reflections on the Founders' ideas about private morality see Thomas L. Pangle, "The Constitution's Human Vision," *Public Interest* 86 (1987): 77–90.

46. *Politics*, bk. I, chap. 2.

47. Besides Pocock, *Machiavellian Moment*, see also Yarbrough, "Republicanism Reconsidered," pp. 70–75.

48. See Herbert J. Storing, ed., "Introduction," in *The Complete Anti-Federalist*, 7 vols. (Chicago: University of Chicago Press, 1981), 1:15–23, 46–47, 73.

49. Wills treats Publius as an ethical sentimentalist but presents scarcely any evidence to justify this (*Explaining America*, pp. 185–92). His argument that Thomas Jefferson was an ethical sentimentalist, presented in *Inventing America: Jefferson's Declaration of Independence* (Garden City, N.Y.: Doubleday, 1978), remains highly controversial.

50. For a careful consideration of the differences between Publius and both the classical and the neoclassical conceptions of civic virtue see also Thomas L.

Pangle, "The *Federalist Papers'* Vision of Civic Health and the Tradition out of Which That Vision Emerges," *Western Political Quarterly* 39 (1986): 577–602.

51. See Lovejoy, *Reflections on Human Nature,* pp. 153–93; and Gerald Stourzh, *Alexander Hamilton and the Idea of Republican Government* (Stanford, Calif.: Stanford University Press, 1970), pp. 95–106.

52. Bernard Mandeville, *The Fable of the Bees; or, Private Vices, Public Benefits,* ed. Douglas Garman (London: Wishart & Co., 1934), p. 230; see Nathan Rosenberg, "Mandeville and Laissez-Faire," *Journal of the History of Ideas* 24 (1963): 183–96.

53. See A. L. Macfie, *The Individual in Society: Papers on Adam Smith* (London: Allen & Unwin, 1967), pp. 53–54, 75–81; and Joseph Cropsey, "Adam Smith and Political Philosophy," in *Essays on Adam Smith,* ed. Andrew W. Skinner and Thomas Wilson (Oxford, Eng.: Clarendon Press, 1975), pp. 132–53.

54. James Madison to George Washington, 16 Apr. 1787, in *The Writings of James Madison,* ed. Gaillard Hunt (New York: G. P. Putnam's Sons, 1900), vol. 2, p. 346. The concept of government as umpire was conventional in Lockean and Scottish thought: see James Conniff, "The Enlightenment and American Political Thought," *Political Theory* 8 (1980): 401. In faculty psychology, the conscience was the umpire over the passions and interests. As Madison used the term in *The Federalist,* the national government would be umpire over the states' "violent factions"—not in the sense of a passive arbitrator but in the sense of a dispassionate, constituted authority, empowered to back up its decisions (43:19).

55. Hume's own psychology, based on the passions, could also be used to construct a model of society, though the result was very different from the one that Publius created using faculty psychology (see Steven Wallech, "The Elements of Social Status in Hume's Treatise," *Journal of the History of Ideas* 45 (1984): 207–18.

56. See Wood, *Creation of the American Republic,* pp. 567–87; John R. Howe, Jr., *The Changing Political Thought of John Adams* (Princeton, N.J.: Princeton University Press, 1966); and Joyce Appleby, "The New Republican Synthesis and the Changing Political Ideas of John Adams," *American Quarterly* 25 (1973): 578–95.

8

"A Republic—
If You Can Keep It"

Terence Ball

INTRODUCTION

Legend has it that as Benjamin Franklin left the Constitutional Convention, a woman asked, "What have you given us, Dr. Franklin?" "A republic," he replied, "if you can keep it." Yet the truth of Franklin's statement was far from self-evident to many of his contemporaries, especially to those who professed to be republicans. Defenders of the new Constitution held it to be the purest distillation of republican principles, while critics claimed that it was republican neither in form nor in spirit. Far from being merely a semantic squabble between partisans, the dispute over the meaning of "republic" assumed a place of central political importance during the debate over the ratification of the Constitution.

The political and conceptual controversies of yesteryear have a way of becoming the historiographical disputes of today. Historians have wrangled with such questions as whether the American founding was a genuinely republican, rather than a protoliberal or perhaps even a Humean-Scottish, one; and there is, to date, no successful resolution in sight.[1] As one commentator has observed with some understatement, "The true nature of early American republican thought remains a topic of fierce dispute among historians."[2]

I propose, not to reopen, much less to resolve, that controversy, but to add a small footnote to it. I want to suggest that the search for "the true nature of early American republican thought" is misguided from the outset, because the true nature of republicanism was itself very much in dispute during the founding. Indeed, it is probably fair to say that no concept was more hotly contested during that period than that of "republic." And for good reason. "Republic" was central to the rhetorical appeals and arguments of all the parties to the dispute over ratification. One's understanding of "tyranny" or "liberty" or "virtue" or "corruption" was deeply dependent upon what one took a "republic" to be. Federalists and Antifederalists alike claimed to be the "real" republicans, and each group decried the other's misunderstanding—or worse, its deliberate and malicious misrepresentation—of what a "republic" really was. Disputants on both sides believed themselves, rightly enough, to be engaged, not in a verbal dispute, but in a political controversy of the highest importance. At issue were not merely the meanings of certain key terms but also the competing conceptions of citizenship, liberty, and civic responsibility, lodged in and constituted by alternative political vocabularies. In the debates over ratification, two competing accounts met in rhetorical and argumentative combat, each vying for the allegiance of an American public that was still politically fluid and very much in the throes of self-formation. Theirs was simultaneously a choice between competing political vocabularies and ways of life, not only for themselves but for many generations to come.

I propose to view that debate as a case study of conceptual change. My aim is to look at this conceptual-cum-political controversy with an eye to discerning the argumentative and rhetorical resources used by both sides to preserve old meanings or, alternatively, to create new ones. For the sake of brevity I shall concentrate upon competing conceptions of "republic" as understood and defended by the Federalist friends and the Antifederalist foes of the new Constitution, focusing primarily upon three questions around which conceptual controversy centered and confining my attentions to the debate between "Brutus" and "Publius" over ratification in New York.[3] The first question is, What bearing does the size or extent of its territory have upon a polity's claim to be a republic? The second, How and by whom are the citizens of a republic to be represented? The third, What is to be the meaning and place of virtue in an American republic? My reason for retreading this oft-trod ground is to bring into bold relief the conceptual dimensions of the controversy over ratification. Finally, I show how the ratification debate took a "linguistic" turn as the protagonists became increasingly aware of the conceptually constituted character of their respective views of politics and citizenship.

FROM REVOLUTION TO RATIFICATION

Immediately before and during the American Revolution, prorevolutionary writers such as Thomas Paine revived and lauded the idea of a "republican" government limited and checked by the power of a virtuous and vigilant citizenry, including its popular or "democratical" part.[4] Revolutionary pamphleteers borrowed republican themes from classical writers; from Machiavelli, Harrington, and Sidney; from eighteenth-century Commonwealthmen such as Trenchard and Gordon; and even from the Tory Bolingbroke, who had turned Old Whig arguments against the "New Whig" ministry of Walpole. The energies, as well as the suspicions, that fueled this ideological ferment were evident in the tone, the tenor, and the provisions of the various state constitutions that were drafted during this period and even in the Articles of Confederation themselves.[5] By the mid 1780s, however, the political climate had begun to alter appreciably. Some people feared that Shays' Rebellion and other local protest movements were parts of a larger and more ominous conspiracy that was being hatched by democrats and debtors. This lent an air of urgency to the call for a convention to amend the Articles of Confederation.[6]

What came out of that meeting, of course, was not an amended version of the Articles but an altogether different document. Despite their differences, the proponents and the critics of the new Constitution were agreed that it would, if adopted, reconstitute the American body politic in a radically new way. The ratification debate of 1787/88 opened a veritable hornets' nest of questions: What is a republic? What are republican liberties? How are they best protected, and how can they be corrupted? How can corruption be stemmed? By what constitutional means might a republic be maintained?

The dispute over ratification was remarkable in many respects. Not the least of these was the way in which political arguments and rhetorical stratagems were deployed by the Federalists and the Antifederalists in their attempts to alter or preserve the meanings of older political concepts. As Gordon S. Wood has correctly noted, "Under the pressure of this transformation of political thought old words and concepts shifted in emphasis and took on new meanings." Thus, for example, "tyranny" ceased to refer to the illegitimate exercise of power by a despotic ruler; instead, it came to refer to "the abuse of power by any branch of the government, even . . . by the traditional representatives of the people." Likewise, "liberty" ceased to mean "public or political liberty, the right of the people to share in the government." "The liberty that was now emphasized," says Wood, "was personal or private, the protection of rights against all governmental encroachments, particularly by the legislature."[7] In addition to "tyranny" and "liberty," other concepts acquired new meanings as they lost their older ones. Not the least of these was the concept of republic itself.

To reconstruct the world of words within which Federalist argued against Antifederalist is to enter a world both different from and formative of the one that we now inhabit.[8] The late Herbert Storing was surely right in suggesting that the new American Republic was the joint creation of Federalists and Antifederalists alike. It was a new political system, not created by the dictates of a lone legislator, but argued into existence and quite literally constituted out of an intense debate between the partisans of different political persuasions and theoretical convictions. During this debate, Antifederalist criticism brought forth Federalist defenses that not only clarified but in some measure constituted the meaning and theoretical justification of the new Constitution. In looking back at that debate, one is bound to be struck by the degree to which it revolved around the meanings of the concepts that were constitutive of republican discourse—liberty, tyranny, virtue, corruption, representation, even "republic" itself. Although the Antifederalists and the Federalists often used the same word, they often meant quite different things by it. Although both groups may be said to have inhabited essentially the same "universe of republican discourse," it is worth noting that while one wished to maintain the boundaries of that universe, the other wished to redraw them.[9]

Even the merest glance at *The Federalist Papers* and at Antifederalist rejoinders is enough to show how centrally important the concept of republic was during the debate over ratification. As one Antifederalist pamphleteer, the pseudononymous Federal Farmer, saw it, the issue was not so much between "federalist" and "antifederalist" as between "real republicans" and "pretended" ones:

> . . . if any names are applicable to the parties, on account of their general politics, they are those of republicans and anti-republicans. The opposers are generally men who support the rights of the body of the people, and are properly republicans. The advocates are generally men not very friendly to those rights, and properly anti republicans.[10]

By the same token, the Federalist defenders of the new design presented it as "wholly and purely republican."[11] And so it was—but only if one had first been persuaded by the Federalists' revision of the concept of republicanism. America, as redesigned and quite literally reconstituted by the Constitution and as defended in *The Federalist Papers*, was not only a new republic but also a new *kind* of republic, the likes of which had not been seen before.

AN EXTENDED REPUBLIC?

Few issues were more heatedly debated than that of the optimal—or rather, perhaps, the permissible—size of any republic deserving of the name. The Federalists and the Antifederalists alike agreed that the

American Republic represented a new wrinkle in the annals of republicanism. It was to be an extended republic, taking in a large territory and an ever-increasing population, with the prospect of still-further extension to the south and west. The Antifederalists were quick to seize upon what they took to be a rank contradiction. An extended republic, they argued, is no republic at all, but a veritable contradiction in terms. Almost all of the Antifederalist critics claimed as much; and almost all of them cited Montesquieu in support of this claim. One of the ablest Antifederalists, New York's Brutus (probably Robert Yates), held that if we consult "the greatest and wisest men who have ever thought or wrote on the science of government," we shall have to conclude that "a free republic cannot succeed over a country of such immense extent, containing such a number of inhabitants, and these encreasing in such rapid progression as that of the whole United States." The first of "the many illustrious authorities" that Brutus cites is none other than Montesquieu, more particularly his observation that "it is natural to a republic to have only a small territory, otherwise it cannot long subsist." Large territories, having heterogeneous populations, diverse interests, and immoderate men of large fortunes, are by their very nature incapable of self-government. They are, therefore, more naturally governed either by monarchs or by despots.[12]

Hamilton and Madison were prepared for attack from this quarter. They had read their Hume and had rehearsed their arguments in advance of Brutus's assault.[13] They soon countered with a one-two punch in *Federalist* numbers 9 and 10, published on the twenty-first and twenty-second of November. Not to be outdone by Brutus's reference to "the science of government," Publius, in number 9, ups the ante, averring that Brutus's science is outmoded, if indeed it is scientific at all. "The science of politics," Hamilton sniffs, "like most other sciences has received great improvement." Thanks to discoveries that had been made in the interim, Rome and Athens can no longer suffice as examples of republican rectitude. And inasmuch as the Roman republic provided Machiavelli's paradigm, Machiavelli and his heirs—English, French, and American—are all equally passé.[14] Publius thus echoes Hume's remark that Machiavelli had lived in too early an age to have been a truly scientific thinker:

> The world is still too young to fix many general truths in politics, which will remain true to the latest posterity. We have not as yet had experience of three thousand years; so that not only the art of reasoning is imperfect in this science [of politics], but we even want [i.e., lack] sufficient materials upon which we can reason. . . . MACHIAVEL was certainly a great genius; but having confined his study to the furious and tyrannical governments of ancient times, . . . his reasonings . . . have been found extremely defec-

tive. . . . [T]he errors of that politician proceed . . . from his having lived in too early an age of the world, to be a good judge of political truth.[15]

Therefore, those who follow in Machiavelli's footsteps—including, eventually, even Montesquieu himself—are still steeped in the ignorance and error of that earlier age.

Hamilton continues to press the claim that his is an age of new developments and novel discoveries. Indeed, he has the temerity to "venture, however novel it may appear to some, to add one more" truth to an already expanding body of scientific knowledge. "I mean the ENLARGEMENT of the ORBIT within which such systems are to revolve."[16] Taking a larger and less localized view of the American political universe, Publius thereby plays Copernicus to the benighted Brutus's Ptolemy. The rhetorical intent is to undercut the force of any appeal to antiquity or to arguments from authority, which Publius disavows, ostensibly because they are unscientific. Publius thereby portrays his opponent as a mere autodidact—an amateur who is describing, after the fact, the scientific discoveries of an earlier age—and himself as a scientist who is adding new contributions to an ever-expanding body of scientific knowledge.

By the time Publius gets around to Brutus's confident reference to "many illustrious authorities" and "the opinion of the greatest men"— including the untouchable Montesquieu—the damage has already been done. "The opponents of the PLAN proposed have with great assiduity cited and circulated the observations of Montesquieu on the necessity of a contracted territory for a republican government," Hamilton allows, with an air of anticlimax. As if his having dismissed their outdated secondhand conception of science were not sufficient rebuke, Publius adds articulate insult to inarticulate injury. The Antifederalists assume an uncritical, indeed an unscientific, attitude toward traditional authority. Even so, the Antifederalists, Brutus most especially, have failed even to read their authorities aright. Although they cite Montesquieu, "they seem not to have been apprised of the sentiments of that great man expressed in another part of his work, nor to have adverted to the consequences of the principle to which they subscribe, with such ready acquiescence."[17]

Publius makes two points. The first is that the Antifederalists cannot legitimately employ Montesquieu's arguments about the restricted size of republics. This is so because, as he notes, Montesquieu's very scale or standard of measurement is, in America, already outdated:

When Montesquieu recommends a small extent for republics, the standards he had in view were of dimensions, far short of the limits of almost every one of these States. Neither Virginia, Massachusetts, Pennsylvania, New-York, North-Carolina, nor Georgia, can by any means be compared with the models, from which he reasoned and to which the terms of his description apply.

From this it follows that Montesquieu's terms of political discourse—including, by implication, his understanding of "republic" itself—are not applicable to America, not only under the new Constitution but even under the Articles of Confederation. Indeed, "if we therefore take his ideas on this point, as the criterion of truth, we shall be driven to the alternative, either of taking refuge at once in the arms of monarchy, or of splitting ourselves into an infinity of little jealous, clashing, tumultuous commonwealths, the wretched nurseries of unceasing discord and the miserable objects of universal pity or contempt."[18] The political choice is thus rhetorically recast in mathematical terms: An unacceptable unity ("monarchy") or an intolerable "infinity." Publius's genius resides in his having shown that the Antifederalist equation can be solved for two unknowns, both of which, when known, prove equally unacceptable. A new standard and a new scale are accordingly called for.

Publius's second point is that this new standard or scale is to be found, ironically, in Montesquieu's notion of a "confederate republic." Had the Antifederalists read their authority aright, they would already have seen what Publius must now show them. Montesquieu, he explains, "explicitly treats of a CONFEDERATE REPUBLIC as the expedient for extending the sphere of popular government and reconciling the advantages of monarchy with those of republicanism." After an extensive citation of the relevant passages—passages that were routinely quoted by the Antifederalists for contrary purposes—Publius admits to having "thought it proper to quote at length these interesting passages, because they contain a luminous abridgement of the principal arguments in favour of the Union." Having turned the Antifederalists' chief ally against them, Hamilton concludes number 9 by turning against Montesquieu, whose authority, however welcome it might be, is not needed after all. Montesquieu's various distinctions and discriminations are, in the end, more scholastic than scientific. The "distinctions insisted upon were not within the contemplation of this enlightened civilian" and must therefore be dismissed as "the novel refinements of an erroneous theory."[19]

Hamilton's countering of the restricted-size argument in *Federalist* number 9 paves the way for the conceptual revision of "republic" that was offered by Madison on the following day in number 10. Without mentioning Montesquieu by name, Madison rejects the heretofore unchallenged Montesquieuan idea that a republic can be democratic. By insisting upon a sharp distinction between a "democracy" and a "republic," Madison redraws the conceptual map in a radically new way. There is nothing novel about his description of democracy as a system of direct rule by an assembly of citizens who inhabit a relatively restricted territory; Montesquieu himself had said as much. What is novel is Madison's twofold insistence that a democracy cannot be a republic and—more striking still—his radical redefinition of "republic" itself. A democracy, in Madison's view, is neither more nor less than a system in which the numerically largest group rules. Calling this ruling part "the majority" does not alter the fact that it is capable of degenerating into a faction that may rule unchecked in its own interest. A "pure Democracy," therefore, "can admit of no cure for the mischiefs of faction." An altogether different form—a republic—"opens a different prospect, and promises the cure for which we are seeking."[20] A republic, as Madison (re)defines it, is characterized by two key features. The first is its system of delegation or representation; the second, its enlarged extent (or "orbit," in number 9).

Madison of course knows, though he omits to mention, that the kind of pure or direct democracy that he is describing—and the kind of democratic republic that Montesquieu described—is practicable only on the scale of a town or a city. But this is scarcely what his Antifederalist foes were alluding to in defending the sovereignty of the several state-republics and in arguing against the new constitution's creation of an extended republic. They were, in fact, defending an entirely different position and performing an altogether different series of speech-acts. Despite the caricature presented by Publius, Brutus and his fellow Antifederalists were hardly simple democrats who were defending direct democracy; many saw themselves, rather, as republicans of a classical stripe.[21] And being good republicans, they posted their warnings about the future by turning to the past. "History," says Brutus, "furnishes no example of a free republic, any thing like the extent of the United States. The Grecian republics were of small extent; so also was that of the Romans." And when they "extended their conquests over large territories of country," they ceased to be republics, "their governments [having] changed from that of free governments to those of the most tyrannical that ever existed in the world."[22] As if "the opinion of the greatest men, and the experience of mankind," were not enough to show how misbegotten is "the idea of an extensive republic," Brutus adds that "the reason and nature of things [are] against it":

> In every government, the will of the sovereign is the law. In despotic governments, the supreme authority being lodged in one, his will is law, and can be as easily expressed to a large extensive territory as to a small one. In a pure democracy the people are sovereign, and their will is

declared by themselves; for this purpose they must all come together to deliberate, and decide. This kind of government cannot be exercised, therefore, over a country of any considerable extent; it must be confined to a single city, or at least limited to such bounds as that the people can conveniently assemble, be able to debate, understand the subject submitted to them, and declare their opinion concerning it.

Brutus goes on to suggest that a "free republic" represents a *via media* between these extremes. It is neither large enough to make despotism necessary nor small enough to make direct democracy possible. The "true criterion between a free government and an arbitrary one" is that the former requires that "the people must give their assent to the laws by which they are governed," and this they do through their representatives.[23]

That is to say, Brutus is defending, not direct democracy, but state sovereignty, while at the same time he is warning his audience about the danger of despotism that extended territory brings to a republic. "I have attempted to shew," he says, "that a consolidation of this extensive continent, under one government, for internal, as well as external purposes, . . . cannot succeed, without a sacrifice of your liberties." Hence, he concludes, "the attempt is not only preposterous, but extremely dangerous."[24] Brutus is warning, in short, about the danger of creating an American empire ruled by despots, rather than a republic governed by duly elected representatives.

TWO CONCEPTS OF REPRESENTATION

Far from being a defense of "direct democracy"—a rhetorical red herring of Madison's own devising—the Antifederalist arguments about size and scale are actually about the conditions under which representative government can be said to be truly representative. Their disagreements about the criterion of true representativeness and about the kind and quality of representation that the new constitution afforded stem from their subscribing to two quite different, indeed incommensurable, theories of representation. Following Hanna F. Pitkin, I propose to call these the "mandate" and the "independence" theories.[25] According to the mandate view, the task of a representative is to mirror the views of those whom he represents; he does as they would do, were they in his place. His function is not merely to represent their interests but to share their attitudes and feelings as well. He is to be their "actual" representative. The independence view, by contrast, holds that the representative is a trustee who must make his own judgments concerning his constituents' interests and how they might be best served. He is to be their "virtual," not their "actual," representative. The constituents' actual feelings and attitudes are, from this perspective, largely irrelevant.[26]

In the main and depending upon which governmental body was being discussed, the Antifederalists subscribed to the mandate view and the Federalists to the independence view. To be sure, they did not all speak with a single voice on this, or on any other, issue. But most of them agreed on at least three points. First, the House of Representatives, if not the Senate, should be a representative cross section, or microcosm, of the larger society. Second, members of the House should be guided by the actual, or "mandate," theory of representation, even if the senators were (or should) not. Third, the House did not in fact meet the first two requirements and was therefore not a genuinely representative body. Like many of his fellow Antifederalists, Brutus believed that the new Constitution created two bodies that were representative in name only. His harshest words were reserved for the House of Representatives, which he thought misnamed. "The more I reflect on this subject, the more firmly am I persuaded, that the representation is merely nominal—a mere burlesque."[27] And, given the master metaphors and controlling imagery of Antifederalist discourse and their theory of representation in particular, this charge comes as no surprise. In attempting to picture the relationship between a constituent and his "actual" representative, mandate theorists often employ the pictorial imagery of "resemblance," "reflection," and "mirroring." Brutus is no exception:

> The very term, representative, implies, that the person or body chosen for this purpose, should *resemble* those who appoint them—a representation of the people of America, if it be a true one, must be *like* the people. It ought to be so constituted, that a person, who is a stranger to the country, might be able to form a just idea of their character, by knowing that of their representatives. They are the *sign*—the people are the thing signified. It is absurd to speak of one thing being the *representative* of another, upon any other principle. . . . [T]hose who are placed instead of the people, should possess their sentiments and feelings, and be governed by their interests, or, in other words, should bear the strongest *resemblance* of those in whose room they are substituted.[28]

From this pictorial, or mandate, view of representation, Brutus derives what he takes to be a mathematically warranted conclusion:

> It is obvious, that for an assembly to be a true likeness of the people of any country, they must be considerably numerous.—One man, or a few men, cannot possibly represent the feelings, opinions, and characters of a great multitude. In this respect, the new constitution is radically defective.[29]

It is important to note that Brutus is not suggesting that representatives should, or even can, represent each of their individual constituents in their uniqueness. Clearly, that would be impossible, because the number of representatives would then equal the number of people represented. The result would then be, not representative government, but direct democracy. And that, as we have already seen, is not the system that Brutus and most of his fellow Antifederalists were defending.

What system, then, were the Antifederalists defending? It was a system of representation resting, as we have seen, upon the mandate theory of "actual" representation, to which is added yet another earlier republican conception—namely, representation, not of individuals, but of "orders" or "ranks" or "classes" (this last not referring to economic classes in the later nineteenth-century sense). As Brutus puts it: "This extensive continent is made up of a number of different classes of people; and to have a proper representation of them, each class ought to have an opportunity of choosing their best informed men for the purpose." If there is to be a "just resemblance" between "the several classes of people" in the society and those whom they elect to speak on their behalf in the representative assemblies—and the House of Representatives in particular—then

> the farmer, merchant, mecanick, and other various orders of people, ought to be represented according to their respective weight and numbers; and the representatives ought to be intimately acquainted with the wants, understand the interests of the several orders . . . , and feel a proper sense and becoming zeal to promote their prosperity.[30]

The mode of election and the system of representation that are mandated by the new Constitution are designed not only to thwart the representation of the various orders or ranks but also to ensure their exclusion:

> The great body of the yeomen of the country cannot expect any of their order in this assembly [i.e., the House of Representatives]—the station will be too elevated for them to aspire to—the distance between the people and their representatives, will be so very great, that there is no probability that a farmer, however respectable, will be chosen—the mechanicks of every branch, must expect to be excluded from a seat in this Body.[31]

The result will be that "in reality there will be no part of the people represented, but the rich, even in that branch of the legislature, which is called democratic." The Federalists' claim that those who are elected will disinterestedly serve all the people, including the "democratical part," is "specious," in the eighteenth-century sense—that is, attractive but erroneous. "The well born, and highest orders in life, as they term themselves," warns Brutus, "will be ignorant of the sentiments of the midling class of citizens, strangers to their ability, wants, and difficulties, and void of sympathy, and fellow feeling." Theirs "will literally be a government in the hands of the few to oppress and plunder the many."[32]

This is republican rhetoric about the recognition and the representation of orders and ranks, not populist rhetoric about how utterly wonderful "the people" or "the masses" are. For all their talk about how important it is that "the democratical part" be represented in a well-ordered republic, most of the Antifederalists were far from sympathetic to pure or direct democracy, much less to narrow partisan politics, and still less to mob rule. To argue otherwise is to accept the caricature painted for partisan purposes by their Federalist opponents. Had the Antifederalists couched their arguments, not in the idiom of classical republicanism, but in that of undifferentiated mass democracy, they would have succeeded only in shooting themselves in their collective foot. During the 1780s, "republic" was by and large a term of approbation and "democracy" a term of opprobrium.[33] Had the Antifederalists been democrats and had their arguments been democratic, they would hardly have called forth, or even required, the concentrated rhetorical firepower of *The Federalist*. But most Antifederalists were not, by their own lights at least, democrats; they were republicans, constructing and propagating republican arguments for an audience that they expected, not without reason, to share their republican sympathies.[34]

It was precisely because the arguments of Brutus and of other Antifederalists were bound to strike deeply resonant republican chords that they had to be met, if not head-on, then at least sideways. Brutus's paper of 15 November was countered one week later by Madison's most powerful broadside, the justly famed *Federalist* number 10. After attempting to tar the Antifederalists with the brush of direct democracy, Madison finally acknowledges that the real choice is not between democratic and republican forms, after all. The choice that Americans are facing is actually between two types of republic and the kinds of representatives that are likely to be chosen in them. Is a small (or classical or Montesquieuean) republic to be preferred to a large (modern or Humean) one? The answer that one gives will, he allows, depend less upon *who* is to be represented than upon *what* is to be represented. The choice is between representing the particular interests of the various orders—which are rhetorically redubbed "factions"—and representing the public good. If we subscribe to the mandate view, he suggests, our legislation will consist of an impure amalgam of narrow factional interests, not a duly filtered distillation of pure public interestedness. Assuming that real republicans will want the latter, rather than the former, the only question remaining is how that result might best be achieved. "The question resulting is," says Madison, "whether small or extensive Republics are most favorable to the election of proper guardians of the public weal." The issue is "clearly decided in favor of the latter" by two considerations, both of which, he allows, are "obvious." The first, which is indeed crashingly obvious, is that the pool of "fit characters" is likely to be larger in a large society than in a small one. The second consideration is rather less obviously true. It amounts to saying that the greater the number of voters in any given election, the more difficult it is for "unworthy candidates to practice with success the vicious arts, by which elections are too often carried."[35]

The point of Madison's argument is to counter the charge of corruption in the event that the wealthy should acquire undue influence. If wealth brings one kind of corruption, as Brutus and the Antifederalists charge, a "numerous representation" would result in corruption of another, far worse, sort. Where Brutus had decried the actions of unrepresentative representatives, Madison decried the stratagems of "unworthy candidates," who were likely to triumph in a popular free-for-all. Bribery, bombast, demagoguery, and the various "vicious arts" would be their stock-in-trade. In other words, while Brutus and the Antifederalists were focusing on what representatives are apt to do after they are elected, Madison and his fellow Federalists were focusing initially on what candidates might do in order to be elected in the first place and secondarily on what wicked and improper projects the candidates might pursue after they had been elected.

The issue of "actual" versus "virtual" representation could not be so easily disposed of, however, and Hamilton returned to face it head-on in number 35. The Antifederalist argument in favor of actual representation he brands as "specious and seducting" and "altogether visionary," consisting only of "fair sounding words" which are "well calculated to lay hold of the prejudices of those to whom [they are] addressed." Hamilton counters with arguments of two sorts. The first we might call the arithmetical argument; the second, the sociological one. The arithmetical argument is simply a reminder that such a system would, by greatly increasing the number of representatives, be well-nigh impossible to put into practice, because if the Constitution should require "an actual representation of all classes of the people by persons of each class," then "each different occupation" would have to "send one or more members" to the Congress. This would require a representative body so large and unwieldly that "the thing would never take place in practice." Not only is such a scheme "impracticable"; it is also "unnecessary," for reasons that we might today call sociological. There is a natural tendency for those of lower social standing to defer to, and to rely upon, those of higher social standing:

> Mechanics and manufacturers will always be inclined . . . to give their votes to merchants in preference to persons of their own professions or trades. Those discerning citizens . . . know that the merchant is their natural patron and friend; and they are aware that however great the confidence they may justly feel in their own good sense, their interests can be more effectually promoted by the merchant than by themselves. . . . We must therefore consider merchants as the natural representatives of all these classes of the community.

To talk only about the efficiency with which their "interests" may be "promoted" might appear to miss the point, as Hamilton acknowledges. The Antifederalists, Hamilton claims, believe it "necessary that all classes of citizens should have some of their own number in the representative body, in order that their *feelings* and interests may be the better understood and attended to." But this, Hamilton says in effect, is to overlook the likelihood that their "feelings" are apt to be ones of inadequacy, inferiority, and incompetence. The lower orders would therefore be understandably reluctant to send people like themselves to Congress to represent their "feelings and interests"! The "altogether visionary" hope of creating a system of actual representation "will never happen under any arrangement that leaves the votes of the people free."[36]

Significantly, however, Hamilton omits to mention, much less to answer, the recurrent Antifederalist charge that the new Constitution would exacerbate and intensify these feelings of civic incompetence and would lead inevitably to popular apathy, political corruption, and the loss of civic virtue.

CORRUPTION AND VIRTUE

The concepts of corruption and virtue, as used by many Antifederalist writers, have deep republican roots. In the republican tradition of discourse, "corruption" refers to a condition in which rulers and citizens have ceased to know or care about the common good, preferring instead to seek their own private (and especially pecuniary) interests. Just as the human body becomes "corrupt" with age, so likewise must the body politic sooner or later lose its unity and organic integrity, as its "parts" thereby become partisan and self-seeking and cease to work together for some greater shared purpose.[37] To have lost interest in the common good is to have ceased to be a citizen—or at any rate a virtuous one. Corruption is, in short, the loss or absence of civic virtue.[38]

The Antifederalist critique echoes many of the themes that are to be found in the earlier republican and radical Whig warnings about the dangers of corruption, especially those sounded by eighteenth-century English "country" party ideologists against the "court" ideology of Walpole and the new Whigs.[39] Thus, for example, the Real Whig warnings about the dangers of political appointees or "placemen" is repeated by Brutus when he decries "that kind of corruption, and undue influence, which will arise from the gift of places of honor and emolument." This, combined with other forms of "influence," is certain to corrupt the executive and the legislature. Indeed,

> when it is considered what a number of places of honor and emolument will be in the gift of the executive, the powerful influence that great and designing men have over the honest and unsuspecting, by their art and address, their soothing manners and civilities, and their cringing flattery, joined with their affected patriotism; when these different species of influence are combined, it is scarcely to be hoped that a legislature, composed of so small a number, as the one proposed by the new constitution, will long resist their force.[40]

Without "an equal and full representation in the legislature," there could be "no security against bribery and corruption."[41]

The corruption of officials or representatives was one thing, but the corruption of the citizenry was another, and even more serious, matter. In the Antifederalist view, these were linked in either of two ways. On the one hand, if the members of the various orders should agree that a "fit character" who was not of their order was by nature or disposition better able to represent their interests, they might then be willing to consign their liberties to the doubtful safekeeping of the "natural aristocracy" of their betters. On the other hand, should the citizens feel themselves to be powerless and voiceless, they would lose interest in public affairs. In either event, they would concentrate on their own purely personal or private affairs and would grow lazy or lax as regards the good of their own order and, by implication, of the common good as well. Either would result inevitably in the corruption of the citizens and, ultimately, in the destruction of their liberties.

The new Constitution, as depicted by Antifederalist critics, embodied both defects. Suspecting a massive Federalist conspiracy against republican values and institutions, many Antifederalists felt that the new Constitution was designed precisely for the dual purpose of making citizens trust their social superiors even as they themselves forgot the Spirit of '76 and became inward-looking and inattentive to matters of common concern. The new Constitution could therefore be viewed, in the parlance of classical republicanism, as a medium or instrument of civic corruption and as a destroyer of the people's liberties.

From the republican perspective of the Antifederalists, a properly constructed constitution is more than a set of rules. Inspiring, informing, and educating the citizenry about their rights and duties, a constitution is also a medium of civic character-formation and public instruction. However hastily drafted and ill-written the various state constitutions may have been, they supposedly fulfilled that educational function. They admonished governors and representatives even as they reminded the citizens that republican liberties are too easily lost when the public is inattentive.[42] From this perspective, one can more readily appreciate the Antifederalists' antipathy toward the document drawn up in Philadelphia.

One of the Antifederalists' main complaints was that the new Constitution sent the wrong sort of message to the citizenry. Not only did its implicit theory of representation imply that their views did not much matter and that the protection of their and the public's interest was best left to an elite; it also failed to inculcate the all-important sense of civic virtue. Many Antifederalists held that these defects were most painfully obvious in the absence of a Bill of Rights. Such an addition would serve as a reminder to all—rulers and citizens alike—that the government's authority was limited by its citizens' inviolable liberties. Did not the Glorious Revolution result in a Bill of Rights that King William agreed to? Did not the still-more-glorious revolution of 1776 deserve no less a guarantee? What was it fought for, if not to preserve American rights and liberties? If they were to be properly protected, the nature and extent of those liberties had to be fixed from the outset. The good will or solicitude of rulers and representatives was not to be relied upon for very long, if at all.[43] Those who have power are bound to abuse it, unless they are checked by the law and by an active and alert citzenry.

Even in a well-ordered republic there exists an inevitable tendency toward corruption. And to Antifederalist eyes, this new American republic seemed to be singularly ill ordered, its tendency toward corruption being hastened at its birth by a constitution that encouraged corruption by empowering the rulers and the representatives at the national or federal level, even as it was emasculating the citizenry at a more local level. This emasculation was effected in part by making the individual citizen and his order smaller by enlarging the scale on which national action was to be taken by an unrepresentative elite. At the very least, then, some "declaration of rights" must be written into the new plan, lest the people be deceived and led into a trap from which there would be no escape.[44] Without such a declaration to protect the rights of "the democratical part," says Brutus, "the plan is radically defective in a fundamental principle, which ought to be found in every free government; to wit, a declaration of rights."[45] Because the arguments in favor of such a declaration are so compelling, its omission is an ominous portent, revealing the true colours of Publius and his fellow Federalists: "So clear a point is this, that I cannot help suspecting, that persons who attempt to persuade people, that such reservations were less necessary under this constitution than under those of the states, are willfully endeavouring to deceive, and to lead you into an absolute state of vassalage."[46] Again and again the Antifederalists hammered this point home with all the repetitive intensity of the "Anvil Chorus": Without a bill of rights, the new system scarcely deserved the name republican.

Finally, in number 84, Publius was compelled to answer, although reluctantly and under the heading of "miscellaneous points," to be dealt with as though they were mere afterthoughts and scarcely on a par with the truly important issues that he had discussed earlier. "The most considerable of these remaining objections is," writes Hamilton, "that the plan of the convention contains no bill of rights." By way of reply he notes that several state constitutions, including New York's, also lack a bill of rights. Acknowledging the force of the Antifederalists' answer to this objection—namely, that no separate bill of rights is needed because provisions for protecting those rights are incorporated into the texts of the state constitutions—Hamilton asserts that the same is true of the new federal Constitution as well. "The truth is, after all the declamation we have heard, that the constitution is itself in every rational sense, and to every useful purpose, A BILL OF RIGHTS."[47] Yet the bill of rights that Hamilton teases out of the text is a rather motley assortment of legal guarantees, prohibitions, and definitions. The "priviledges" of *habeas corpus* and jury trials are affirmed, even though there is no requirement that the jury be composed of one's peers; "treason" is defined; and the prohibition of titles of nobility, about which Madison had made so much in number 39, is again presented as proof positive of the republican character of the new constitution: "Nothing need be said to illustrate the importance of the prohibition of titles of nobility. This may truly be denominated the corner stone of republican government; for so long they are excluded, there can never be serious danger that the government will be any other than that of the people."[48]

Hamilton, who was well aware that "A Countryman" and other Antifederalists had earlier denied that there was any necessary connection between republican government and the granting of titles of nobility,[49] then goes on to play his ace. The Antifederalists had often charged their opponents with attempting to alter the meanings of key concepts. Now it is Hamilton's turn. Playing the part of conceptual conservative, Hamilton turns the tables by charging the Antifederalists with having attempted to alter the very meaning of the concept of a bill of rights—a concept as old as Magna Carta and as recent as the Bill of Rights to which William of Orange had agreed. Because "bills of rights are in their origin, stipulations between kings and their subjects," says Hamilton, they have no place in a republican charter. "Here, in strictness, the people surrender nothing, and as they retain every thing, they have no need of particular reservations." The Preamble, he sniffs, affords "a better recognition of popular rights than volumes of those aphorisms . . . in several of our state bills of rights, and which would sound much better in a treatise of ethics than in a constitution of government."[50]

In thus downplaying "ethics," Publius did not so much deny the importance of virtue and character as he proposed to *relocate* them. Henceforth, virtue would be, not an individual, but a systemic property. It is the virtue and character of the *system*, not the citizenry, that Publius praises repeatedly. The citizen is, at best, a weak reed, bending easily before the wind of self-interest. If the individual be weak, the system must be strong. "Ambition must be made to counteract ambition." The appropriate "policy" must therefore be one "of supplying by opposite and rival interests, the defect of better motives."[51] Here again Publius is following Hume, who wrote:

> Political writers have established it as a maxim, that, in contriving any system of government, and fixing the several checks and controuls of the constitution, every man ought to be supposed a knave, and to have no other end, in all his actions, than private interest. By this interest we must govern him, and, by means of it, making him, notwithstanding his insatiable avarice and ambition, co-operate to public good.[52]

The corruptibility of the citizenry is, in short, to be stemmed by the incorruptibility of the system. In thus relocating virtue, Publius redefines its role and changes its meaning. And in changing the meaning of "virtue" and its proper place within a "republic," Publius partially reconstituted the concept of a republic.

PUBLIUS'S LINGUISTIC TURN

These and other conceptual changes can hardly be discounted, much less dismissed, as so much semantic quibbling or rhetorical window dressing; they were, instead, rational strategies in a hard-fought concep-

tual-cum-political struggle. And as the debate over ratification inten-
sified, the protagonists focused not only upon individual issues but also,
and increasingly, upon the appropriate language in which to frame and
discuss these very issues. Madison, in particular, recasts the conflict
over ratification as a competition between tongues, languages, and
voices. "Hearken not," he admonishes, "to the voice which petulantly
tells you that the form of government recommended for your adoption
is a novelty in the political world; that it has never yet had a place in the
theories of the wildest projectors; that it rashly attempts what it is
impossible to accomplish." In an uncharacteristically emotional appeal,
the calm and "candid" Madison adds: "No my countrymen, shut your
ears against this unhallowed language." Even this might not seem so
odd, were it not that Madison then goes on to take that very language
for his own. He admits that the critics are right, after their fashion: The
system *is* new; it is untried. "But why," he asks, "is the experiment of
an extended republic to be rejected merely because it . . . is new?"[53]

But since the Antifederalists had not objected to the new constitution merely because it was new and untried but also because it was,
according to their lights, not truly "republican," Publius returns repeatedly to the defense of his and the new Constitution's republican
bona fides. In *Federalist* number 14, Madison once again felt compelled to
defend the distinction drawn in number 10 between a democracy and a
republic; but this time he used a new logical-cum-linguistic twist that
was to become even more pronounced as the ratification debate wore on
throughout the waning months of 1787 and well into 1788. Due to a
"fallacy" stemming from "the confusion of names," Madison avers, "it
has been an easy task to transfer to a republic, observations applicable to
a democracy only," including the oft-heard contention that a republic
"can never be established but among a small number of people, living
within a small compass of territory." "Such a fallacy," he adds on an
apparently conciliatory note, "may have been the less perceived as most
of the governments of antiquity were of the democratic species." What
he omits to note, of course, is what Machiavelli and Montesquieu had
accepted without question, namely, that those "democracies" were in
fact "republics." Without mentioning either of these republican theorists by name, Madison reiterates and reinforces the "Humean" point
made by Hamilton in number 9: earlier thinkers—Machiavelli and
Montesquieu among them—lived in too early an age to see what can
now be seen clearly by all but the most benighted and prejudiced. Not
wishing to pit any of the founders against those republican paragons, he
attributes this new "discovery," not to the genius of any man or small
band of men, but to that of an entire nation. "America," says Madison,
"can claim the merit of making the discovery [of "the great principle of

representation''] the basis of unmixed and extensive republics.''[54] Thus, Madison invokes the classical republican notion of "glory," not for the framers, as Publius had proclaimed in number 9, but now for the people themselves. "Is it not the glory of the people of America," he asks, "that whilst they have paid a decent regard to the opinions of former times and other nations, they have not suffered a blind veneration for antiquity, for custom, or for names, to overrule the suggestions of their own good sense . . . ?" It is to this forward-looking "manly spirit" of innovation that "posterity will be indebted.''[55] Madison fails to mention that the innovation is above all a *conceptual* one, for it is, after all, the concept of republic itself that he (like Hume before him) has subtly if not altogether convincingly tried to transform.

It is scarcely surprising, then, that Brutus and other critics were quick to charge Publius with having abused the hallowed language of republicanism.[56] Madison responded by taking his own version of the linguistic turn. All language, republican or otherwise, he complains, is an inherently imperfect medium. His exasperation is especially evident in number 37, where he decries the opacity and recalcitrance of language itself:

> [T]he medium through which the conceptions of men are conveyed to each other, adds a fresh embarrassment. The use of words is to express ideas. Perspicuity therefore requires not only that the ideas should be distinctly formed, but that they should be expressed by words distinctly and exclusively appropriated to them. But no language is so copious as to supply words and phrases for every complex idea, or so correct as not to include many equivocally denoting different ideas. Hence, it must happen, that however accurately objects may be discriminated in themselves, and however accurately the discrimination may be considered, the definition of them may be rendered inaccurate by the inaccuracy of the terms in which it is delivered. And this unavoidable inaccuracy must be greater or less, according to the complexity and novelty of the objects defined.

Imprecision and "inaccuracy" are "unavoidable," the more so as "the objects defined" are complex or novel, or both. The object of an extended republic having been admitted (in number 14 and elsewhere) to be both novel and complex, Madison reflects upon the difficulty that faces any conceptual innovator. Machiavelli and Rousseau had asked how a human but godlike legislator could hope to communicate with ordinary mortals, given the limitations of their language.[57] Madison wonders aloud whether God Almighty Himself might fail to make His meaning clear, were He to speak to us even in our own tongue: "When the Almighty himself condescends to address mankind in their own language, his meaning, luminous as it must be, is rendered dim and doubtful, by the cloudy medium through which it is communicated.''[58]

Madison goes on to list "three sources of vague and incorrect definitions"—namely, "indistinctness of the object, imperfection of the organ of conception, [and] inadequateness of the vehicle of ideas"—any one of which "must produce a certain degree of obscurity." In remarking that the framers of the new plan had "experienced the full effect of them all," Madison implied that mere mortals had been saddled, as Rousseau had remarked, with the responsibility of gods. In Madison's hands, however, this was not a proclamation of superiority; it was a plea for sympathy and for understanding the difficulties faced by legislators who are also conceptual innovators. Not the least of these difficulties involved the problems presented by Publius's newly minted concept of republic.

Madison therefore felt compelled to return, in number 39, to the bold promise that Hamilton had made in number 1 and to the question that Madison himself had attempted to answer in numbers 10, 14, and 37. In number 1, Publius had promised to demonstrate "the conformity of the proposed constitution to the true principles of republican government."[59] In number 10 he had offered "a Republican remedy for the diseases most incident to Republican Government."[60] In number 14 he had reiterated and reinforced the argument of number 10. And in number 37 he had adverted to the inadequacy of language as a medium of political communication. One senses in his linguistic turn a growing sense of desperation. During the six weeks that had passed since the appearance of the first number of *The Federalist*, he had failed to convince his critics that the new government would be republican in form and spirit; and he could only fear that his wider audience must share their skepticism.

And so, already nearly halfway though the series, Madison begins number 39 with a question that should have been settled already. "The first question that offers itself is, whether the general form and aspect of the government be strictly republican?" For, he admits,

> it is evident that no other form would be reconcileable with the genius of the people of America; with the fundamental principles of the revolution; or with that honorable determination, which animates every votary of freedom, to rest all our political experiments on the capacity of mankind for self-government. If the plan of the Convention therefore be found to depart from the republican character, its advocates must abandon it as no longer defensible.[61]

The stakes are higher now. Madison must either prove the republican character of the new constitution or repudiate it. But how?

Publius's twofold strategy might best be characterized as a linguistic or conceptual counterattack. His first task is to show that the term "republic" has been applied indifferently and indiscriminately, even by the greatest authorities and thus, by implication, by those lesser authorities who cite them, the Antifederalists. This done, he can then defend not only the legitimacy but also the superiority of his alternative understanding. He begins by asking what "the distinctive characters of the republican form" are. He then proceeds to show that there is no single feature or set of features that have been shared by all polities designated as "republics." Holland, Venice, Poland, and England have all been called republics at one time or another. Yet "these examples, which are nearly as dissimilar to each other as to a genuine republic, shew the extreme inaccuracy with which the term has been used in political disquisitions."[62]

About Madison's first move we might pause to note two objections that his Antifederalist opponents did not, and indeed could not, have raised. The first is that Madison's criticism is, from a linguistic point of view, misconceived, not to say misleading. It is a little like asking, as Wittgenstein does in another context and for another purpose, what single feature or set of features is common to all the things we call games. What do board games, games played on fields, with and without balls or other objects, by teams or by individuals or by solitary players, and so forth, have in common? The answer, of course, is nothing— and everything. There are, as Wittgenstein remarks, "family resemblances" between and among all those things that we call "games."[63] Just as no single feature—nose shape, hair color, complexion, and so forth—is shared by all members of one family, so too, we might say, no single feature is shared by all those polities called republics. To raise this objection would, however, be unfair, not to say anachronistic.

A second objection, however, suffers from neither of these liabilities. Translated into more modern terms, it amounts to this: there is today no political system that has not been described by someone somewhere as "democratic." Chile, South Africa, South Korea, North Korea, East Germany, West Germany, the Soviet Union, and the United States have all been described as "democracies." From this fact, neither of two conclusions follows. The first—namely, that their systems of government are essentially similar if not identical—is quite obviously absurd. The second—that the term "democracy" is meaningless—does not follow either. The most that can be concluded from this fact is that "democracy" is a "contested concept" whose criteria of application are disputed by partisans of different political persuasions.[64] And as is the case with "democracy" in our day, so too was the case with "republic" in Publius's time.

Were this the sum and substance of Publius's argument in number 39, the case for the "republican character" of the plan would hardly have been proved. But once again, Madison has warmed up, so to speak, by setting fire to a straw man. His second and weightier argument is about the priority of principles in political discourse. Names and labels, he maintains, count for less than principles. The former are applied by partisans of various ages in the heat of passion and political intrigue; the latter, by contrast, constitute the acid test of the validity of those claims. Thus, if we try to define a republic, "not by recurring to principles, but in the application of the term by political writers, to the constitutions of different States, no satisfactory one would ever be found."[65]

But when, in number 39, Publius sets out to "define a republic" in "principled" terms, he downplays the ostensibly crucial distinction—which he had introduced in number 10 and reiterated in number 14—between "democracy" and "republic." Those particular institutional forms, he admits, apparently have no essential bearing upon the defining "principle" of republicanism:

> [W]e may define a republic to be, or at least may bestow that name on, a government which derives all its powers directly or indirectly from the great body of the people; and is administered by persons holding their offices . . . for a limited period, or during good behaviour. It is *essential* to such a government, that it be derived from the great body of the society, not from an inconsiderable proportion, or a favored class of it; otherwise a handful of tyrannical nobles, exercising their oppressions by a delegation of their powers, might aspire to the rank of republicans, and claim for their government the honorable title of republic. It is *sufficient* for such a government, that the persons administering it be appointed, either directly or indirectly, by the people.[66]

There would now appear to be no reason "in principle" why a democracy could not be a republic (though perhaps not a very harmonious or long-lived one, as Hamilton had charged in number 9) and every reason why a system ruled by "tyrannical nobles" could not be. Publius must then show that contrary to the charges leveled by some Antifederalists, the new system would not be a tyrannical aristocracy, either in principle or in practice. Publius points out that all the officers in the new government have their terms in office limited either by periodic elections or by good behavior and adds that any of them can be removed from office at any time. Even the president can be impeached. And, as though this were not enough, Publius offers a final and apparently conclusive proof. "Could any further proof be required of the republican complextion of this system," he maintains, "the most decisive one might be found in its absolute prohibition of titles of nobility, both under the Federal and the State Governments; and in its express guarantee of the republican form to each of the latter."[67]

The only decisive proofs in politics derive, says Publius, not from our language, but from those principles whose meanings our language tries, too often in vain, to capture and hold. Even though the meaning of the word "republic" may be mutable, Madison contends, the principles of republicanism are timeless and above the partisan fray. Ironically, in maintaining that principles, unlike terms, are timeless, Madison echoes John Toland's contention that "men may change, and words may change, but principles never."[68] What neither Toland nor Madison saw—or admitted—is that "words" are no more mutable than "principles," for there can be no principle that is not expressed in words. In revising the meaning of "republic," Publius had not merely changed the meaning of a word. He had constituted a world. Whether or in what sense that world was any longer recognizably "republican" continues to be a matter of dispute.

NOTES

I am grateful to Garry Wills, Gerald Stourzh, Donald Moon, Russell Hanson, and James Farr for criticizing an earlier version of this essay.

Abbreviations used in the notes:

FP   *The Federalist Papers,* ed. Garry Wills (New York: Bantam Books, 1982)

CAF   *The Complete Anti-Federalist,* ed. Herbert J. Storing, 7 vols. (Chicago: University of Chicago Press, 1981)

AF   *The Anti-Federalist,* abridged 1-vol. ed. of *CAF,* ed. Murray Dry (Chicago: University of Chicago Press, 1985)

WMQ   *William and Mary Quarterly,* 3d series

1. The literature is vast and growing. The thesis of a Lockean-liberal American founding, propounded by Louis Hartz in the mid 1950s but discredited by Bernard Bailyn, Gerald Stourzh, Gordon S. Wood, J. G. A. Pocock, Lance Banning, and other proponents of a "republican synthesis" during the late 1960s and 1970s, has been revived of late by Joyce Appleby, Isaac Kramnick, and John Patrick Diggins. Douglass Adair's claim that the American founding owes a large debt to Hume and other thinkers of the Scottish Enlightenment has recently been revived and defended by Garry Wills and has been disputed by Ronald Hamowy. See, *inter alia,* Louis Hartz, *The Liberal Tradition in America* (New York: Harcourt Brace, 1955); Bernard Bailyn, *The Ideological Origins of the American Revolution* (Cambridge, Mass.: Harvard University Press, 1967), chap. 2; Gordon S. Wood, *The Creation of the American Republic, 1776–1787* (Chapel Hill: University of North Carolina Press, 1969), chaps. 1–3; Gerald Stourzh, *Alexander Hamilton and the Idea of Republican Government* (Stanford, Calif.: Stanford University Press, 1970), chaps. 1–3; J. G. A. Pocock, "Machiavelli, Harrington, and English Political Ideologies in the Eighteenth Century," *WMQ* 22 (1965), and *The Machiavellian Moment: Florentine Political Thought and the Atlantic Republican Tradition* (Princeton, N.J.: Princeton University Press, 1975), chap. 15; Lance

Banning, *The Jeffersonian Persuasion: Evolution of a Party Ideology* (Ithaca, N.Y.: Cornell University Press, 1978) and "Jeffersonian Ideology Revisited: Liberal and Classical Ideas in the New American Republic," *WMQ* 43 (Jan. 1986): 3–19; and the useful overviews and assessments by Robert E. Shalhope, "Toward a Republican Synthesis: The Emergence of an Understanding of Republicanism in American Historiography," *WMQ* 29 (Jan. 1972): 49–80, and "Republicanism and Early American Historiography," *WMQ* 39 (Apr. 1982): 334–56; and Jean Yarbrough, "Republicanism Reconsidered: Some Thoughts on the Foundation and Preservation of the American Republic," *Review of Politics* 41 (Jan. 1979): 61–95. This emerging republican synthesis has come under attack by, *inter alia*, Isaac Kramnick, "Republican Revisionism Revisited," *American Historical Review* 87 (1982): 629–64; and Joyce Appleby, "Republicanism and Ideology," *American Quarterly* 37 (1985): 461–73, and "Republicanism in Old and New Contexts," *WMQ* 43 (Jan. 1986): 20–34. The thesis of a Humean-Scottish founding has been advanced and defended by Douglass Adair, *Fame and the Founding Fathers*, ed. Trevor Colbourn (New York: Norton, 1974); and by Garry Wills, *Inventing America: Jefferson's Declaration of Independence* (Garden City, N.Y.: Doubleday, 1978) and *Explaining America: The Federalist* (Garden City, N.Y.: Doubleday, 1981). The thesis has been criticized by Ronald Hamowy, "Jefferson and the Scottish Enlightenment: A Critique of Garry Wills' *Inventing America*," *WMQ* 36 (1979): 503–23.

2. Keith Thomas, "Politics as Language," a review of J. G. A. Pocock's *Virtue, Commerce and History*, in the *New York Review of Books*, 27 Feb. 1986, p. 39.

3. Of course, not all Antifederalists spoke with one voice. For a discussion of their differences see James H. Hutson, "Country, Court, and Constitution: Antifederalism and the Historians," *WMQ* 38 (1981): 337–68.

4. See Wood, *Creation of the American Republic*, chap. 2; Willi Paul Adams, *The First American Constitutions: Republican Ideology and the Making of the State Constitutions in the Revolutionary Era*, trans. Rita Kimber and Robert Kimber (Chapel Hill: University of North Carolina Press, 1980), chap. 4, and his "Republicanism in Political Rhetoric before 1776," *Political Science Quarterly* 85 (1970): 397–421.

5. See Zera S. Fink, *The Classical Republicans: An Essay in the Recovery of a Pattern of Thought in Seventeenth-Century England* (Evanston, Ill.: Northwestern University Press, 1945); Caroline Robbins, *The Eighteenth Century Commonwealthman* (New York: Atheneum, 1968; first published in 1959); Bailyn, *Ideological Origins*; Wood, *Creation of the American Republic*, chaps. 1–3; Pocock, *Machiavellian Moment*, chap. 15; Banning, *Jeffersonian Persuasion*, chaps. 1–3; Michael Lienesch, "In Defence of the Antifederalists," *History of Political Thought* 4 (Feb. 1983): 65–87; Adams, *First American Constitutions* and "Republicanism in Political Rhetoric before 1776."

6. The degree to which Shays' Rebellion can be accounted a cause of, or at least a reasonable pretext for, the calling of the Philadelphia convention is disputed by historians. The conventional view—that it was the condition *sine qua non* for the Philadelphia meeting—is defended by Robert A. Feer, "Shays' Rebellion and the Constitution: A Study in Causation," *New England Quarterly* 42 (1969): 388–410, but disputed by Gordon S. Wood, "Interests and Disinterestedness in the Making of the Constitution," in *Beyond Confederation: Origins of the Constitution and American National Identity*, ed. Richard Beeman, Stephen Botein, and Edward C. Carter III (Chapel Hill: University of North Carolina Press, 1987), pp. 69–109, at 73. It was, Wood insists, "good old American

popular politics, . . . especially as practiced in the state legislatures, that lay behind the founders' sense of crisis." No doubt; but it bears mentioning that Shays' Rebellion is the only contemporary political event decried early on and by name in *The Federalist* (*FP* 6, p. 23).

7. Wood, *Creation of the American Republic*, pp. 608–9. Cf. also Michael Kammen, *Spheres of Liberty: Changing Perceptions of Liberty in American Culture* (Madison: University of Wisconsin Press, 1986).

8. Herbert J. Storing, *What the Anti-Federalists Were "For,"* vol. 1 of *CAF*, p. 3.

9. See Russell L. Hanson, *The Democratic Imagination in America: Conversations with Our Past* (Princeton, N.J.: Princeton University Press, 1985), pp. 58, 64–83; and Banning, *Jeffersonian Persuasion*, p. 106.

10. *CAF* 2.8.72; *AF*, pp. 67–68.

11. *FP* 73, p. 374.

12. *CAF* 2.9.11; *AF*, p. 113. Brutus's attack, which appeared on 18 Oct. 1787, was almost certainly on Madison's mind as he drafted *FP* 10 (see n. 13, below).

13. An earlier version of the argument for an extended republic had been rehearsed earlier at the Philadelphia convention and had been sharpened subsequently in private correspondence (see, e.g., Madison to Jefferson, 24 Oct. 1787, in *The Origins of the American Constitution: A Documentary History*, ed. Michael Kammen [New York: Penguin Books, 1986], esp. p. 71).

14. *FP* 9, pp. 37–38.

15. David Hume, "Of Civil Liberty," *Essays Moral, Political, and Literary*, ed. Eugene F. Miller (Indianapolis, Ind.: Liberty Classics, 1985), pp. 87–88.

16. *FP* 9, p. 38.

17. Ibid., p. 39.

18. Ibid.

19. Ibid., p. 42.

20. *FP* 10, p. 46.

21. *Contra* Charles Beard, Jackson Turner Main, and Gordon S. Wood, who with respectively increasing degrees of sophistication make the Antifederalists into agrarian democrats-cum-populists. *Contra* also Storing's assertion that "the Anti-Federalists are liberals—reluctant and traditional, indeed—in the decisive sense that they see the end of government as the security of individual liberty, not the promotion of virtue or the fostering of some organic common good" (*CAF* 1, p. 83 n. 7).

22. *CAF* 2.9.12; *AF*, p. 113.

23. *CAF* 2.9.13–14; *AF*, p. 114.

24. *CAF* 2.9.36; *AF*, pp. 122–23.

25. Hanna Fenichel Pitkin, *The Concept of Representation* (Berkeley and Los Angeles: University of California Press, 1967), chap. 7.

26. The *locus classicus* of the "independence" view is Burke's "Letter to the Sheriffs of Bristol" (1777), in *Edmund Burke: Selected Writings and Speeches*, ed. Peter J. Stanlis (Garden City, N.Y.: Anchor Books, 1963), pp. 186–208. Publius's source appears to be Hume, "Of the First Principles of Government," in *Essays*, pp. 32–36; cf. also "Of the Independency of Parliament," ibid., pp. 42–46. See, further, Frederick G. Whelan, *Order and Artifice in Hume's Political Philosophy* (Princeton, N.J.: Princeton University Press, 1985), p. 352; and Wills, *Explaining America*, chaps. 27 and 28.

27. *CAF* 2.9.44; *AF*, p. 126.

28. *CAF* 2.9.42; *AF*, pp. 123–25; emphasis added. Cf. the similar strictures adduced by the Federal Farmer, *CAF* 2.8.97–100; *AF*, pp. 74–78; also see Banning, *Jeffersonian Persuasion*, p. 108.

29. *CAF* 2.9.42; *AF,* p. 125.

30. Ibid.

31. Ibid., p. 126.

32. Ibid.

33. See Willi Paul Adams, *First American Constitutions* and "Republicanism in Political Rhetoric before 1776."

34. To put the matter in dichotomous terms—"republican" vs. "democratic"—is already to adopt the Madisonian distinction that was by no means widely shared, even by Madison's fellow Federalists (see Hanson, *Democratic Imagination,* esp. pp. 85–88). Also see n. 21 above.

35. *FP* 10, p. 47.

36. *FP* 35, pp. 167–68; emphasis supplied.

37. See my "Party," in *Political Innovation and Conceptual Change,* ed. Terence Ball, James Farr, and Russell L. Hanson (Cambridge, Eng.: Cambridge University Press, 1988), chap. 7.

38. See J. Peter Euben, "Corruption," in *Political Innovation and Conceptual Change,* chap. 11.

39. Although, as Pocock notes, America during the colonial and confederation period "constituted a Country without a Court" (*Machiavellian Moment,* p. 509). That, of course, is just the way the Antifederalists hoped to keep it, even as they feared that the new Constitution was seeking to serve the interests of an emerging commercial or court party. See, further, John Murrin, "The Great Inversion, or Court versus Country: A Comparison of the Revolution Settlements in England (1688–1721) and America (1776–1816)," in *Three British Revolutions: 1641, 1688, 1776,* ed. J. G. A. Pocock (Princeton, N.J.: Princeton University Press, 1980), pp. 368–453; and Hutson, "Country, Court and Constitution."

40. *CAF* 2.9.47; *AF,* pp. 128–29.

41. *CAF* 2.9.46; *AF,* p. 128.

42. See Wood, *Creation of the American Republic,* chaps. 4–6; Lienesch, "In Defence of the Antifederalists"; and Adams, *First American Constitutions,* chap. 4.

43. *CAF* 2.9.42–43; *AF,* p. 126.

44. *CAF* 2.9.33; *AF,* p. 122.

45. *CAF* 2.9.36; *AF,* pp. 122–23.

46. *CAF* 2.9.33; *AF,* p. 122.

47. *FP* 84, p. 438.

48. Ibid., p. 436.

49. *CAF* 6.7.8.

50. *FP* 84, pp. 436–37.

51. *FP* 51, pp. 262–63.

52. Hume, "Of the Independency of Parliament," *Essays,* p. 42.

53. *FP* 14, p. 66. Madison later admits—"candidly," as is his wont—that "what immediately strikes us" in the idea of an extended republic is its "novelty" (*FP* 37, p. 177).

54. *FP* 14, p. 63.

55. Ibid., pp. 66–67.

56. See, e.g., John DeWitt, "To the Free Citizens of the Commonwealth of Massachusetts," *CAF* 4.3.7.

57. Machiavelli, *Discourses,* bk. 1, chap. 11; Rousseau, *Social Contract,* bk. 2, chap. 7. Both maintain that the "translation problem" may be resolved by the

legislator's reliance upon the religious idiom of divinely ordained laws and revealed truths.

58. *FP* 37, pp. 179–80.
59. *FP* 1, p. 5.
60. *FP* 10, p. 49.
61. *FP* 39, p. 189.
62. Ibid., p. 190.
63. See Ludwig Wittgenstein, *Philosophical Investigations,* trans. G. E. M. Anscombe (Oxford: Basil Blackwell, 1967), paras. 66–70.
64. See W. B. Gallie, "Essentially Contested Concepts," *Proceedings of the Aristotelian Society* 56 (1955–56), and the subsequent qualifications and modifications introduced by Hanson, *Democratic Imagination,* chap. 1, and William E. Connolly, *The Terms of Political Discourse,* 2d ed. (Princeton, N.J.: Princeton University Press, 1983), chap. 1.
65. *FP* 39, p. 190.
66. Ibid.
67. Ibid., p. 191.
68. John Toland, *The State-Anatomy of Great Britain* (London, 1716), p. 18.

9

"Commons" and "Commonwealth" at the American Founding: Democratic Republicanism as the New American Hybrid

Russell L. Hanson

I

Revolutionary movements are notoriously difficult to sustain, and successful movements are perhaps most difficult of all, especially when, as is usually the case, the movements combine diverse opponents of the status quo. The desire for freedom unites the various factions that compose such movements, causing them to submerge their differences in the interest of defeating a common foe. Once the old regime has been toppled, however, these differences rise to the surface in efforts to complete the revolution, as each faction understands that task. In the ensuing struggle over the proper interpretation and implementation of revolutionary ideals, factions accuse each other of having betrayed the original aims of the movement, while claiming for themselves the right to finish the job of revolution. Such contests are rarely resolved without violence.

The American Revolution was concluded peaceably, making it an exception to this general tendency. This extraordinary outcome cannot reasonably be attributed to the absence of postindependence factionalism, the claims of "consensus" historians to the contrary notwithstanding. Other scholars have clearly identified a serious split in the American independence movement. An older group of state politicians, such as George Clinton, Patrick Henry, George Mason, and Elbridge Gerry, had advocated revolution as a way of ensuring the autonomy of states. They were not interested in establishing a strong central government; they were willing to let the union wither, once independence had been achieved and the need for a united military front had diminished. For such men, most of whom later became staunch Antifederalists, the Treaty of Paris signaled the end of the Revolution.[1]

Members of a younger generation, which included George Washington, Alexander Hamilton, James Madison, Robert Morris, James Wilson, and John Jay, were initially more reluctant to declare independence, but their experiences in the army, in Congress, and in the administration and financing of the war effort had given them a "continental vision" of America and its possibilities. For these men, independence was a prelude to nationhood, and the establishment of a central government capable of realizing this vision was part of the purpose of the Revolution. The frustration of their ambition under the Articles of Confederation made them advocates of a stronger central government and earned them the name of "Federalists."

The efforts by the Federalists—first to rouse the Confederal Congress to action, then to reform the Articles of Confederation, and finally to replace the Articles with an altogether different arrangement of political power—culminated in the debates with the Republicans during the 1790s over the proper exercise of power by the central government. As several scholars have noted, these debates parallel the seventeenth-century contest between "country" and "court" politicians in England.[2] However, the American version of this dispute between country and court decisively altered the tradition of republican politics in which it originated.[3]

Nowhere is this more evident than in the language of republicanism itself and in the very uses to which words such as "republic" and its cognates ("republicanism," "republican") were put. The meaning of these key words shifted dramatically during this period, and in the ensuing pages, I describe some of the terminological changes that were an integral part of the new understanding of politics that emerged at this time. As I hope to make clear, such linguistic innovations not only recorded the ideological ferment of the Founding but also constituted that ferment, at least partially. That is to say, it was in and through political discourse itself that American conceptions of politics were reshaped, producing a *novus ordo seclorum*.

The fact that these changes were effected by an appeal to reason, without resort to arms, is all the more extraordinary when the extent of them is considered. Americans moved from a dominant conception of republicanism, in which government was limited or held in check by the people, to one in which popular government itself was limited, if not altogether stymied, by its constitution. The former conception, which was known as "democratic republicanism," understood governance to be a precarious balance between rulers and those who were ruled; and it assigned rulers the job of serving the *res publica,* or the commonweal. For their part, those who were ruled were obliged to exercise vigilance in keeping rulers from abusing their powers—that is, using them for purposes antithetical to the commonweal.

This conception, which I sketch out in more detail in the third and fourth sections below, gave way to a new conception of governance, associated with the Federalists, one that eschewed democracy. This is discussed in section V, where I analyze the dilemma of those who proposed a popular government in which the overriding concern was to prevent the people, or at least a majority of them, from abusing their power through government. The rhetorical strategy by which this argument was presented to the people themselves for their approbation is the focus of my concern there, for it is remarkable that a people ostensibly lacking the virtue necessary for democratic republican governance were nevertheless persuaded of their own weakness in this regard and convinced of the need to accept a reduced role in republican politics.

In the last two sections, I discuss the inherent susceptibility of this kind of republican politics to charges about its undemocratic (or at least its insufficiently democratic) nature. A popular government explicitly differentiated from democracy turned out to be the Federalists' Achilles heel. The fortunes of the party declined fairly quickly after its success in winning ratification, because it proved incapable of surviving under a constitution of its own making. Before that story can be told, however, it is necessary to describe the rise of ''republican'' politics at the time of independence, as it was within this context that the entire debate took place.

II

The centrality of republicanism to American politics during the last twenty-five years of the eighteenth century is undeniable, even though few Americans would have predicted that in the years immediately preceding independence. Until 1776, most citizens denied any allegiance to republican principles. They subscribed to theories of mixed government and therefore accepted the legitimacy of limited monarchy. Hence the ascendance of republicanism on the eve of independence was noted by Thomas Jefferson with some amazement, when in 1777 he observed that Americans ''seem to have deposited the monarchical and taken up the republican government with as much ease as would have attended their throwing off an old and putting on a new suit of clothes.''[4]

The ease and speed with which this change was accomplished has amazed scholars, even those who now stress the disproportionate influence of English republicans on American thought—for example, Bernard Bailyn and Gordon Wood.[5] J. R. Pole explains this by saying that "the American colonies developed characteristics of what would later be known as a republican form of government many years before they were to claim to be republican in principle."[6] Thus, the rise of republicanism was a change of name only, not a change of heart, if I may depart from Jefferson's sartorial metaphor.

Of course the same is true of the Real Whigs themselves, who were reluctant to accept the republican designation for fairly obvious reasons. The "republican" charge recalled the tumultuous "world turned upside down" of the Puritan Commonwealth. The bulk of eighteenth-century Englishmen preferred to mark time with reference to the Glorious Revolution, a peaceful and successful effort to establish their political liberties on a firm constitutional basis. They saw no need to hark back to the earlier, more violent, and ultimately unsuccessful experiment in republican government associated with the Civil War. Indeed, most denied any connection between the Commonwealth period and the later struggle to exclude James Stuart and secure the Glorious Revolution; therefore they rejected outright the radicalism of republican politics.[7]

Occasionally, radical opponents of the Crown in England owned up to their republican heritage. For the most part, however, Real Whigs refrained from calling themselves republicans; instead, they spent considerable energy trying to show that they were *not* republicans or Commonwealthmen, their opponents' charges notwithstanding. Robert Molesworth, for example, lamented "the heavy Calumny thrown upon us, that we are all Commonwealth's-Men: which (in the ordinary Meaning of the Word) amounts to *Haters* of *Kingly* government." He accepted the appellation only after carefully noting the republican affinity for balanced government, with its implicit acceptance of monarchy.[8]

Molesworth was not able to put the issue to rest; members of the court party continued to accuse their country opponents of disloyalty and even sedition. John Trenchard and Thomas Gordon were vilified for having propagated republican sympathies in *Cato's Letters,* and James Burgh, writing in 1775, still felt it necessary to observe:

> Now I am mentioning republican government, I take this opportunity of entering a express caveat against all accusations of a desire to establish republican principles. I do not think a friend to this nation is obliged to promote a change in the constitution. The present form of government by king, lords, and commons, if it could be restored to its true spirit and efficiency, might be made to yield all the liberty, and all the happiness, of which a great and good people are capable in this world.[9]

The same was true of American dissidents, who claimed liberties that had been secured by the Glorious Revolution when they expressed their dissatisfaction with colonial rule under George III. The continuity of the Americans' cause with that of English dissenters during the exclusion controversy of the 1680s was so easily assumed by Congress that it called its own statement of principles "A Bill of Rights," after the Parliamentary document of 1689.[10] In the time-honored fashion of English politics, Congress merely asserted liberties that were enjoyed by Englishmen and petitioned for the redress of grievances that were associated with the Coercive Acts. Hence, when independence was declared after the petition had failed, Charles James Fox could say that "the Americans have done no more than the English did against James II" when their petition was rejected.[11]

The patriots' invocation of the Glorious Revolution was matched by their opponents' recollection of the days of Cromwell. Representatives of the Crown, as well as loyalists in the colonies, followed the lead of their court-party brethren and branded such demands "republican" and occasionally "democratic," hoping thereby to explode their opponents by what Robbins has aptly called "missile words."[12] Reports to the Crown about political unrest in the colonies repeatedly characterized the American dissidents as "republicans" and referred to the "licentious" spirit of republicanism as the underlying cause of resistance to colonial rule.

Such charges assumed that the constitutions of the colonies were, like that of Britain, made up of mixed elements and that the commons, who were represented in the assembly, had gained too much influence.[13] This denied the legitimacy of the patriots' grievances and undercut their strategy of reenacting, as it were, the Glorious Revolution, because that revolution had supposedly established a true balance in favor of liberty. The rise to prominence of the assemblies and the weaknesses of the royal executives therefore represented a political imbalance in the colonies, or so the king's men argued, even as country opponents and their American devotees pointed to the imbalance in England that arose from the corruption associated with cabinet government.[14]

Loyalists persisted in this line of attack until the very eve of war; advertisements for Samuel Seabury's *The Republican Dissected: or, the Anatomy of an American Whig* appeared a week before the skirmish at Lexington, even though the book was never published and circulated. But Seabury's opinions were quite well known, because he elsewhere depicted the Continental Congress as an assembly of Republicans, likening it to the Long Parliament and worrying that by its actions "will our happy constitution be destroyed, and a REPUBLIC raised on its ruins."[15] Likewise, Jonathon Boucher warned southern delegations to the Continental Congress about the "infuriate politics of the Republicans of the North"—a "wild Republic of mad Independents"—who were certain to treat the Church of England in America and its members badly, even as the reign of Charles I had been cut short and the Puritan Commonwealth established.[16]

The publication of Thomas Paine's *Common Sense* in January 1776, which was followed quickly by a longer version in February 1776, confirmed the worst fears of American loyalists. Although Paine dealt little with the nature of republican government in *Common Sense*, his attack on the English constitution and its vaunted balance was extremely vigorous. Paine observed that the English monarch was able to circumvent the Glorious Revolution by dispensing places and pensions and that "the *will* of the king is as much the *law* of the land in Britain as in France, with this difference, that instead of proceeding directly from his mouth, it is handed to the people under the most formidable shape of an act of parliament. For the fate of Charles the First, hath only made kings more subtle—not more just."[17]

The plain truth of the matter, Paine averred, "is, that it is wholly owing to the constitution of the people, and not to the constitution of the government that the crown is not as oppressive in England as in Turkey." The only true security for English liberties was the House of Commons, the "new republican materials" which, compounded with the "base remains of two ancient tyrannies," one monarchical and the other aristocratic, made up the English constitution. These forms of hereditary privilege, far from protecting liberty by checking the excesses of the people, were in fact the greatest threat to liberty, and only the vigilance of the people and their representatives kept these orders from encroaching on the rights of Englishmen.[18]

Paine's denunciation of balanced government as the bulwark of liberty, along with his hyperbolic remarks on the tyrannical tendencies and genetic shortcomings of hereditary rule, reminded loyalists, not of the Glorious Revolution, but of the Civil War. This parallel between Paine and the "mad Independents" of the Commonwealth period was explicitly drawn in Charles Inglis's (1775) response to *Common Sense*, wherein he excoriated Paine as "an avowed, violent Republican utterly averse and unfriendly to the English constitution."[19]

Inglis went on to note that Paine's rudimentary sketch of republican government strongly resembled Harrington's rota, which Montesquieu scorned as the wildly impractical design of a theoretician. Along the same lines, Inglis recalled the well-known impossibility of republican government on an extended scale, but he also claimed that the genius of the American people made them especially unsuited for republican governments:

The Americans are properly Britons. . . . But Britons never could bear the extremes, either of monarchy or republicanism. Some of their kings have aimed at despotism, but always failed. Repeated efforts have been made towards democracy, and they equally failed. Once indeed republicanism triumphed over the constitution; the despotism of one person ensued; both were finally expelled. The inhabitants of Great-Britain were quite anxious for the restoration of royalty in 1660, as they were for its expulsion in 1642, and for some succeeding years.[20]

But Americans in 1776 were apparently in the mood for expelling royalty, and they embraced with a vengeance Paine's scorn for those who evinced loyalist sympathies. For the patriots, "republicanism" was the watchword of revolution, and the principle of popular sovereignty became the cornerstone of American politics. In the process, republicanism transcended the confines of mixed government and came to be associated with wholly popular forms of government that had previously been known as "democratic." The relationship between republicanism and democracy therefore became a crucial issue in American political discourse, as we shall see in the following section.

III

The defeat of Britain's army was a "republican" triumph. Yet it was something of a hollow victory, insofar as the meaning of republicanism was far from evident once the war was over. In the context of colonial rule and the drive for independence, "republican elements" were pitted against the "base remains" of hereditary rule, to use Paine's language. Defined in opposition to monarchy and aristocracy, "republicanism" had a distinctly radical edge, as its opponents had always known.

Once independence had been accomplished, this edge was dulled, and the very meaning of "republicanism" was called into question. It could no longer be understood as being in opposition to hereditary rule, because the war had ostensibly ended that. Only patriots who feared the return of aristocracy continued to use the term in this way, when, as in the case of the Cincinnati, they saw evidence of a conspiracy to reestablish hereditary privilege. Instead, patriots turned to the difficult task of formulating a positive notion of republicanism. Not surprisingly, several different strains of republicanism emerged, some of which enjoyed a local or regional hegemony and others of which were peculiar to certain occupations or "classes."[21] As a result, the meaning of republicanism was hotly contested during this time.

In the midst of this ideological diversity and uncertainty, it was perhaps natural that "democracy" and "republic" came to be seen as equivalent. One example—and there are many—appeared in the *Providence* (R.I.) *Gazette*, which reported in August 1777 that "by a *democracy* is meant, that form of government where the highest power of making laws is lodged in the common people, or persons chosen out of them. This is what by some is called a republic, a commonwealth, or free state, and seems so the most agreeable to natural rights and liberty."[22]

The rhetorical interchangeability of "democracy" and "republic" reflected customary English usage, except that the connotations were no longer negative.[23] In the American context, the only viable form of governance was what Montesquieu referred to as a democratic republic—that is, a republic in which "the body of the people is possessed of the supreme power."[24] After all, it was evident that Americans were interested only in republican government, having already ruled out monarchy and, of course, despotism. Nor were many of them interested in establishing an aristocratic republic, although the desire for the moderating effects of aristocracy clearly informed proposals for instituting bicameral state legislatures. According to Montesquieu's typology, that left only a democratic republic as a possible model for state government, and a confederation of such republics as a model for continental governance. In that sense, "democracy" and "republic" really were equivalent shorthand expressions for a wholly popular kind of government.

Even those who tried to differentiate a democracy from a republic found it difficult to maintain the distinction. For example, Philodemus argued that "in a true commonwealth or democratic government, all authority is derived from the people at large, held only during their pleasure, and exercised only for their benefit."[25] This anticipation of Lincoln's definition of democracy as "government of the people, by the people, and for the people" went on to distinguish democracy from a republic, observing that "every constitution that has hitherto existed under that name [republic, R.L.H.] has partaken more or less of the nature of an Aristocracy." Furthermore, "it is this aristocratic leaven that has generally occasioned disorders and tumults in every republican government, and has so far brought the name into disrepute, that it is become a received opinion, that a Commonwealth, in proportion as it approaches to Democracy, wants those springs of efficacious authority which are necessary to the production of regularity and good order, and degenerates into anarchy and confusion."

Lamentably, this imputation to democracy of evils that are caused by aristocratic remnants failed to recognize the injustice that lies behind popular rebellion against oppression: the people "have a just claim to perfect political equality, and it is ungenerous and base to deny them justice, and at the same time to load them with reproaches." For this reason it should come as no surprise "that a government *approaching* to

Democracy"—that is, one in which democratic and aristocratic elements are mixed—"is apt to be disorderly," because "the people have a right to complain, so long as they are robbed of any portion of their freedom." They may legitimately take matters into their own hands to rectify this injustice.[26] This good democrat then concludes that South Carolinians ought to do away with the vestiges of aristocratic rule in order to arrive at a government that would be founded upon "pure republican principles," thereby undoing the whole distinction between democracy and republic.[27]

The precise form that popular government should take was, of course, a matter of dispute, particularly insofar as Americans retained a strong commitment to the idea of mixed government. The state constitutional conventions debated the very possibility of having a mixed government in a democratic republic that lacked noble and royal orders. These conventions struggled to devise institutions—for example, senates—that could counterbalance popular assemblies without frustrating the principle of popular sovereignty. Not a few statesmen despaired of this and instead opted for the simple government advocated by Paine, one that consisted of a single body of elected representatives. Indeed, Hamilton himself defended the idea of "representative democracy" embodied in simple government against those who preferred some version of "mixed government." Using arguments similar to those of Philodemus, Hamilton disputed the claim that democracy was inherently unstable; he asserted that "a strict examination of history" would show that the apparent instability of democratic regimes stemmed from their being mixed with other elements. The evil was not democracy; rather, it was compound governments; and the solution therefore was a simple legislature.[28]

Questions about the best method of representation understandably dominated such discussions, which ranged over the issues of suffrage, apportionment, the frequency of election, tenure in office, eligibility for reelection, the desirability of binding instructions, and provisions for recall. All reflected the preoccupation of citizens with establishing effective popular control over government, so as to minimize the risk of tyranny and to provide for a speedy and effective remedy when that failed. As Zabdiel Adams noted, "government by deputation does not consist with that plenitude of liberty in the people that they might enjoy, could they give their suffrages personally. However, when our representatives are regularly chosen, are amenable to our tribunals, and their election is not of long duration, then we may be said to be as free as the state of the world will commonly admit. To be deprived of the power of chusing our rulers, is to be deprived of self dominion."[29] Or as a well-known maxim of the time stated, "Where annual elections end, Tyranny begins."

The unrelenting fear of tyranny grew out of the belief that sovereignty was absolute and indivisible.[30] Government, whatever its form, was limited only in the sense that rulers must not stray from the purpose of government, as established in the sort of political compact so important to the political thinking of this period. Usually, the purpose of government was tied to promoting men's happiness. As Pole comments, "by the mid-century something of a consensus was emerging that government owed to the people the obligation of creating and defending the conditions of their happiness. Not their happiness itself: given freedom, that was their own affair."[31]

One such condition was liberty; and in this way, the *purpose* of government was linked to securing the otherwise precarious liberties of men in a state of nature. For that the *powers* of government were, in principle, unlimited.[32]

> As in a state of nature much happiness cannot be enjoyed by individuals, so it has been conformable to the inclinations of almost all men, to enter into a political society so constituted, as to remove the inconveniences they were obliged to submit to in their former state, and, at the same time, to retain all those natural rights, the enjoyment of which would be consistent with the nature of a free government, and the necessary subordination to *the supreme power of the state.*[33]

Because the powers of government were limited only by its purpose, the danger posed by the abuse of powers by rulers was great, as was the need for constructing a remedy short of, but not excluding, armed rebellion. Locating sovereignty close to the people—at the state level—and subjecting it to an intricate set of "democratic" controls was the preferred solution, so that within a state, the abuse of powers by rulers might be checked or limited by the vigilance of those who were ruled. In this way, too, the language of "balanced government" could be invoked in a context where distinctions among social orders were no longer widely accepted. Such language made obvious sense in the English context, but with the repudiation of hereditary privilege, the people became an undifferentiated "commons." Only by construing rulers as being susceptible to corruption, thereby posing a threat to the commonweal, could sociopolitical tensions be reconceived in a way that would make liberty hang "in the balance," as classical republicanism held that it did.[34]

IV

The idea that democratic republican government entailed elaborate mechanisms of popular control was, therefore, established early in the states. The overriding consideration was the preservation of liberty against *governmental* tyranny; and state governments, over a small extent of territory and subject to intricate popular controls, were assumed to be the bulwark of liberty. The sovereignty that they enjoyed vis-à-vis the national legislature under the Articles reinforced this bulwark, enabling state governments to interpose themselves between Congress and the people, protecting citizens in one state or region from those in another who might use Congress to further their own interests at the expense of others in matters pertaining to the apportionment of troops and imposts and the disposition of western lands.[35]

This throws a different light on the Antifederalists' later objections to the Constitution. When the Antifederalists argued against the consolidating tendencies of the Constitution, they were at the same time defending a confederated republic, not simply as a philosophical ideal, but also as an accomplished fact. Similarly, when they complained about the absence of a specific enumeration of powers in the Constitution and about the elasticity of the "necessary and proper" clause, they had in mind the sort of detailed listing of granted and denied powers that was such a prominent feature of state constitutions of the time. And when they complained about the inadequacy of representation under the Constitution, they were making an invidious comparison to the schemes of apportionment that were already in existence in the several states.

Because a confederation of democratic republics was widely presumed to be the best guarantee of liberty, it is not surprising that the leitmotif of Antifederalist writings is the charge of consolidation that they laid against the Federalists—that is, the claim that the latter's proposal would diminish liberty by weakening state governments. "A Federal Republican" urged the Pennsylvania convention to amend the proposed Constitution by including the language of the second Article of Confederation, which asserted the "sovereignty, freedom and independence" of state governments over and against the national government.[36] The failure to incorporate this amendment would mean an end to liberty, said a "Democratic Federalist," who was not convinced by James Wilson's assertion that powers not granted to the national government were reserved to the states and people, because

the federal rulers are vested with each of the three essential powers of government—their laws are to be *paramount* to the laws of the different States, what then will there be to oppose to their encroachments? Should they ever pretend to tyrannize over the people, their *standing army*, will silence every popular effort, it will be theirs to explain the powers which have been granted to them; Mr. Wilson's distinction will be forgot, denied or explained away, and the liberty of the people will be no more.[37]

Thus, A Federal Farmer insisted on the need to preserve the sovereignty of state governments as the bulwark of liberty and opposed the Constitution for consolidating power in a "federal head," far removed from the web of popular controls that had so painstakingly been woven about state governments:

> It is the essential characteristic of a confederal republic, that this head be dependent on, and kept within limited bounds by, the local governments; and it is because, in these alone, in fact, the people can be substantially assembled or represented. It is, therefore, we very universally see, in this kind of government, the congressional powers placed in a few hands, and accordingly limited, and specifically enumerated: and the local assemblies strong and well-guarded, and composed of numerous members. Wise men will always place the controuling power where the people are substantially collected by their representatives.[38]

A Federal Farmer emphasized the inviolability of state sovereignty in a way that distinguished him from other Antifederalists, because he observed that this argument was not based on a technical complaint about the inadequacy of the proposed scheme of representation: "Nor do I conceive, that as full a representation as is practicable in the federal government, will afford sufficient security: the strength of the government, and the confidence of the people, must be collected principally in the local assemblies; every part or branch of the federal head must be feeble, and unsafely trusted with large powers."[39]

The problem was aggravated, other Antifederalists noted, by the "feebleness" of representation, as well as the grant of apparently unlimited powers of taxation and conscription. These removed the federal government from the close control of the people; and that would increase the risk of tyranny, even as the expansion of national power would enlarge its danger. James Warren, the Speaker of the Massachusetts General Assembly and the husband of Mercy Otis Warren, peevishly summarized the argument by interpreting the Preamble of the Constitution to mean

> We the people . . . do relinquish that security for life, liberty and property, which we had in the Constitutions of these States, and of the Union—do give up governments which we well understood, for a new system which we have no idea of—and we do, by this act of ratification and political suicide, destroy the new system itself, and prepare the way for a despotism, if agreeable to our rulers. All this we do, for the *honour of having a system of consolidation formed by us the people.*[40]

For the Antifederalists, then, the Revolution was over. The Articles of Confederation, along with the state constitutions, provided a democratic republican framework of governance that was well suited to the preservation of liberty. Amendments to that framework would, in the view of the Antifederalists, invite tyranny, particularly if these amendments involved any diminution of "democratic" mechanisms of popular control or a relocation of political authority.

No one understood this position better than James Wilson, a Pennsylvania Federalist, who repeatedly urged the delegates at the Philadelphia convention to provide for the popular election of both representatives and senators, which they did not do. Wilson was a vigorous supporter of a strong central government, but he sensed that democratic concessions would be necessary in order to win popular approval for the proposed expansion and relocation of power. A people accustomed to democratic politics would insist that national policy makers be subject to the same sort of controls that bound state governments, or as he later put it, "The pyramid of government—and a republican government may well receive that beautiful and solid form—should be raised to a dignified altitude: but its foundations must, of consequence, be broad, and strong, and deep. The authority, the interests, and the affections of the people at large are the only foundation, on which a superstructure, proposed at once to be durable and magnificent, can be rationally erected."[41]

A broad, popular "base" was not only essential for "raising high the pyramid of government." It would also give the new government a legitimacy at least as great as the one enjoyed by state governments and would enable it to resist efforts by the states to interpose themselves between the citizens and the national government—a singularly important advantage in Wilson's view. But the Antifederalists, who might otherwise have agreed on the need for a broad representation, feared this would do away with state governments. Men such as John Smilie in Pennsylvania and Patrick Henry in Virginia pointed to the Preamble of the Constitution—which employed the language of "We, the people," instead of "We, the states"—as unmistakable evidence of the consolidating tendency of the Constitution. They were not convinced by Wilson's demonstration of the formal dependence of the general government upon state governments for the selection of officers. The fact that state legislatures would define suffrage requirements for elections to the House of Representatives and that they would select senators, as well as determine the methods for the indirect election of the president, was little consolation to them,

> for, Sir, it is the silent but certain operation of the powers, and not the cautious, but artful tenor of the expressions contained in this system, that can excite terror, or generate oppression. The flattery of language was indeed necessary to disguise the baneful purpose, but it is like the dazzling polish bestowed upon an instrument of death; and the visionary prospect of a magnificent, yet popular government, was the most specious mode of

rendering the people accessory to the ruin of those systems which they have so recently and so ardently labored to establish.[42]

According to Wilson, these men had failed to understand the popular origins of *state* sovereignty itself and were therefore unable to see that the loss of state powers to the federal government was in fact a reaffirmation of popular sovereignty. "When the principle is once settled that the people are the source of authority, the consequence is that they may take from the subordinate governments powers with which they have hitherto trusted them, and place those powers in the general government, if it is thought that there they will be productive of more good."[43] Therefore, those who objected to the Federalist proposal in the name of states' rights were misconstruing the nature of state sovereignty itself and were even setting state governments over and against the people.

In this way, Wilson neatly turned the Antifederalist objections about the Preamble's use of the language "We, the People" back upon his opponents:

> I am astonished to hear the ill-founded doctrine, that States alone ought to be represented in the federal government; these must possess sovereign authority forsooth, and the people be forgot! No: let us *reascend* to first principles. That expression is not strong enought to do my ideas justice. Let us RETAIN first principles. The people of the United States are now in the possession and exercise of their original rights, and while this doctrine is known and operates, we shall have a cure for every disease.[44]

Wilson eventually concluded that this principle required a broader suffrage, averring that

> representation is the chain of communication between the people and those, to whom they have committed the exercise of the powers of government. If the materials which form this chain, are sound and strong, it is unnecessary to be solicitous about the very high degree, to which they are polished. But in order to impart to them the true republican lustre, I know no means more effectual, than to invite and admit the freemen to the right of suffrage, and to enhance, as much as possible, the value of that right. . . . I cannot, with sufficient energy, express my own conceptions of the value and dignity of this right. In real majesty, an independent and unbiased elector stands superior to princes, addressed by the proudest titles, attended by the most magnificent retinues, and decorated with the most splendid regalia. Their sovereignty is only derivative, like the pale light of the moon; his is original, like the beaming splendor of the sun."[45]

Staunch nationalist that he was, Wilson may have been convinced that an unorganized electorate posed little threat to energetic government, compared to the obvious danger inherent in sovereign state governments. But other Federalists were less sanguine about the capacity of the electorate; in their view, citizens who were not independent and not unbiased might well succeed in diverting government from serving the commonweal. Madison, for one, sought to avoid this possibility by devising a scheme of representation that might allow for the "refinement of opinion" by establishing the central government upon a popular base that was much narrower than the one envisioned by Wilson. The means by which Madison advanced this position against the conventional democratic republican wisdom of the day are the subject of the next section.

V

If the Antifederalists desired a popularly limited government, the Federalists advanced the idea of a limited popular government. This stemmed from their discontent with state governments, which, in their view, were entirely too democratic and hence subject to the distempers of popular rule. As Madison listed them in his *Vices of the Political System of the United States,* these were: the failure of the states to comply with constitutional requisitions; encroachments by the states on the federal authority; violations by the states of the laws of nations and treaties; trespasses by the states on the rights of each other; the lack of concert in matters where common interest requires it; the lack of any guaranty in states' constitutions and laws against internal violence; the lack of sanctions to the laws and of coercion in the government of the confederacy; want of ratification by the people of the Articles; the multiplicity of laws in the several states; the mutability of states' laws; and the injustice of states' laws.[46]

Madison levels the same indictment of the states in his letter to Jefferson, in which he apparently rehearsed the argument that would appear a month later as *Federalist* number 10.[47] In number 10, however, he played down complaints about state government in favor of arguments that focused on the inadequate "energy" allowed to Congress under the Articles of Confederation. That is, Madison chose to attack the Articles, rather than the state governments, whose actions were responsible for the paralysis of Congress and which enacted internal legislation obnoxious to the "public good." This surely reflected Madison's assessment of the political problem that was facing the Federalists, who wanted to do away with constitutional arrangements that were widely held to be republican, in order to replace them with a frame of government that was admittedly less popular in orientation and therefore not so obviously republican in character.

Because popular sentiment overwhelmingly favored republican government, only one rhetorical strategy was open to the Federalists: to show that the *form* of the proposed government was "republican" and also that it was better suited to the *ends* of republican politics than were the Articles of Confederation. Conversely, the Federalists argued that politics under the Articles was democratic in form; by constantly sacrificing the public good to the interests of faction, it was antithetical to the ends of republican government.

The success of this strategy turned on a new interpretation of republican government, one that sharply distinguished it from democracy, thereby denying the interchangeability of the two or the Antifederalists' easy conjoining of them. The Federalists strove mightily to educate the public on the differences between a democracy and a republic, so as to reserve the virtues of popular government for their own cause and to lay its vices on their opponents' heads. In so doing, they capitalized on a lingering suspicion about the instability of "democratic" politics, as evidenced in Shays' Rebellion and the mutability of state laws governing debts and other property rights. "Democracies," Madison noted in *Federalist* number 10, "have ever been spectacles of turbulence and contention; have ever been found incompatible with personal security, or the rights of property; and have in general been as short in their lives, as they have been violent in their deaths." And in number 14, Madison names the Greek democracies and modern Italy, which most other commentators have mentioned as examples of small *republics*, as typical of this tendency.

By "democracy" Madison meant what we now call "direct democracy," in which citizens assemble to make their laws or, as Madison put it in *Federalist* number 14, in which "the people meet and exercise the government in person." As such, democracy is practicable only when it is limited to an area over which citizens might conveniently travel to meetings of the committee of the whole. In both numbers 14 and 37, Madison uses this definition to exculpate republican government from the evils associated with democracy but erroneously attributes it to popular government per se: "Under the confusion of names, it has been an easy task to transfer to a republic, observations applicable to a democracy only, and among others, the observation that it can never be established but among a small number of people, living within a small compass of territory."[48]

Representation, however, makes republican government over a more extensive territory possible, and as Madison argued in *Federalist* number 10, it has the additional advantage of allowing for a "refinement of opinion." While there is no guarantee that only the most enlightened and public spirited men will be selected as representatives, Madison claims that this is more likely to happen in polities that have a numerous citizenry, because the number of true statesmen is likely to be greater and because it will be harder for unworthy candidates to practice the "vicious arts" by which elections are sometimes carried. Furthermore, by keeping the number of representatives small in proportion to the citizenry, the odds in favor of electing these wise men can be enhanced.[49]

When representatives stand for larger constituencies, they are also more likely to be insulated from popular pressure and, therefore, free to exercise their wisdom. Larger constituencies tend to be more diverse and hence more divided in their opinions, thus permitting representatives to follow their conscience in making laws. Indeed, Madison elevates this tendency into a full-blown argument in favor of the extended republic, seeing in that republic a remedy for the mischief of faction to which popular governments, especially those of a democratic stripe, are prone. As he put it to Jefferson, "The great desideratum in Government is, so to modify the sovereignty as that it may be sufficiently neutral between different parts of the Society to controul one part from invading the rights of another, and at the same time sufficiently controuled itself, from setting up an intense adverse to that of the entire Society."

The solution to this problem, Madison avers, is somewhat perverse: "Divide et impera (divide and rule), the reprobated axiom of tyranny, is under certain qualifications, the only policy, by which a republic can be administered on just principles."[50] That is because a majority cannot be contained in a government that is wholly popular. But if majorities do not form, except on issues that are clearly consistent with justice and the common welfare, the problem does not arise.

The formation of unjust majorities bent on "tyranny" can be impeded and perhaps even prevented by extending the republic so as to include numerous interests. Madison explained:

> If then there must be different interests and parties in Society; and a majority when united by a common interest or passion can not be restrained from oppressing the minority, what remedy can be found in a republican Government, where the majority must ultimately decide, but that of giving such an extent to its sphere, that no common interest or passion will be likely to unite a majority of the whole number in an unjust pursuit.[51]

Extending the republic is not the only safeguard against unruly majorities that are bent on injustice. The "separation of powers" at the national level was quite asymmetrical under the Constitution, which would make it much easier to halt the progress of popularly inspired action than to mobilize popular sentiment against the actions of executives and judges. This, plus the fact that these executives would be chosen by doubly indirect methods, and that judges were unelected, did not go unnoticed.[52] One Antifederalist, Montezuma, composed an artful letter purporting to explain the precautions that Federalists had taken against popular rule; he noted that "our judicial power is a strong work, a masked battery, few people see the guns we can and will ere long play off from it; for the judicial power embraces every question which can arise in law or equity, under this constitution and under the laws of 'the United States.'" As if that were not enough, Montezuma innocently asks:

> What have we to fear armed with such powers, with a president at our head who is captain-general of the army, navy, and militia of the United States, who can make and unmake treaties, appoint and commission ambassadors and other ministers, who can grant or refuse reprieves or pardons, who can make judges of the supreme and other continental courts, in short who will be the source, the fountain of honor, profit and power, whose influence like the rays of the sun will defuse itself far and wide, will exhale all *democratical vapours* and break *clouds of popular insurrection?*

Furthermore, Montezuma confides to his erstwhile Federalist fellow conspirators:

> We have thought meet to indulge them in something like a democracy in the new constitution, which part we have designated by the popular name of the House of Representatives; but to guard against every possible danger from this *lower house*, we have subjected every bill they bring forward, to the double negative of our upper house and president—nor have we allowed the populace the right to elect their representatives annually, as usual, lest this body should be too much under the influence and controul of their constituents.[53]

To the contrary, James Wilson argued that in the Constitution "*all authority, of every kind, is derived by* REPRESENTATION *from the* PEOPLE, *and the* DEMOCRATIC PRINCIPLE *is carried into every part of government.*"[54] But John Dickinson openly admitted the "unpopularity" of the proposed regime in the *Letters of Fabius*, number 5, in which he described the Constitution as "a single republic with one democratic branch in its government." And Madison insisted on the undemocratic, but nonetheless republican credentials of the new regime.

What was it that qualified the proposed government as "republican"? Madison is resigned to the fact that "the genius of Republican liberty, seems to demand on one side, not only that all power should be derived from the people; but, that those entrusted with it should be kept in dependence on the people, by a short duration of their appointments; and, that, even during this short period, the trust should be placed not in a few, but in a number of hands."[55] Furthermore, he admits that "if the plan of the Convention therefore be found to depart from the republican character, its advocates must abandon it as no longer defensible.''[56] On the surface this concedes much to the Antifederalists, but in number 39 it becomes evident that Madison is quite content to interpret the "genius of Republican liberty" in very narrow terms:

> If we resort for a criterion, to the different principles on which different forms of government are established, we may define a republic to be, or at least may bestow that name on, a government which derives all its powers directly or indirectly from the great body of the people; and is administered by persons holding their offices during pleasure, for a limited period, or during good behaviour. It is *essential* to such a government, that it be derived from the great body of the society, not from an inconsiderable proportion, or a favored class of it; otherwise a handful of tyrannical nobles, exercising their oppressions by a delegation of their powers, might aspire to the rank of republicans, and claim for their government the honorable title of republic. It is *sufficient* for such a government, that the persons administering it be appointed, either directly or indirectly, by the people; and that they hold their appointments by either of the tenures just specified; otherwise every government in the United States, as well as every other popular government that has been or can be well organized or well executed, would be degraded from the republican character.

The fact that it is "*essential* to such a government, that it be derived from the great body of the society, not from an inconsiderable proportion, or a favored class of it" meant that mixed regimes—for example, that in England—were not republican, though they were commonly held to be. Instead, the "republican" accolade was reserved for wholly popular regimes. Then, to distinguish republican from democratic popular government, as Madison desires, "It is *sufficient* for such a government, that the persons administering it be appointed, either directly or indirectly, by the people; and that they hold their appointments by either of the tenures just specified."

Although this may seem to be a weak condition, Madison was no foe of popular government, as he understood it. He and other like-minded Federalists assumed that the citizens were capable of choosing their rulers and of submitting to their rule. However, this "honorable determination" in favor of popular rule emphatically did not mean that citizens were capable of self-rule in a democratic sense. That required virtue beyond what could safely be assumed in the constitution of politics. In that sense, Madison's interpretation departs from Montesquieu's assertion that virtue is the underlying principle of republican government. As Epstein says, for Madison it is "not the expectation that political life will be an arena of selflessness, but the attractiveness of political life as an occasion for an honorable self-assertion" that informs republicanism, or at least this brand of it.[57]

The connection with Fame and its pursuit then seems natural. The energetic use of power in service to the commonweal was simultaneously a way of satisfying personal ambition. The pursuit of Fame, understood as an honorable self-assertion, was a motivating force drawing members of a natural aristocracy to public service. Yet it was also essential to provide *opportunities* for exercising individual talents in government, and that depended upon an attenuation of popular control. A certain amount of independence was, therefore, an essential component of good government, because without it, the leaders would not serve the common interest but would cater to the interests of the commons. Yet this independence would also increase the risk of tyranny, or so the opponents of the Federalists feared, and as I will show in the next section, the Antifederalists fiercely resisted the Federalists' attempt to sever the connection between democracy and republicanism.

VI

The "wholly republican" Constitution established a limited popular government, but one that would be capable of acting with great energy. Indeed, it was partly *because* popular control was weak and concentrated in the House of Representatives that the executive could function as the driving force in national policy making. The powers of the executive were broad, especially in economic matters, where the authority to conduct foreign affairs and military operations were vitally important. Furthermore, "checks" on the exercise of this power were relatively weak, centered as they were in an indirectly elected Senate, and often would not come into play until after the effective exercise of power by the executive.

Nor was this merely a theoretical possibility. Alexander Hamilton was determined to use the powers of the federal government to establish the foundations of a commercial empire similar to that of Great Britain. The various elements of his program, which included the creation of a Bank of the United States, the assumption by the federal government of outstanding state and national debts, and the creation of a revenue system, were all designed to provide a favorable climate for the increase of manufactures and trade. Hamilton also called for a strong army and navy to protect American economic interests from foreign interference.[58]

The Jeffersonian Republicans attacked these policies, which, they alleged, had "greatly encreased the spirit and enterprize of speculators, and occasioned in this way the most detestable and enormous frauds, and promoted a depravity of morals and a great decline of republican virtue."[59] Even Madison, in his *Letters of Halvidius*, objected to the imperialistic and expansive nature of this use of executive power, although he was certainly less concerned about the corrupting effects that this commercial strategy might have on virtue.

During the course of this debate over the proper extent and use of political power, many of the "democratic republican" themes of popular control that were so prominent in the 1780s were reintroduced. In turn, this called forth Federalist exegeses on the nature of citizenship and its duties, especially those of obedience and quiescence. As one Federalist pastor fulminated, "Those, who choose their civil magistrates, do voluntarily pledge their obedience, whether they take the oath of allegiance or not. By putting power into the hands of their rulers, they put it out of their own; by choosing and authorizing them to govern, they practically declare, that they are willing to be governed; and by declaring their willingness to be governed, they equally declare their intention and readiness to obey."[60]

Indeed, Federalists went so far as to claim that "the people never act, in their sovereign capacity, but either in framing or dissolving a constitution. While the constitution is in force, the people are either subjects or agents of the constitution."[61] This left very little room, short of rebellion, for popular participation, and to the extent that citizens engaged in political action *under* the constitution, it was only because, as one Federalist sarcastically commented, "we are blessed with a group of government levellers, who cultivate those all-preserving, democratic virtues, jealousy and ingratitude."[62] These levelers confused liberty with license under the "indefinite phrase" the Rights of Man and desired to replace the rule of law by a reign of terror, as in France.

These sentiments were frankly expressed in a famous letter to Joseph Priestley from Noah Webster, who explained the American usage of these terms, emphasizing the illegality of efforts to influence duly elected representatives:

> By democracy is intended a government where the legislative powers are exercised directly by all the citizens, as formerly in Athens and Rome. In our country this power is not in the hands of the people but of their representatives. The powers of the people are principally restricted to the direct exercise of the rights of suffrage. Hence a material distinction between our form of government and those of the ancient democracies. Our form of government has acquired the appellation of a *Republic*, by way of distinction, or rather of a *representative Republic*.
>
> Hence the word Democrat has been used as synonymous with the word Jacobin in France; and by an additional idea, which arose from the attempt to control our government by popular associations, the word has come to signify a person who attempts an undue opposition to or influence over government by means of private clubs, secret intrigues, or by public popular meetings which are extraneous to the constitution. By Republicans we understand the friends of our Representative Governments, who

believe that no influence whatever should be exercised in a state which is not directly authorized by the Constitution and laws.[63]

The Democratic-Republican Societies that sprang up in support of the French Revolution strongly resisted this rather narrow and passive characterization of republican citizenship, claiming

> that the People, upon having formed a government, are implicitly to resign themselves to the Agents and Delegates appointed by them, is a doctrine calculated to undermine the foundations of Freedom, and to erect on her ruins, the fabric of Despotism . . . it is the right and duty of every Freeman, to watch with the vigilance of a faithful centinel, the conduct of those, to whom is entrusted the administration of Government, that they pass not the sacred barriers of the Constitution.[64]

The need for the societies was quite clear to their members, who included such esteemed men as David Rittenhouse:

> All governments are more or less combinations against the people; they are states of violence against individual liberty, originating from man's imperfection and vice, and as rulers have no more virtue than the ruled, the equilibrium between them can only be preserved by proper attention and association; for the power of government can only be kept within its constituted limits by the display of a power equal to itself, the collected sentiment of the people.[65]

The "collected sentiment of the people" was represented in the expressions of the Democratic-Republican Societies themselves, which were supposed to function in an educational capacity. Members were to come "together for the purpose of gaining and communicating information on the affairs of their country, to express with decency and firmness, their sentiments respecting the measures adopted by their Delegates, and to offer their opinions with candour on matters of political concernment."[66] In this way, a "spirit of liberty, like every virtue of the mind, is to be kept alive only by constant action."[67]

The Federalists attempted to discredit the societies by denouncing them as "democratic," hoping thereby to associate them with the excesses of Jacobinism. Many of the clubs gladly obliged the Federalists in this matter. Of the forty-two societies listed by Link, and the four additional clubs mentioned by Foner, sixteen used the word Democratic in their official titles, sixteen used Republican, two used Democratic-Republican, and four employed labels such as Committee of Correspondence and French Society.[68]

At the same time, the Federalists laid plans to recapture the republican label for their own use. The name Federalist had served them well in the ratification debate, as Mercy Otis Warren recalled, when she said that the proposed Constitution was

> a many headed monster; of such motley mixture, that its enemies cannot trace a feature of Democratick or Republican extract; nor have its friends the courage to denominate it a Monarchy, an Aristocracy, or an Oligarchy, and the favoured bantling must have passed through the short period of its existence without a name, had not Mr. *Wilson*, in the fertility of his genius, suggested the happy epithet of a *Federal Republic*.[69]

Had the second term in the epithet been retained, it would have been far more difficult for the Federalists' opponents to appropriate the label for their own partisan purposes. This they were able to do, and Fisher Ames, in a letter to John Rutledge, emphasized the need to "wrench the name *republican* from those who have unworthily usurped it. . . . Names and appearances are in party warfare arms and ammunition. It is particularly necessary to contest this name with them now."[70]

Initially, the Federalists' strategy seemed well taken. The Whiskey Rebellion of 1794, which was widely attributed to the subversive activities of the societies, made plausible the Federalists' dire predictions of democratic distemper. It brought the immense prestige of Washington to bear against the societies and the principles for which they stood. But after a brief respite during the deliberation over the highly unpopular Jay Treaty, which they had opposed from the start, the societies began to wither under the continuous attacks of the Federalist-dominated press. The notorious XYZ affair, as well as the passage of the Alien and Sedition Act of 1798, then signaled their demise.

VII

In the long run, the Federalists' strategy of denouncing democracy backfired. In trying to show that they were the sole and rightful heirs to the republican tradition of the American Revolution, the Federalists attempted to identify republicanism with a particular set of institutional arrangements, as Webster's letter to Priestley suggests. To the extent that their educational program succeeded, republicanism came to be associated more with a particular form of government and less with the characteristic purpose or aim of government, as it had been during the war years. And in becoming more concrete, it lost some of its moral force, even as it became vulnerable to criticism from those who were dissatisfied with the constitutionally provided avenues of representation.

"Democracy," on the other hand, was proceeding in the opposite direction. Whereas it had referred previously to a particular form of government, it began to acquire more abstract and positive connotations. The Democratic-Republican Societies and the Jeffersonian Republicans succeeded in neutralizing the more odious connotations of "mob rule" through their countereducational efforts and the "responsible" opposition to Federalist policies. They also initiated the process by which the rhetorical links between democracy and ideas of popular sovereignty and political equality were forged.

This was particularly true of the debates at the state level over the extension of suffrage, which took place during the first two decades of the nineteenth century. Precisely because the Federalists advanced the idea that political participation by ordinary citizens ought to be confined to the selection of leaders, the breadth of suffrage became an important issue. Efforts to broaden the suffrage were common and were often advanced under the language of the Rights of Man. These arguments proved quite popular, and at the same time they were quite easily generalized to other forms of political participation, in addition to voting. By the presidency of Andrew Jackson, the deference by commoners to natural aristocrats, upon which the Federalists depended, had largely been eroded. A participant political culture more consonant with mass parties capable of mobilizing the electorate had emerged. Democracy, it seems, had proved irresistible. Madison's carefully wrought distinction between democratic and republican forms of popular government had broken down, and the work of the Revolution had truly been completed.[71]

NOTES

1. Louis Hartz, in *The Liberal Tradition in America* (New York: Harcourt, Brace, 1955), represents the consensus point of view. The opposite perspective is outlined by Merrill Jensen in *The Articles of Confederation: An Interpretation of the Social-Constitutional History of the American Revolution, 1774–1781* (Madison: University of Wisconsin Press, 1940) and by Stanley M. Elkins and Eric McKitrick in "The Founding Fathers: Young Men of the Revolution," *Political Science Quarterly* 76, 2 (June 1961): 181–216.

2. On this point see J. G. A. Pocock, *The Machiavellian Moment: Florentine Political Thought and the Atlantic Republican Tradition* (Princeton, N.J.: Princeton University Press, 1975), and especially Lance Banning, *The Jeffersonian Persuasion: Evolution of a Party Ideology* (Ithaca, N.Y.: Cornell University Press, 1978).

3. The spirit of this debate over the historical relation between republican and liberal thought in America is captured in the exchange between Joyce Appleby, "Republicanism in Old and New Contexts," *William and Mary Quarterly* 43, 1 (Jan. 1986): 20–34, and Lance Banning, "Jeffersonian Ideology Revisited: Liberal and Classical Ideas in the New American Republic," *William and Mary Quarterly* 43, 1 (Jan. 1986): 3–19.

4. The quotation is from a letter to Benjamin Franklin, 3 Aug. 1777, reported in Gordon S. Wood, *The Creation of the American Republic, 1776–1787* (New York: W. W. Norton, 1972), p. 92. For earlier commentaries see George M. Dutcher, "The Rise of Republican Government in the United States," *Political Science Quarterly* 55, 2 (June 1940): 199–216, and Cecelia Kenyon, "Republicanism and Radicalism in the American Revolution: An Old-fashioned Interpretation," *William and Mary Quarterly* 12, 1 (Jan. 1962): 3–43.

5. Bernard Bailyn, *The Ideological Origins of the American Revolution* (Cambridge, Mass.: Harvard University Press, 1967); Wood, *Creation of the American Republic.*

6. J. R. Pole, *The Seventeenth Century: Sources of Legitimate Power* (Charlottesville: University of Virginia Press, 1969), p. 69.

7. Caroline Robbins, *The Eighteenth-Century Commonwealthman: Studies in the Transmission, Development and Circumstance of English Liberal Thought from the Restoration of Charles II until the War with the Thirteen Colonies* (Cambridge, Mass.: Harvard University Press, 1961).

8. The quotation is from Molesworth's preface to *Franco Gallia* and is taken from Willi Paul Adams, "Republicanism in Political Rhetoric before 1776," *Political Science Quarterly* 85 (Sept. 1970): 397–421, at p. 403, whose account informs this section of my paper.

9. "Political Disquisition," I, 9, as reported in Adams, "Republicanism in Political Rhetoric," p. 404.

10. Garry Wills, *Inventing America: Jefferson's Declaration of Independence* (New York: Random House, Vintage Books, 1978), p. 54.

11. Wills, *Inventing America,* p. 64.

12. In 1768, Thomas Gage wrote to Viscount Hillsborough that there was very little government in Boston and that "the constitution of the province leans so much to democracy, that the governor has not the power to remedy the disorders which happen in it" (see J. R. Pole, "Historians and the Problem of Early American Democracy," *American Historical Review* 67 (Apr. 1962): 626–46, at p. 633.

13. Pole, "Historians and the Problem of Early American Democracy," pp. 634–36, rightly notes that the preponderance of power in the hands of the assembly did not necessarily mean that the people ruled, in some modern democratic sense. The assemblies were often under the control of colonial oligarchs who obstructed popular pressures as zealously as they resisted English rule.

14. Bernard Bailyn, *The Origins of American Politics* (New York: A. A. Knopf, 1968).

15. The quotation is from "An Alarm to the Legislature of the Province of New-York" (1775); it is taken from Adams, "Republicanism in Political Rhetoric," pp. 408–9.

16. Ibid., p. 410.

17. Thomas Paine, *Common Sense* (Harmondsworth, Eng.: Penguin Books, 1986 [1776]), p. 71.

18. Ibid., p. 71.

19. Charles Inglis, *The True Interest of America Impartially Stated in certain Strictures on a Pamphlet intitled "Common Sense"* (Philadelphia, 1775), p. vii.

20. Ibid., p. 52.

21. The burgeoning literature on varieties of republicanism, which is too broad to cite here, is well summarized by Robert E. Shalhope in "Republicanism

and Early American Historiography," *William and Mary Quarterly* 39, 2 (Apr. 1982): 334–56. Several works deserve special mention for their careful analyses of the dynamic qualities of republican thought, which they trace to the conflict between divergent interpretations of the meaning of republicanism: Alfred F. Young, ed., *The American Revolution: Explorations in the History of American Radicalism* (DeKalb: Northern Illinois University Press, 1976); Gary Nash, *The Urban Crucible: Social Change, Political Consciousness and the Origins of the American Revolution* (Cambridge, Mass.: Harvard University Press, 1979); Drew R. McCoy, *The Elusive Republic: Political Economy in Jeffersonian America* (Chapel Hill: University of North Carolina Press, 1980); and Rhys Isaac, "Dramatizing the Ideology of Revolution: Popular Mobilization in Virginia, 1774–1776," *William and Mary Quarterly* 33 (July 1976): 357–85.

22. Willi Paul Adams, *The First American Constitutions: Republican Ideology and the Making of the State Constitutions in the Revolutionary Era* (Chapel Hill: University of North Carolina Press, 1980), p. 107.

23. This interchangeability was noted by Robert W. Shoemaker, "'Democracy' and 'Republic' as Understood in Late Eighteenth-Century America," *American Speech* 41 (May 1966): 83–95, and analyzed by Adams, *First American Constitutions.*

24. "Lorsque, dans la république, le peuple en corps a la soveraine puissance, c'est une Démocratie," in *The Spirit of the Laws*, bk. 2, chap. 2. Montesquieu goes on to explain that in a democratic republic, "there can be no exercise of sovereignty, but by their [the people's, R.L.H.] suffrages, which are their own will; now the sovereign's will is the sovereign himself." Compare "Agrippa," in the *Massachusetts Gazette*, 22 Jan. 1788: "Republicks are divided into democraticks and aristocraticks," in Herbert J. Storing, *The Complete Anti-Federalist*, 7 vols. (Chicago: University of Chicago Press, 1981), vol. 4, pp. 102–4, at p. 103. See also John Adams, *The Works of John Adams*, ed. Charles Francis Adams (Boston: Little, Brown & Co.), vol. 10, p. 378: "The strict definition of a republic is, that in which the sovereignty resides in more than one man. A democracy, then, is a republic, as well an aristocracy, or any mixture of both."

25. Philodemus, "Conciliatory Hints, Attempting, by a Fair State of Matters, to Remove Party Prejudice," at Charleston, 1784, reprinted in Charles S. Hyneman and Donald S. Lutz, *American Political Writing during the Founding Era*, 2 vols. (Indianapolis, Ind.: Liberty Press, 1983), pp. 606–30, at p. 612. Philodemus was Thomas Tudor Tucker (1745–1828), who studied medicine at Edinburgh, served as a surgeon in the war, and was a member of the Continental Congress in 1787/88, and the House of Representatives from 1789 to 1793.

26. Philodemus, "Conciliatory Hints," at pp. 612, 615-16, 617.

27. Actually the distinction is not completely lost: "pure republican principles" (or "democracy") might still be contrasted with common usage of "republic" to refer to mixed regimes that harbored aristocratic elements, thus pointing to a corruption of language.

28. Cf. Wood, *Creation of the American Republic*, pp. 224–25; Adams, *First American Constitutions*, p. 107. In bk. 2, chap. 3, of *Rights of Man*, Paine also referred to this scheme as representative democracy, which he took to be the most appropriate form of republican government for a nation: "Simple democracy was society governing itself without the use of secondary means. By ingrafting representation upon democracy, we arrive at a system of government capable of embracing and confederating all the various interests and every extent of territory and population; and that also with advantages as much

superior to hereditary government, as the republic of letters is to hereditary literature" (see Thomas Paine, *Rights of Man* [New York: Willey Book Co., 1942 (1792)], p. 171 ff.).

29. "An Election Sermon," Boston, 1782, in Hyneman and Lutz, *American Political Writing*, pp. 539–64, at pp. 543–44.

30. Bailyn, *Ideological Origins*.

31. J. R. Pole, *The Gift of Government: Political Responsibility from the English Restoration to American Independence* (Athens: University of Georgia Press, 1983), p. 32.

32. This was a point to which the Federalists would later return with great effect, justifying the expansion of powers for a central government with reference to its responsibilities. This argument was crucial to their discussion of the need for a standing army and the justification of taxing authority for the Congress.

33. Theophilus Parsons, "The Essex Result," Newburyport, Mass., 1778, reprinted in Hyneman and Lutz, *American Political Writing*, pp. 480–531, quotation at pp. 484–85, with my emphasis.

34. Just because rulers were likely to become corrupt, direct democracy was the preferred arrangement, but this was acknowledged to be impractical in a society of any great extent.

35. Madison later came to see the merit of this argument, when in his "Report on the Virginia Resolutions" he stoutly defended the third Virginia Resolution, which argued that "in case of a deliberate, palpable, and dangerous exercise of other powers, not granted by the said compact (i.e., the Constitution, R.L.H.), the states who are parties thereto have the right, and are in duty bound, to interpose, for arresting the progress of the evil, and for maintaining, within their respective limits, the authorities, rights, and liberties appertaining to them" (see Marvin Meyers, *The Mind of the Founder: Sources of the Political Thought of James Madison*, rev. ed. [Hanover, Mass.: Brandeis University Press, 1981], p. 232). Note also Madison's admission in his letter to Jefferson on 24 Oct. 1787 that if the republic were to become too extensive, "a defensive concert may be rendered too difficult against the oppression of those entrusted with the administration" of the national government (see Michael Kammen, ed., *The Origins of the American Constitution: A Documentary History* [New York: Penguin Books, 1986], p. 73).

36. "A Review of the Constitution Proposed by the Late Convention by a Federal Republican," a pamphlet published on 28 Oct. 1787, reprinted in Storing, *Antifederalist*, 3:65–88, at p. 85.

37. "Essay of a Democratic Federalist," in the *Pennsylvania Herald*, 17 Oct. 1787. This was probably Richard Henry Lee, according to Storing, *Antifederalist*, 3:58–64, at p. 59.

38. "Letter XVII of a Federal Farmer," 23 Jan. 1788, in Storing, *Antifederalist*, 2:330–39, at p. 336. Herbert Storing, in *What the Anti-Federalists were "For": The Political Thought of the Opponents of the Constitution* (Chicago: University of Chicago Press, 1981), pp. 23–26, discusses the dispute among scholars over the authorship of these letters; he concludes that the evidence for attributing them to Richard Henry Lee is thin.

39. Ibid., p. 338.

40. "Letters of a Republican Federalist," which appeared in the *Massachusetts Centinel* from Dec. 1787 to Feb. 1788, reprinted in Storing, *Antifederalist*, 4:162–90, at p. 178.

41. *Lectures on Law:* "Of the Legislative Department," in James Wilson, *The Works of James Wilson,* ed. James DeWitt Andrews, 2 vols. (Chicago: Callaghan & Co., 1896 [1790–92]), 2:10.

42. John Smilie of Fayette County, on Wednesday 28 Nov. 1787, in the Pennsylvania ratification convention (see John Bach McMaster and Frederick D. Stone, eds., *Pennsylvania and the Federal Constitution, 1787–1788* [Lancaster: Historical Society of Pennsylvania, 1888], pp. 267–68).

43. James Wilson, on Saturday 1 Dec. 1787, in the Pennsylvania ratification convention, in McMaster and Stone, *Pennsylvania,* p. 302.

44. James Wilson, on Tuesday 4 Dec. 1787, in the Pennsylvania ratification convention, in McMaster and Stone, *Pennsylvania,* p. 341.

45. Wilson, *Works,* 2:10.

46. "Vices of the Political System of the United States," Apr. 1787, in Meyers, *Mind of the Founder,* pp. 57–65.

47. Madison's letter to Thomas Jefferson, 24 Oct. 1787, in Kammen, *Origins of the American Constitution,* pp. 65–76.

48. In *Federalist* no. 37, Madison discusses the problem of terminological confusion: "The use of words is to express ideas. Perspicuity therefore requires not only that the ideas should be distinctly formed, but that they should be expressed by words distinctly and exclusively appropriated to them." He goes on to admit that no language is sufficiently well stocked with words and phrases to cover all complex ideas, but he leaves no doubt that in this case, "republic" and "democracy," used properly, describe distinct ideas.

49. Richard W. Krouse, " 'Classical' Images of Democracy in America: Madison and Tocqueville," in *Democratic Theory and Practice,* ed. Graeme Duncan (Cambridge, Eng.: Cambridge University Press, 1983), pp. 58–78.

50. Letter to Jefferson, 24 Oct. 1787, in Kammen, *Origins of the American Constitution,* p. 73.

51. Ibid., p. 71. At times this process is presented as if it had no known limits, as Pocock observes in *Machiavellian Moment,* p. 522. However, as I mentioned in note 35, Madison himself believed that a republic could become so extensive as to make it difficult to oppose governmental tyranny.

52. Federalism, which created the "compound republic" and established a "double security," was another mechanism, which I neglect here (see *Federalist* no. 51).

53. "Letter of Montezuma," which appeared in *Independent Gazetteer* (Philadelphia), 17 Oct. 1787; reprinted in Cecelia Kenyon, ed., *The Antifederalists* (Indianapolis, Ind.: Bobbs-Merrill, 1966), pp. 61–67, at pp. 64–65, 64, 62.

54. James Wilson, on Tuesday 4 Dec. 1787, in the Pennsylvania ratification convention, in McMaster and Stone, *Pennsylvania,* p. 344.

55. *Federalist* no. 37. Indeed, the whole second volume of *The Federalist* was entitled "The Conformity of the Proposed Constitution to the True Principles of Republican Government."

56. *Federalist* no. 39.

57. David F. Epstein, *The Political Theory of "The Federalist"* (Chicago: University of Chicago Press, 1984), p. 126.

58. Gerald Stourzh, *Alexander Hamilton and the Idea of Republican Government* (Stanford, Calif.: Stanford University Press, 1970).

59. John Zvesper, *Political Philosophy and Rhetoric: A Study of the Origins of American Party Politics* (Cambridge, Eng.: Cambridge University Press, 1977), p. 146.

60. Nathanael Emmons, "A Discourse Delivered on the National Fast," Wrentham, Mass., 1799, in Hyneman and Lutz, *American Political Writing*, pp. 1023–41, at 1027.

61. Alexander Addison, "Analysis of the Report of the Committee of the Virginia Assembly," Philadelphia, 1800, in Hyneman and Lutz, *American Political Writing*, pp. 1055–98, at 1058.

62. Jonathan Maxcy, "An Oration," Providence, R.I., 1799, in Hyneman and Lutz, *American Political Writing*, pp. 1042–54, at 1045.

63. *The Letters of Noah Webster*, ed. Henry Warfel (New York: Library Publishers, 1953), pp. 207–8.

64. "Declaration of the Massachusetts Constitutional Society," Boston, 13 Jan. 1794, in Philip S. Foner, *The Democratic-Republican Societies, 1790–1800: A Documentary Sourcebook of Constitutions, Declarations, Addresses, Resolutions, and Toasts* (Westport, Conn.: Greenwood Press, 1976), pp. 257–58.

65. Henry Kammerer to the *Philadelphia Gazette and Universal Daily Advertiser*, 29 Dec. 1794, in Foner, *Democratic-Republican Societies*, pp. 60–63, at 62.

66. "Declaration of the Massachusetts Constitutional Society," Boston, 13 Jan. 1794, in Foner, *Democratic-Republican Societies*, pp. 257–58.

67. Henry Kammerer to the *Philadelphia Gazette and Universal Daily Advertiser*, 29 Dec. 1794, in Foner, *Democratic-Republican Societies*, pp. 60–63, at 62.

68. Eugene P. Link, *The Democratic-Republican Societies, 1790–1800* (New York: Octagon Books, 1942); Foner, *Democratic-Republican Societies*, pp. 257–58.

69. "Observations on the New Constitution, and on the Federal and State Conventions," by a Columbian Patriot, Boston, 1788; reprinted in Storing, *Antifederalist*, 4:270–87, at 275. The jibe at Wilson apparently refers to his definition of a "Federal Republic" as "a species of government which secures all the internal advantages of a republic, at the same time that it maintained the external dignity and force of a monarchy" (see McMaster and Stone, *Pennsylvania*, p. 221).

70. Regina Ann Markel Morantz, " 'Democracy' and 'Republic' in American Ideology, 1787–1840" (Ph.D. diss., Columbia University, 1971), p. 145.

71. This paper was originally prepared for presentation at a conference on "Conceptual Change and the Constitution of the U.S.," jointly sponsored by the Conference for the Study of Political Thought and the Folger Institute Center for the History of British Political Thought, Washington, D.C., 15–17 Apr. 1987. Tom Horne and Gerald Stourzh provided helpful comments at that time. Presentations by Peter Onuf and Garry Wills caused me to revise the fifth section of my paper. The last section is drawn from chapter 2 of Russell L. Hanson, *The Democratic Imagination in America: Conversations with Our Past* (Princeton, N.J.: Princeton University Press, 1985).

10

Some Second Thoughts on Virtue and the Course of Revolutionary Thinking

Lance Banning

Opponents of the Constitution, one of its supporters said, supposed that Congress would abuse its trust as often as it could.

> If this were a reasonable supposition, their objections would be good. I consider it reasonable to conclude that they will as readily do their duty as deviate from it; nor do I go on the grounds mentioned by gentlemen on the other side—that we are to place unlimited confidence in [national officials] and expect nothing but the most exalted integrity and sublime virtue. But I go on this great republican principle: that the people will have virtue and intelligence to select men of virtue and wisdom. Is there no virtue among us? If there be not, we are in a wretched situation. No theoretical checks, no form of government, can render us secure. To suppose that any form of government will secure liberty or happiness without any virtue in the people is a chimerical idea.[1]

The sentiment many sound conventional enough, but something, surely, is amiss. The stage for these remarks was the Virginia state convention. The speaker was James Madison. And it is Madison on whom we customarily rely for an insistence that the Federalists were moved by a pervasive fear of a *collapse* of virtue, Madison to whom a host of analysts have turned in order to support discussions of a new republican regime "which did not require a virtuous people for its sustenance."[2]

A little ingenuity, of course, can handle this apparent contradiction. Some interpreters might simply brush the speech aside as a debater's ploy or an anomalous intrusion of an older mode of thought into a changing situation, though they would also have to sweep aside some other statements in which Madison apparently affirms that even an enlarged republic must rest on virtue.[3] Other analysts might argue that the speech concedes no more than that the people have to know to whom they should defer, which was to drain the Revolutionary concept of its content. Here again, however, there are many passages in which Madison makes it clear that he did not envision a republic in which popular participation would be limited to choosing proper rulers.[4] A better strategy, accordingly, might follow Gordon S. Wood, who makes two subtle points that have been often overlooked. In the first place, Wood describes a Madison who was, at once, a pioneer of modern thinking and a thinker who did not depart as far from eighteenth-century patterns as some of his contemporaries did.[5] In the second, Wood observes that the depreciation of the need for virtue was as yet "sporadic," "premature," and less the current rule than the beginning "of a fundamental shift in thought."[6] Although Wood identifies the explanation and defense of the completed Constitution as a vital moment in the substitution of a politics of interest for a politics of virtue, he is well aware that this was not a moment's work. John Pocock chose his words with care when he suggested that it was "less in contradiction than in correction" (or perhaps in amplification) that I and others tracked the influence of the older values and concerns into the new republic, where Jeffersonians and Federalists continued to pursue the old antithesis of virtue and corruption.[7]

But it is not my purpose here to recapitulate the current controversy over liberal and classical dimensions of early nineteenth-century thinking.[8] Rather, I propose a tentative, decidedly preliminary effort to articulate some thoughts about another worry that has troubled me increasingly for several years. For there is yet-another possibility inherent in the way that Madison's remarks seem radically at odds with dominant interpretations of the movement of republican opinion. It is possible that we have not precisely understood or have not precisely managed to convey what even early Revolutionaries meant by "virtue"—early Revolutionaries and their eighteenth-century sources. And if this is so, then we have pushed our pens into a thicket of confusions that might best be cleared away by clarifying eighteenth-century usage of this term.

Since *The Creation of the American Republic*, "virtue" has become an organizing theme for histories of Revolutionary thinking. In this masterwork itself, Wood tells us that the colonists' decision to declare their independence was related to their fear that they could not remain a free and healthy people if they continued to be bound to a corrupt and corrupting Britain. Independence was simultaneously a grim necessity, in order to defend the virtue that was threatened in a myriad of ways by the connection with Great Britain, and a revolutionary opportunity to buttress liberty and to achieve regeneration as a people by creating new republics, which would rest upon and nurture the impressive public spirit that had been displayed in the American resistance.

Americans, Wood says, did not embark upon their revolutionary enterprise without some reservations. While the people's spirited defense of liberty suggested that they were, indeed, "the stuff" of which "republicans are made," there were already many signs of "luxury and corruption"; virtue was, almost by definition, rare and constantly endangered.[9] On balance, nonetheless, the striking fact about the early Revolution was the optimistic faith with which its leaders looked to the regenerative powers of republics, trusted in the people's virtue, and anticipated countless benefits from the creation of an order in which office would depend exclusively on talent and elections. Thus, the story of the movement of elite opinion from the Declaration of Independence to the Constitution can be told, to a significant degree, in terms of a progressive testing of this faith. The disillusionment and discontents resulting from the final weary years of war and from the local legislation that was prompted by the postwar economic troubles were fundamental to the movement for a sweeping alteration of the federal system. The times seemed full of faction, indolence, extravagance, and dissipation. The failure of the people to display the public spirit on which all republics were assumed to rest produced a crisis of the Revolution. The reformers felt compelled to make and justify a new political arrangement that would guarantee good government " 'even in the absence of political virtue,' . . . to establish a republican government even though the best social science of the day declared that the people were incapable of sustaining it."[10]

In *The Jeffersonian Persuasion*, I suggested, in effect, that Wood may have gone too far in his discussion of the early Revolutionary break with eighteenth-century constitutional opinion, as well as in his early dating of an end of classical concerns.[11] I nevertheless accepted—and I still accept—the fundamental thrust of his interpretation, along with most of its details. I still believe that *The Creation of the American Republic* is the proper starting point for subsequent discussions, that Wood is much more nearly right than wrong in his description of the course of Revolutionary thinking. But if he swings the pendulum too far, there may be aspects of the book that have contributed to current controversies and confusions: the paradigm may need repairs. This, indeed, now seems to me the case. There are some passages in *The Creation* that suggest—or, at the least, have frequently been taken to imply—that early Revolutionaries meant by "virtue" something more than, and different from, what I believe that most of them were saying. And especially when Wood's sophisticated presentation is compacted by his followers and critics, we can easily become entangled in a serious misunderstanding, both of early Revolutionary thought and of the Federalists' departures from new and old traditions.[12]

Wood himself is undeniably a careful, subtle analyst of "virtue"— so much so that I will often be objecting less to his discussion than to how he has been read. I do not intend, by any means, to quarrel with the burden of his comments: "Frugality, industry, temperance, and simplicity—the rustic traits of the sturdy yeoman—were the stuff that made a society strong. The virile martial qualities—the scorn of ease, the contempt of danger, the love of valor—were what made a nation great." What sickened it was luxury. "The love of refinement, the desire for distinction and elegance eventually weakened a people and left them soft and effeminate, dissipated cowards, unfit and undeserving to serve the state. 'Then slumbers that virtuous jealousy of public men and public measures, which was wont to scrutinize not only actions but motives: then nods that active zeal, which, with eagle eye watched, and with nervous arm defended the constitution.' "[13]

This paragraph repays repeated reading for the clarity with which it captures the association of "virtue" with "virility" and "vigilance," which were among its closest synonyms, and places it in opposition to a fear of softness, effeminacy, and slumber, which were antonyms attributed most commonly to the debilitating spread of luxury and refinement.[14] Every specialist has taken pains to warn against the feminine associations that "virtue" has acquired since Revolutionary times. And yet there still remains a strong temptation to associate the word with self-surrender, a temptation that is easy to give in to as we read the sentences that follow. "The sacrifice of individual interests to the greater good of the whole formed the essence of republicanism," Wood writes, "and comprehended for Americans the idealistic goal of their Revolution. . . . By 1776 the Revolution came to represent a final attempt, perhaps—given the nature of American society—even a desperate attempt, . . . to realize the traditional Commonwealth ideal of a corporate society, in which the common good would be the only objective of government." In a republic, the people were to be conceived of as

> a single organic piece . . . with a unitary concern that was the only legitimate objective of governmental policy. This common interest was not . . . simply the sum or consensus of the particular interests that made up the community. It was rather an entity in itself, prior to and distinct from the various private interests of groups and individuals.
> . . . Ideally, republicanism obliterated the individual.

In a monarchy each man's desire to do what was right in his own eyes could be restrained by fear or force. In a republic, however, each man must somehow be persuaded to submerge his personal wants into the greater good of the whole. This willingness of the individual to sacrifice his private interests for the good of the community—such patriotism or love of country—the eighteenth century termed "public virtue."[15]

This language seems to me more problematic. On the one hand, it imparts a graphic sense of the American rejection of "the base remains" of a hereditary order, the Revolutionary faith in the capacity of democratic polities to make the world anew.[16] Early Revolutionaries did contrast the unity of interests among a democratic people, as well as the identity of interests between the people and their rulers, with the divisiveness and irresponsibility of aristocrats and kings. They did expect abundant benefits from the creation of a new political society in which no individual or group would have either a permanent, hereditary place in government or a persistent interest that was necessarily distinct from that of others. On the other hand, we ought to keep it constantly and firmly fixed in mind that eighteenth-century talk about public virtue and corruption started—for most Anglophones at least—with a profound commitment to a mixed or balanced constitution, a commitment that *assumed* that individuals and groups possess potentially conflicting interests and will take advantage of opponents if they can. Eighteenth-century British advocates of balanced constitutions did not deny that conduct will relate to selfish interests. This, they thought, is why men need a government to start with; it is also why no government except a balanced one is likely to assure the good of all. Thus, it seems to me that Carter Braxton's often-quoted doubt that any people could display "a disinterested attachment to the public good, exclusive and independent of all private and selfish interest," might best be taken to deny what very few Americans would ever have affirmed.[17] Plainly, the majority of Revolutionary leaders disagreed with Thomas Paine's conclusion that the simplest form of government is best. Plainly, too, there was a great deal in their heritage, as well as in the context of their lives, that warned them that it was impossible, in theory or in practice, to dissociate men's conduct from their interests.

Remember Harrington's discussion of the serving girls and the division of the cake? In order to divide it fairly, one (who represents the few) will cut the pieces; the other (symbolizing, in this case, the many) will choose between the parts.[18] Equity results from a decision in which each *asserts* her interest but does so in the knowledge that the other must agree. Each pursues her interest knowing that she has to take the other's interest and the other's power into account. The common good emerges as a mutually respectful act of two autonomous, inherently self-interested people. Indeed, in the tradition for which Harrington was an important source, to act politically in terms of someone else's interests, rather than one's own—as servants, it was thought, would necessarily reflect the wishes of their masters—was corrupt. The citizen was self-reliant and assertive. He was expected to contribute to political decisions precisely on the basis of his independent understanding of his needs, choosing what is good for him as well as for the whole. He was not expected to *surrender* his particular self-interest. Instead, he was thought of as pursuing his particular desires while still remaining conscious of the interests of his peers and of participating in a collectivity of equals. Quoting Revolutionary sources, Wood conveys this process neatly when he writes: "Every one must consult his neighbour's happiness, as well as his own," and "each individual gives up all private interest that is not consistent with the general good, the interest of the whole body."[19] Where Wood has emphasized the sacrifice, however, I would call renewed attention to the self who must perform it.

What, then, did the Revolutionaries usually intend by their repeated calls for the sacrifice of selfish interests, for a commitment to the public good (for these were not less prominent than Wood suggests)? Not, if I am right thus far, a generally disinterested pursuit of general needs, not the continuous foreswearing of personal self-interest. On the contrary, a vigorous and vigilant defense of one's own liberties and interests, as several of the quoted sources say, was an essential characteristic of the republican citizen; it was his contribution of his virtue to the public. Far from demanding that a man forget himself and think only of the public, Revolutionary thinkers ordinarily assumed that citizens neither could nor should act selflessly.[20] The Revolutionary thinkers expected individuals to differ, clash, and even threaten one another's rights—especially if they were rulers. This helps to explain why most of them rejected simple forms of government and wanted bills of rights. The great departure that the Revolutionaries made from eighteenth-century thinking was not to call for, or expect, a conscious and continuing self-abnegation, but, instead, to conclude that in a polity that did not have legal and hereditary distinctions, no individual or group could have a *permanent* interest that was distinguishable from the well-considered interest of all. Individuals, who would inevitably assert their personal demands when making political decisions, might mistake the public good; but none could possibly escape involvement in the public fate, and none should ever forget that the public fate would be his own.

Commitment to the public good meant vigilant, continuous attention to the public life. It meant, as well, submission to the will of the community—obedience to law—and this submission had to be a conscious, voluntary act, because sound republics were assumed to be incapable of rigorous, continuing coercion.[21] In these senses, "self-immersion," if we understand that term to mean absorption in one's private goods to the neglect of public duty, *was* profoundly dangerous to a republic. In these senses, individual desires and private interests would clearly have to be "subordinated" to the public interest, even "sacrificed" to public needs. And in these senses, too, the individual's particular desires must certainly give way to the decisions and demands of the community, which might call upon a man to sacrifice his property or, in a war, his life itself, to public needs or wishes. But the sacrifice of self was to occur primarily in an individual's submission to community decisions or in taking time from personal enjoyments and pursuits in order to attend to public business. It would seldom happen in the *making* of political decisions, where citizens would be "restrained" by the consciousness of others, but where they neither should nor could "forego" their own self-interests.

These distinctions, I believe, are critical to understanding the development of Revolutionary thinking. They suggest that Wood exaggerated the degree to which the early Revolutionaries held a fully classical, perhaps a Montesquieuan, concept of the public good in a republic and that he then exaggerated the degree to which the Federalists rejected early Revolutionary thinking. In part, perhaps, because his presentation tended to abstract "the Whig science of politics"—the concerns that were most characteristic of eighteenth-century British oppositions—from the commitment to theories of balanced government, in which they were embedded, his discussion may have under-emphasized the contemporary recognition of the inherently self-interested nature of man. He may have gone too far toward reading in a call for "selflessness" where early Revolutionaries really hoped for vigorous assertions of the self within a context of communal consciousness and a willingness to live by the community's decisions. He may thus have left too little room for comprehending Madison's continued insistence on the indispensability of virtue.[22]

In none of this, again, is it my purpose to reject the central thrust of Wood's interpretation. I do not deny that Revolutionary thinking changed in much the manner that Wood describes or that the Constitution was a product of a crisis of republican convictions. I argue, rather, that this crisis can be better understood, confusions cleared away, and needless controversies partially resolved by clarifying what it was that late and early Revolutionaries meant by "virtue," what was classical and what was not classical in this conception and what was changing over time. Here I need to turn again to Pocock—always hoping, to be sure, that I have read him correctly.

Pocock says that classical republicanism and its early-modern derivatives viewed the republic as a means of associating and combining the particular virtues of distinguishable types of men in such a fashion that the particular virtues of each must contribute to a common pursuit of a general good. Each individual attains his highest good—becomes most fully human—by contributing his virtue to decisions in which he is simultaneously restrained by and aware of the power and the virtue of others. Sound republican decisions are cooperative—rather like the girls' division of the cake. They are reached in such a way that every citizen is conscious both of ruling and of being ruled, of being one of a community of equals, of contributing his fallible opinion to a process in which every judgment will be checked by others. Virtue is a matter both of an autonomous participation in community decisions and of according due authority to the virtue of others. For eighteenth-century Englishmen—indeed, for Harrington himself—this often meant electing those distinguished by their superior wisdom, talents, and public service.[23]

Persistent ambiguities or tensions, Pocock notes, were present in these concepts; and I suspect that these inherent tensions grew more tense as eighteenth-century Anglophones adjusted to the rise of commerce and incorporated a contractual component in their thinking. The individual was not a citizen, according to civic-humanist opinion, unless he was pursuing his particular good in a public forum; and yet, the subordination of the public good to his particular desires, absorption in his private interests to the point of losing sight of what was universal, was corrupt. The citizen might be conceived of, Pocock writes, either as an Athenian or as a Spartan; but the relationship between the private and the public was always problematic. Paradoxically, moreover, because the citizen was always thought of as at once deferring to and receiving deference from his fellows, as a member either of the many or of the few, and sometimes either as a ruler or as a subject, citizenship was always thought of as an equal relationship between unequals.[24]

Pocock considers Wood to be correct—and so do I—when Wood maintains that the Federalists, in completing the rejection of the concept of a people who could be qualitatively differentiated into social groups, severely modified the eighteenth-century concepts of deference and civic virtue. A civic-humanist conception of the citizen in a republic was so intimately tied to the idea of mutual deference between the many and the few, each of which possessed distinctive virtues, that demands for virtue called for something rather different as the American Revolution progressed. Democratic citizens were not expected to identify the different virtues of contrasting social groups, nor were they expected to contribute differentially according to their different social personalities—except, perhaps, in the relationship between electors and elected.[25] Thus, a truly classical conception of the virtue of the citizen broke down. "If the people could not be differentiated into separately-characterized groups," Pocock writes, "there could be no ascribing to them that higher virtue of respecting (or, if you like, deferring to) the virtues of others who in their turn defer, which is at the root of both the Polybian concept of mixed government and the Aristotelian concept of citizenship. . . . An undifferentiated people could not be a virtuous people" in this sense.[26]

And yet, as Pocock quickly notes, there was a great deal more to eighteenth-century talk of virtue than the concept of mutual deference between the many and the few—which itself, as Wood has recently repeated, continued to perform a central role in Federalist conceptions of relationships between the people and the sort of men who were best qualified to lead them.[27] "Deeply entrenched in eighteenth-century agrarian classicism," Pocock writes, "was an image of the human personality, at once intensely autonomous and intensely participatory," which "staked everything on a positive and civic concept of the individual's virtue."[28] "If Americans had been compelled to abandon a theory of constitutional humanism which related the personality to government directly and according to its diversities, they had not thereby given up the pursuit of a form of political society in which the individual might be free and know himself in his relation to society."[29]

We can go a good deal further, though in doing so it may be necessary to depart significantly from Pocock as well as from Wood. We might remark that even in the eighteenth century, opposition calls for virtue were seldom (at least overtly) calls for mutual deference. " 'Virtue,' " Pocock writes, "consisted as much in the civic independence of the arms-bearing freeholder from private patron or governmental interest, as of his membership in one of a hierarchy of orders who respected and deferred to one another."[30] "Autonomy, and virtue, [were assumed to] rest on material as well as moral prerequisites," both of which were thought to be endangered by the instruments of oligarchic rule: standing armies, patronage, and public debts.[31] Condemnations of corruption were, in largest part, denunciations of this system: condemnations of the multiple dependencies that it forged, of its misuse of public treasure, of the degeneration of the balanced constitution, of the killing enervation and quiescence fostered by the unearned luxury with which it favored some at the expense of the impoverishment of many. In all these ways, the oligarchic system undermined the economic preconditions and the moral spirit that were necessary if the citizen was to contribute independently to public life; the system corrupted the gainers and the losers, both of whom might be "demoralized by an exclusive concern with private or group satisfactions."[32] Virtue, for the eighteenth-century British opposition, lay especially in independence from this system and in vigilance against it; and much of what the early Revolutionaries sought was the replacement of the system by a polity and a social order free from the dependencies that it entailed. Men might still be different and unequal in their faculties and possessions, but every citizen would be autonomous in his participation in the public life.

Autonomous participation in the public sphere, awareness of one's membership in a community of equals, a self-denying spirit to resist immersion in the private life of acquisition and enjoyment—all were elements of early Revolutionary or of eighteenth-century opposition talk about public virtue. But—it bears repeating—there was little in this talk that clearly called for self-effacing, totally disinterested regard for an abstracted general good, little to suggest that citizens' decisions would or should be made without consideration for their interests, and little to suggest a Spartan uniformity of individual conditions. A balanced government was necessary to control men's differences, no less than to conjoin their virtues, and a qualified assertion of self-interest was demanded even in the antithesis of virtue and corruption. The dependent man was not a citizen because it was another's interests, rather than his own, from which he had to act. Self-interest was to be restrained by a regard for the community and for one's peers. It was to be restrained, additionally, by voluntary willingness to sacrifice one's private interests to community decisions, by obedience to laws, by consciousness of being ruled as well as ruling. But it would always enter into every individual's decisions, and those decisions would be made, we need to note, within the confines of a *representative* governmental system.

All these points, it seems to me, bear stressing. All are necessary if we are to understand how different even early Revolutionary thinking was from classical conceptions of the citizen and the polis or from Montesquieu's discussion of the spirit of republics.[33] Here, however, Pocock's writings, much like Wood's, present some difficulties that have been compounded by his followers and critics. Even as Pocock's writings serve—again like Wood's—as an essential starting point for further explorations, they contain some themes that can engender serious confusion when we think about the Federalist achievement and about the Federalists' departures from prevailing modes of eighteenth-century thought.

One of these confusions, we may hope, is on its way to resolution. Pocock argued that the central theme of eighteenth-century British discourse—the fulcrum on which fundamental changes turned—was its preoccupation with the dangers posed to virtue by the growing role of commerce. This argument became most troublesome when later writers oversimplified what "commerce" means in such a formulation, and much of the confusion might be ended simply by accepting Pocock's warning that he never said "that republican virtue was [considered] incompatible with trade and industry."[34]

A second difficulty lies, however, in recurring protests that Pocock's monumental works portray the eighteenth century as more consistently and more fully classical than was in fact the case. In this complaint, there seems to me to be more substance, although we ought to bear in mind that Pocock has himself insisted that his "tunnel" through the eighteenth century does not exhaust its treasures. *The Machiavellian Moment* reaches back to Aristotle and ahead to Richard M. Nixon, focusing throughout upon a language that early-modern westerners used in order to grapple with the secular or temporal dimensions of their polities' existence. To this language, Pocock argued, Locke made little contribution, and the old fixation on the advent and centrality of "modern," "liberal" ideas appeared to him to be not merely partial but also the principal impediment to understanding that the most important changes in received ideas were generated by a dialogue concerning virtue and corruption, a dialogue that Locke ignored. But Pocock's effort to construct a history sans Locke—a history that would be emancipated from a single-minded "Whiggish" search for a direct, uncomplicated line into the present—seems to many to create a new imbalance. His recent essays toward a history of two distinctive, intertwining languages of liberty—one civic humanist, the other civil jurisprudential—have not attempted, yet, to bring Locke back into the picture. And despite his warnings that contemporaries did not see these languages "as distinct and ideologically" opposing, the very effort to construct two separate tunnels—necessary and defensible as it may be—may foster an impression that they were.[35] This impression interferes in a variety of ways with our attempt to comprehend the Federalists' relationship with earlier opinion.

No republic could be fully classical, as Pocock notes, once individuals had receded from their full, direct participation in the public forum and had begun to be conceived of as contributing their virtue largely—or exclusively, as some elitists hoped—to the selection of their sovereign rulers. Pocock therefore joins with Wood and others to remark that Madison accomplished an amazing feat of intellectual and verbal daring when he redefined republics as governments in which the people *do not* "meet and exercise the government in person" but "administer it by their representatives and agents."[36] This was to turn the classical, or Montesquieuan, image of republics nearly on its head. It not only recognized and clarified a difference between the new American republics and the archetypal Grecian cities; it opted unequivocally for the superiority of modern representative regimes.[37] And yet, what seems to have been wholly overlooked in emphasizing Madison's departure from the ancients is that he departed not at all from early Revolutionary views. The English-speaking peoples, after all, had made their peace with this concession to modernity a hundred years before the American Revolution, whose early leaders never planned on anything *except* a representative republic. And Madison, in turn, was hardly casting off the Anglophonic civic-humanist tradition when he praised this modern innovation. Thus, when we remark that Thomas Jefferson regretted the departure from the ancients far enough to sketch his scheme for ward democracies, which would allow for greater popular participation, we also ought to note that Madison's rejection of a wholly national regime, along with his elaboration of a theory in which representatives were not to be conceived of as sovereign, can also be regarded as attempts to limit the concession that modernity required.[38] It will be helpful, too, to note that even Jefferson admitted that his countrymen would never be content with Spartan portions of "a double mess of porridge."[39]

Again, in truly classical, or Montesquieuan, images of the republic, there was little room, as critics of the Pocock-Wood interpretation sometimes gleefully announce, for an antithesis of liberty and power. In the polis, the community's decision could be nothing other than the product of the liberty and the virtue that every citizen contributed to public business. But here, too, as neither Wood nor Pocock really fails to see, the water had been muddied many years before by the acceptance of representation and by the influence of a modern politics of natural rights. In representative, contractual republics, liberty and power could so easily collide that an insistence on the need for public virtue often called, more loudly than for any other thing, for vigilance against the separate interests and ambitions of elected rulers.

John Adams wrote:

> Mankind have been . . . injured by insinuations that a certain celestial virtue, more than human, has been necessary to preserve liberty. . . . The best republics will be virtuous and have been so, but we may hazard a conjecture that the virtues have been the effect of the well ordered constitution rather than the cause. And perhaps it would be impossible to prove that a republic cannot exist even among highwaymen by setting one rogue to watch another; and the knaves themselves may in time be made honest men by the struggle.[40]

How many times have we reverted to this passage or to Hamilton's denial of the possibility of Spartan virtue in order to explain the movement of American opinion? How often have we noted Madison's insistence on the differences between the classical democracies and modern representative republics? And yet, like Carter Braxton, Hamilton and Adams may have been rejecting concepts that few Americans had ever held; and Montesquieu's discussion of republics may have been most useful to the Revolutionaries, as they groped toward a clearer understanding of the character of citizens who might be capable of public life, while still being plainly modern. Even in the first full flush of Revolutionary optimism, I submit, only a minority of the Revolutionaries ever hoped for superhuman, self-effacing, and totally disinterested participation in political affairs—in other words, for Montesquieu's heroic virtue. On the other hand, however, the need for virtue—if we use the word without these connotations—may have been denied by just as few when the Revolutionaries faced the crisis of the postwar years.

At this point, if I am right, we should be able to revert to Madison's remarks at the Virginia state convention, prepared to understand more clearly what he had in mind. For Madison, I would suggest, the really frightening conclusions of the postwar years did not result from a discovery (or a rediscovery) that men were factious, that they are often tempted to pursue their selfish interests at other men's expense.[41] With very few exceptions, I suspect—and it is possible that these exceptions might be found primarily among New England's most enthusiastic Christians—English-speaking politicians never did count much on a disinterested attention to the public good (not, at least, among the body of the people). With few exceptions, too, most Revolutionaries knew that their societies did not suggest—and should not seek—a Spartan uniformity of interests. The crisis came, for Madison at least, when he was forced to recognize that under poorly balanced constitutions, the majority itself could be a "faction," willing and imposing policies that were persistently at odds with private rights or long-term public needs, and when an armed minority resisted the majority in Massachusetts. In Shays' Rebellion and in many other things, Madison indeed saw many signs of insufficient virtue, and these were all the more alarming at a time when liberty and union both appeared to be at risk. Too many people seemed to lack any regard for their relationship with others, to be neglectful of the public business, or to be unwilling to submit themselves to the community's decisions.[42] But the solution did not lie, as Madison conceived it, in denying the necessity of virtue or in doubting that the body of the people possessed enough virtue to maintain the Revolutionary order. The solution could be found in an enlarged compound republic, in governmental mechanisms that were calculated to impose additional restraints on passion, and in governmental policies that would correct the economic difficulties that were at the source of moral and political malaise. A flood of foreign luxuries, together with restricted foreign markets for domestic goods, was threatening the economic preconditions of a virtuous participation in the public life, making citizens incapable of looking further than their hardships or their wants. But if these constitutional and economic weaknesses could be repaired, the people's underlying virtue could be reasserted.[43]

"Virtue," to be sure, did not connote to Madison the superhuman quality that Hamilton and Adams mocked. Madison did not believe that men were angels, nor did he imagine that the United States was any kind of Sparta. But if few Americans had ever held a "Montesquieuan" concept of republican society, then Madison was rejecting early Revolutionary concepts less decisively than has been thought.

When Madison insisted on the indispensability of virtue, he plainly meant, as Wood and Pocock both suggest, a certain deference by the many to the few: a recognition of and a preference for the public-minded, wiser men who were best qualified to lead. For Madison, moreover, this elective, wholly natural aristocracy—to use a term that he himself consistently avoided—would continually defer, in turn, to popular opinion, although, again, these terms are inappropriate for representatives who were to come entirely *from* the body of the people.[44] Nor was even this the whole of what he meant when he insisted on the need for virtue. "Virtue" also meant, for Madison as clearly as for eighteenth-century critics of the British Whig regime, a jealous, vigilant commitment to the public life: continuing participation in a politics that trusted only limited responsibilities to national officials and demanded, even so, that these officials be continuously watched for any signs of an appearance of a separate set of interests. Slothful inattention to the public business and an enervated and debauched indulgence in a merely private life still seemed to Madison to be as dangerous to commonwealths as they had ever seemed to Bolingbroke or Burgh. And Madison insisted too, as strongly as these neo-Harringtonians had done, that liberty was incompatible with standing armies, overgrown executives, and swollen public debts.[45] If "virtue" did not signify for Madison what it had signified for Montesquieu, for Rousseau, or for the ancients, it still undoubtedly denoted most of what it had implied for eighteenth-century British oppositions and their early Revolutionary heirs. For most Americans, this may have been its most essential meaning all along.

NOTES

I wrote this essay while a fellow at the National Humanities Center. I am deeply grateful to the center for its generous support and for the seminars and private talks in which the other fellows criticized an early draft and taught me much about republicanism in its many different contexts.

1. Jonathan Elliot, ed., *The Debates in the Several State Conventions on the Adoption of the Federal Constitution* . . . , 5 vols. (Washington, D.C., 1854), 3:536 37.

2. Gordon S. Wood, *The Creation of the American Republic, 1776–1787* (Chapel Hill: University of North Carolina Press, 1969), p. 475.

3. See Jacob E. Cooke, ed., *The Federalist* (Middletown, Conn.: Wesleyan University Press, 1961), no. 55, p. 378; no. 57, 387: "As there is a degree of depravity in mankind which requires a certain degree of circumspection and distrust: So there are other qualities in human nature, which justify a certain portion of esteem and confidence. Republican government presupposes the existence of these qualities in a higher degree than any other form. Were the pictures which have been drawn by the political jealousy of some among us, faithful likenesses of the human character, the inference would be that there is not sufficient virtue among men for self-government; and that nothing less than the chains of despotism can restrain them from destroying and devouring one another." What will prevent the national representatives from passing inequitous or dangerous laws? "I answer . . . above all the vigilant and manly spirit which actuates the people of America, a spirit which nourishes freedom, and in return is nourished by it. If this spirit shall ever be so far debased as to tolerate a law not obligatory on the Legislature as well as on the people, the people will be prepared to tolerate anything but liberty."

4. The clearest examples of Madison's insistence on a continuing role for popular participation and public opinion came after 1789, especially in his essays for the *National Gazette*, but I am prepared to argue that he articulated here assumptions that had guided him throughout the 1780s. See the essays on "Consolidation," "Public Opinion," "Government," "Charters," and especially "Government of the United States": "In bestowing the eulogies due to the partitions and internal checks of power, it ought not the less to be remembered, that they are neither the sole nor the chief paladium of constitutional liberty. The people, who are the authors of this blessing, must also be its guardians. Their eyes must be ever ready to mark, their voice to pronounce, and their arm to repel or repair aggressions on the authority of their constitutions." Relevant passages can be found in William T. Hutchinson, Robert A. Rutland, et al., eds., *The Papers of James Madison* (Chicago: University of Chicago Press, 1962-), 14:138–39, 178, 179, 192, 218; see also David F. Epstein's argument that Madison as "Publius" assumed continuous participation, in *The Political Theory of "The Federalist"* (Chicago: University of Chicago Press, 1984), p. 195 and passim.

5. See, esp., Wood, *Creation of the American Republic*, pp. 411–13, 501–6.

6. Ibid., p. 612.

7. *The Political Works of James Harrington*, ed. J. G. A. Pocock (Cambridge, Eng.: Cambridge University Press, 1977), p. 150.

8. For this see Banning, "Jeffersonian Ideology Revisited: Liberal and Classical Ideas in the New American Republic," *William and Mary Quarterly*, 3d

ser., 43 (1986): 3–19; Joyce Appleby, "Republicanism in Old and New Contexts," ibid., pp. 20–34; John Ashworth, "The Jeffersonians: Classical Republicans or Liberal Capitalists?" *Journal of American Studies* 18 (1984): 425–35; and James T. Kloppenberg, "The Virtues of Liberalism: Christianity, Republicanism, and Ethics in Early American Political Discourse," *Journal of American History* 74 (1987): 9–33.

9. Wood, *Creation of the American Republic*, p. 93.

10. Ibid., p. 429. The primary quotation here is not from Madison, although the text and compound footnote may leave that impression.

11. Lance Banning, *The Jeffersonian Persuasion: Evolution of a Party Ideology* (Ithaca, N.Y.: Cornell University Press, 1978), pp. 84–90 and chap. 4.

12. I think this may be clearly seen in John Patrick Diggins, *The Lost Soul of American Politics: Virtue, Self-Interest, and the Foundations of Liberalism* (New York: Basic Books, 1984), and in two excellent articles by John T. Agresto: "Liberty, Virtue, and Republicanism: 1776–1787," *Review of Politics* 39 (1977): 473–504, and " 'A System without a Precedent'—James Madison and the Revolution in Republican Liberty," *South Atlantic Quarterly* 82 (1983): 129–44.

13. Wood, *Creation of the American Republic*, p. 52.

14. On this point see also Edmund S. Morgan, "The Puritan Ethic and the American Revolution," *William and Mary Quarterly*, 3d ser., 24 (1967): 1–43.

15. Wood, *Creation of the American Republic*, pp. 53–54, 58, 61, 68.

16. "Common Sense," in *The Complete Writings of Thomas Paine*, ed. Philip S. Foner, 2 vols. (New York: 1945), 1:6–9 and below. A superb discussion of this pamphlet is Bernard Bailyn's "Common Sense," in *Fundamental Testaments of the American Revolution*, Library of Congress Symposia on the American Revolution no. 2 (Washington, D.C.: 1973), pp. 7–22.

17. Braxton's *Address to the Convention of . . . Virginia* is quoted and discussed by Wood, *Creation of the American Republic*, pp. 96–97.

18. "The Commonwealth of Oceana," in *Political Works of James Harrington*, p. 172.

19. Wood, *Creation of the American Republic*, pp. 60–61.

20. I mean to make allowance for exceptions and for language quoted from such individuals as Samuel Adams and Benjamin Rush (ibid., pp. 61, 118). But even Rush and Adams spoke in different terms at different times.

21. "In a republic there was no place for fear; there could be no sustained coercion from above" (ibid., p. 66). To trivialize a bit, consider traffic regulations: What if no one stopped on red except when fearing enforcement?

22. Carefully considered, I submit, few of the quotations in part 1 of *The Creation of the American Republic* actually suggest that many early Revolutionaries ever expected or demanded the sort of self-abnegation and disinterestedness that I am writing about. There may be some validity in this regard in the critique of Wood's subchapter on "The Public Good" in Gary J. Schmitt and Robert H. Webking, "Revolutionaries, Antifederalists, and Federalists: Comments on Gordon Wood's Understanding of the American Founding," *Political Science Reviewer* 9 (1979): 195–229. This article, however, criticizes Wood for what he never said and serves as an additional example of the way in which problems are compounded by misreadings. For a criticism more congruent with my own, as well as for a helpful argument that Pocock's civic humanists were far from strictly classical in their desires, see Jean Yarbrough, "Republicanism Reconsidered: Some Thoughts on the Foundation and Preservation of the American Republic," *Review of Politics* 41 (1979): 61–95. As I did in "Jeffersonian Ideology

Revisited," which was written in ignorance of this earlier essay, Yarbrough argues that the Revolutionary generation did not *choose between* modern liberal and classical republican ideas (p. 63).

23. See, esp., J. G. A. Pocock, *The Machiavellian Moment: Florentine Political Thought and the Atlantic Republican Tradition* (Princeton, N.J.: Princeton University Press, 1975), pp. 71, 115–16; *Political Works of James Harrington*, pp. 64–69.

24. Pocock, *Machiavellian Moment*, pp. 73–74.

25. Ibid., pp. 523–24.

26. Pocock, "Virtue and Commerce in the Eighteenth Century," *Journal of Interdisciplinary History* 3 (1972): 124–25.

27. Ibid., pp. 124, 126, 133; Gordon S. Wood, "Interests and Disinterestedness in the Making of the Constitution," in *Beyond Confederation: Origins of the Constitution and American National Identity*, ed. Richard Beeman et al. (Chapel Hill: University of North Carolina Press, 1987), pp. 69–109.

28. Pocock, "Virtue and Commerce," p. 134.

29. Pocock, *Machiavellian Moment*, p. 527.

30. Pocock, "Virtue and Commerce," p. 133.

31. *Political Works of James Harrington*, p. 145.

32. Pocock, "Virtue and Commerce," p. 121.

33. Montesquieu, in his discussion of virtue as the "spring" or fundamental principle of a republic, is less unambiguous than many American histories might suggest. He opens by associating virtue with a consciousness of membership in a community within which rules of equity apply, with a consciousness (among the magistrates as well as others) of being subject to the laws. Virtue's opposites, he writes, include ambition in the magistrates, resentment of the public treasury's demands, and "thirst of gain" in all (bk. 3, chap. 3, pp. 20–22). Americans, if I am right, were saying much the same thing and would have readily agreed when he defined the concept "as the love of the laws and of our country" (bk. 4, chap. 5, p. 34). "But virtue," Montesquieu continued, "is a self-renunciation." It "requires a constant preference of public to private interest" (ibid.). Here, I am suggesting, he may well have been proceeding onto ground where relatively few Americans (or Englishmen) would follow, although it is precisely at this point that several writers introduce his influence. Montesquieu believed that a republic called for "heroic virtues which we admire in the ancients, and to us are known only by tradition" (bk. 3, chap. 5, p. 23). He regarded Sparta as an archetype and made it clear that no such polity could be successfully revived without imposing a "community of goods," withdrawal from commerce (or placing it in public rather than private hands), disuse of money, and perhaps a nearly absolute equality of wealth (bk. 4, chap. 6, quotation at p. 34; bk. 5, chaps. 3–5). But even Montesquieu conceded that democracies that were founded on commerce could tolerate the acquisition of great fortunes (bk. 5, chap. 6; bk. 7, chap. 2). And Americans would readily have comprehended and approved his explanation that equality "does not imply that everybody should command, or that no one should be commanded, but that we obey or command our equals." In "a well-regulated democracy, men are equal only as citizens" (bk. 8, chap. 3, p. 111). Citations are to *The Spirit of the Laws*, trans. Thomas Nugent, with an introduction by Franz Neumann, "Hafner Library of Classics" (New York: Hafner, 1966; originally published in 1949).

34. Pocock, *Virtue, Commerce, and History: Essays on Political Thought and History, Chiefly in the Eighteenth Century* (Cambridge, Eng.: Cambridge University Press, 1985), p. 272.

35. See, esp., Pocock, "The Varieties of Whiggism from Exclusion to Reform: A History of Ideology and Discourse," ibid., pp. 215–310, and "Cambridge Paradigms and Scotch Philosophers: A Study of the Relations between the Civic Humanist and the Civil Jurisprudential Interpretation of Eighteenth-Century Social Thought," in *Wealth and Virtue: The Shaping of Political Economy in the Scottish Enlightenment*, ed. Istvan Hont and Michael Ignatieff (Cambridge, Eng.: Cambridge University Press, 1984), pp. 235–52. The quotation is from the latter at 251.

36. *The Federalist* no. 14, p. 84; see also no. 10, p. 62.

37. See Pocock, *Virtue, Commerce, and History*, p. 271. Other recent essays that make much of Madison's terminological legerdemain include Jean Yarbrough, "Madison and Modern Federalism," in *How Federal is the Constitution*, ed. Robert A. Goldwin and William A. Schambra (Washington, D.C.: American Enterprise Institute, 1987), pp. 84–108; and Daniel W. Howe, "The Language of Faculty Psychology in *The Federalist Papers*," chap. 7 in this volume.

38. I do not dispute Yarbrough's valuable suggestion in "Republicanism Revisited" that Madison and the other Framers made inadequate institutional provision for popular participation and that they underestimated the enormous dangers posed to it by the enlargement of the size of the republic, in part because the context led them to assume that the perpetuation of vigorous popular involvement was the least of their problems. I do suggest, however, not only that Madison's party building after 1789 was consciously addressed to the problem of participation but also that we should emphatically reemphasize that Madison (and most of the other Founders) consistently assumed that most political decisions would continue to be made in the states and local communities, whose governments were closer to the people. On the role of federalism in Madison's thinking, Yarbrough and I are far apart. See also her "Rethinking '*The Federalist's* View of Federalism,'" *Publius* 15 (1985): 31–53.

39. Harold C. Syrett and Jacob E. Cooke, eds., *The Papers of Alexander Hamilton*, 26 vols. (New York: Columbia University Press, 1960–79), 3:103; Jefferson to John Jay, 23 Aug. 1785, in *Thomas Jefferson: Writings*, ed. Merrill D. Peterson (New York: Library of America, 1984), pp. 818–20. Recent studies of the Scots, such as those in *Wealth and Virtue*, are making it increasingly apparent how peculiar Samuel Adams was in wishing that America could be a Christian Sparta.

40. "A Defense of the Constitutions of Government of the United States of America," in *The Works of John Adams*, ed. Charles Francis Adams, 10 vols. (Boston, 1850–56), 6:219.

41. The contrary appears to be suggested by Jack N. Rakove in "The Great Compromise: Ideas, Interests, and the Politics of Constitution Making," *William and Mary Quarterly*, 3d ser., 44 (1987): 424–57.

42. In the early Revolutionary constitutions, Madison suggested, "a provision for the rights of persons was supposed to include of itself those of property, and it was natural [for himself as well as others, I suggest] to infer from the tendency of republican laws, that these different interests would be more and more identified." But injustices deriving from this error, together with "the multiplicity and mutability of laws" encouraged by the early constitutions, had brought into question "the fundamental principle of republican Government, that the majority who rule in such Governments, are the safest Guardians both of public Good and of private rights" ("Observations on Jefferson's Draft of a

Constitution for Virginia," 15 Oct. 1788, and "Vices of the Political System of the United States," Apr. 1787, in *Papers of Madison*, 11:287 and 9:354).

43. "Most of our political evils may be traced up to our commercial ones, as most of our moral may to our political" (to Jefferson, 18 Mar. 1786, ibid., 8:502). On this matter see Drew R. McCoy, *The Elusive Republic: Political Economy in Jeffersonian America* (Chapel Hill: University of North Carolina Press, 1980), chap. 3. And note how many of the sources quoted in Wood's section on the "Political Pathology" of the 1780s (pp. 413-25) appear to be condemning the sort of self-indulgence that leads men to forget that they are citizens and parts of a community; see also the sources quoted on p. 100: luxury unmans a man and renders him incapable of being vigilant or of forgoing immediate gratifications even under an immediate threat; poverty reduces men to beasts, enslaving them to want.

44. See, esp., *Federalist* no. 57.

45. Before as well as after Hamilton presented his reports on public credit; see, esp., his speech of 29 June in Max Farrand, ed., *The Records of the Federal Convention of 1787*, rev. ed., 4 vols. (New Haven, Conn.: Yale University Press, 1966; originally published in 1937), 1:464-65; *Federalist* no. 41, pp. 273-74; and Elliot, *Debates in the Several State Conventions*, 3:382.

About the Contributors

TERENCE BALL, coeditor of this volume, is professor of political science at the University of Minnesota. His most recent book is *Transforming Political Discourse* (1988); he is also the editor of *Political Theory and Praxis* (1977) and *Idioms of Inquiry* (1987) and a coeditor and contributor to *After Marx* (1984) and *Political Innovation and Conceptual Change* (1988). He is currently working on a book about our obligations to future generations.

LANCE BANNING is professor of history at the University of Kentucky. He is the author of *The Jeffersonian Persuasion: Evolution of a Party Ideology* (1978) and of many articles and essays on James Madison, republican ideas, and the making and ratification of the Constitution. His second book, *James Madison and the Founding*, will be completed shortly.

JAMES FARR is associate professor of political science at the University of Minnesota. He is a coeditor of *After Marx* (1984) and *Political Innovation and Conceptual Change* (1988). He has also published essays on political theory and on the history and philosophy of the social sciences. He is currently working on studies in the American science of politics.

RUSSELL L. HANSON is associate professor of political science at Indiana University. He is the author of *The Democratic Imagination in America* (1985) and articles about political theory and the welfare state. He is also a coeditor and a contributor to *Political Innovation and Conceptual Change* (1988).

DANIEL WALKER HOWE is professor of history at the University of California, Los Angeles. His publications include *The Unitarian Conscience: Harvard Moral Philosophy, 1805–1861* (1970; 2d ed., 1988), *The American Whigs: An Anthology* (1973), *Victorian America* (1976), and *The Political Culture of the American Whigs* (1980).

PETER S. ONUF is professor of history at Southern Methodist University. He is the author of *The Origins of the Federal Republic: Jurisdictional Controversies in the United States, 1775–1787* (1983) and *Statehood and Union: A History of the Northwest Ordinance* (1987).

J. G. A. POCOCK, a coeditor of this volume, is Harry C. Black Professor of History at Johns Hopkins University. He is the author of *The Ancient Constitution and the Feudal Law* (1957; reissued 1987), *Politics, Language and Time* (1971), *The Machiavellian Moment* (1975), *Virtue, Commerce, and History* (1985), and is the editor of *The Political Works of James Harrington* (1977). He is currently working on studies of Edmund Burke and Edward Gibbon.

GERALD STOURZH is professor of history at the University of Vienna. The author of many works written in German, he is also the author of *Benjamin Franklin and American Foreign Policy* (1954) and *Alexander Hamilton and the Idea of Republican Government* (1971) and is a co-editor of *Readings in American Democracy* (1959).

GARRY WILLS is the Henry R. Luce Professor of American Culture and Public Policy at Northwestern University. The author of *Cincinnatus: George Washington and the Enlightenment, Inventing America: Jefferson's Declaration of Independence, Explaining America: The Federalist,* and other books, he is now working on a book about James Wilson.

Index